OUR BROKEN AMERICA

*To my husband, Jimmy, and our children, Maggie and Robert.
I am so grateful for you three. Without you, I would be adrift in a
sea of nothingness. You are my anchor and safe harbor.*

OUR BROKEN AMERICA

Why Both Sides Need to Stop Ranting and Start Listening

JACKIE GINGRICH CUSHMAN

FOREWORD BY

NEWT GINGRICH

CENTER
STREET

NEW YORK   NASHVILLE

Center Street
Hachette Book Group
1290 Avenue of the Americas, New York, NY 10104
centerstreet.com
twitter.com/centerstreet

First Edition: September 2019

Center Street is a division of Hachette Book Group, Inc. The Center Street name and logo are trademarks of Hachette Book Group, Inc.

The publisher is not responsible for websites (or their content) that are not owned by the publisher.

The Hachette Speakers Bureau provides a wide range of authors for speaking events. To find out more, go to www.HachetteSpeakersBureau.com or call (866) 376-6591.

Library of Congress Cataloging-in-Publication Data has been applied for.

ISBNs: 978-1-5460-8488-4 (hardcover), 978-1-5460-8486-0 (ebook)

Printed in the United States of America

LSC-C

10 9 8 7 6 5 4 3 2 1

CONTENTS

FOREWORD
by Newt Gingrich

This is a book with a powerful message of hope for American renewal and an amazing number of specific examples and insights. It is a serious contribution to the conversation we must have if we are to bring our country back together again.

I am proud of the citizen that my daughter Jackie Cushman has become, and I am most proud of the time and energy she and her husband, Jimmy Cushman, have put into their two children: Maggie, now a sophomore at Davidson College; and Robert, now the senior class president at his high school. It has been fascinating to watch Jackie study and learn as her children went through the various stages of childhood and adolescence and are now emerging as solid, thoughtful, and admirable young adults.

It was by talking with Jackie over the years about the different ways Maggie and Robert deal with life that I began to realize just how constantly she learns and how many different places she goes to for information. She was constantly bringing up the newest thinking about childhood or education, or grappling with the challenges of life.

About fifteen years ago, Jackie began writing columns. Her thoughtful approach to writing columns carried her from personal topics (such as remembering her mother) to insights into the raising of children, to education, to religious liberty, to the lessons of history and current events. During that period, she also wrote two books. The one we wrote together, *5 Principles for a Successful Life: From Our Family to Yours*, is as relevant today as when we collaborated on it more than a decade ago.

It was while Jackie was thinking through the current tensions, hostility, and bitterness that are splitting the country that she began to develop an important notion. She determined that persuading Americans to take personal responsibility for emphasizing the positive was the key to getting America out of its current decline into vicious, unrelenting political partisanship.

Jackie's insights into the importance of being positive—and her ability to cite psychological studies on the upward spiral of energy, confidence, and cooperation versus the downward spiral of hostility, alienation, and gridlock—create a significant framework for getting America back on a positive track.

Both Democrats and Republicans would profit from reading Jackie's analysis. The current infighting has real negative consequences for the future of America, and even small positive steps could build a reinforcing cycle of accomplishment.

In some ways, Jackie represents a revival of a deeply American positivism, which grew from Benjamin Franklin, Abraham Lincoln, the two Roosevelts, and Ronald Reagan. Historically, Americans have held a deep belief that the future will be better, that we can help make that future better, and that the key was, in Dr. Norman Vincent Peale's bestselling phrase, "the power of positive thinking." (It is no accident that the Trump family routinely attended services at Dr. Peale's church and learned the importance of having faith in a better future while working to make it come true.) This combination of optimism about the future and a willingness to work—both as individuals and in voluntarily formed collaborations—was a key part of Alexis de Tocqueville's analysis in his 1835 classic, *Democracy in America*.

Jackie has had the great advantage of living what she is recommending. She and Jimmy have a deep commitment to the

Atlanta community. Jimmy has served on the boards of the Atlanta Botanical Garden, the Atlanta History Center, and the Arts Alliance. They have supported Our House (which provides shelter for homeless children and their families so they can live, learn, and thrive). Jackie and Jimmy have also supported activities at Pace Academy, the school their children attended. Every time I chat with them, Jackie and Jimmy have a civic engagement underway. They are also deeply engaged in their church, where Jimmy serves on the vestry.

Jackie also serves on the CFA Society Atlanta Foundation (which focuses on financial literacy), the Trust for Public Land Advisory Council, and the Georgia Early Education Alliance for Ready Students (GEEARS), which focuses on learning for children from birth to the age of five. Jackie is also an avid tennis player (Atlanta has the largest tennis association in the United States).

I mention all those activities so you will understand that when she advocates local involvement and local citizenship, she is living what she is preaching.

Jackie's belief that local volunteerism is better than national bureaucracy is a restatement of the classic American position. She understands Friedrich Hayek's principle—expressed in his classic work *The Road to Serfdom*—that a centrally planned and implemented system inevitably involves the massive loss of freedom. She has absorbed George Orwell's warning that a totalitarian system must inevitably eliminate individuality and coercively force obedience to the whims of the central system.

This warning that socialism and left-wing totalitarianism are both roads to loss of freedom is timely. We have a younger generation that has not learned the lessons of history. We have a news media that does not want to describe the lessons of Venezuela, Cuba, Zimbabwe, and other economic failures pulled down by failed socialist ideas. Jackie is combining the lessons of American history, the warnings of great economists and writers, and just plain common sense.

What makes me especially interested in this book is Jackie's clarity that the long-range future is not conservative centralism versus left-wing centralism. Any centralism is inherently dangerous. In this approach, Jackie is exactly in the tradition of the Founding Fathers. She cites example after example of the great leaders who believed in freedom and understood that defending liberty required courage and a deep sense of personal responsibility.

Finally, this book is so inherently American. As the author of *The Essential American: 25 Documents and Speeches Every American Should Own*, Jackie is especially well prepared to emphasize the core values and history that have made America an exceptional nation.

She understands that the Founding Fathers created a system of exceptional freedom designed to protect liberty from the human propensity to slide into dictatorship of one form or another. She correctly emphasizes that the belief that our rights come from God and not from the state is what makes America exceptional. For virtually all of human history, rights have come from those with power—whether a chieftain, a dictator, a king, or whatever form upon which power was centered.

The generation that wrote the Declaration of Independence knew from their study of history that human institutions tended to decay, that power was corrupting, and that the powerful operated out of self-interest rather than patriotism.

That founding generation believed its duty was to design a machine that could prevent tyranny. In 1776, in the Declaration of Independence, they first established that we owed our rights to God, not government. They insisted that we had been guaranteed life, liberty, and the pursuit of happiness by that God.

In 1787, in the Constitution, they established the machinery of government, which has lasted for 232 years. This machinery was deliberately made so inefficient that no would-be dictator could force it to work. In fact, the founders did such a good job of creating inefficiency by sharing power among different institutions that we can barely get it to work voluntarily.

American Exceptionalism comes from this focus on individual liberty and God-given rights. It has allowed more people from more countries with extraordinarily diverse backgrounds and cultures to come together in the pursuit of happiness.

Jackie understands that this remarkable achievement is under attack and that saving it requires a cultural response more than a political response. It requires personal responsibility more than government responsibility.

This is an important, timely book that offers hope and practical suggestions in a period of hostility, divisiveness, and tribalism.

After you read it, tell your friends and those concerned about the survival of America about it and continue this essential conversation.

INTRODUCTION

Who Am I, Why I Care—Why You Should, Too

I am tired of the politically polarized environment of America. How about you? This environment is being enabled by politicians, news organizations, social media, and even my friends and family. I am not alone. According to an Associated Press–NORC Center for Public Affairs Research poll, over half of Americans believe "the political polarization of the nation is extremely or very threatening, and another 34 percent say it is moderately threatening."[1] Combined, 86 percent of us believe our polarizing political environment is a threat.[2]

And we are right—the great divide is a threat to our nation; our nation is broken. We must work together to counter division by transforming this threat into a call to action. A call for us to work together—no matter how hard or frustrating that may be—to make our country better.

People from all political stripes are worried about the high level of polarization, and you have probably noticed that it's virtually impossible to have a civil discussion about politics. In the past, all too often, I steered conversations away from politics to avoid getting trapped in political discussions. This polarization has become so prevalent that it has silenced people and stopped them from engaging with each other.

I, too, was scared to engage in debate. I was scared people wouldn't like me.

I was so paranoid about these terribly polarizing discussions that I often wouldn't tell people that my father is former Speaker of the House Newt Gingrich. His name alone is polarizing to some. People love him or hate him, without even knowing anything about him as a person. Often, when they find out that he is my father, they are surprised. Some say, "I love him, he's so smart." Others say, "But you're so nice" (as if he can't have a nice daughter).

My sister has been turned down for jobs due to the employers' disdain of our dad. After three rounds of interviews that she thought had gone well at one company, she finally met with the company president, who told her, "Well, of course you interview well, your dad is Newt Gingrich."

He then walked her out, telling her she would not get the job.

I have had salespeople yell at me, telling me how much they hated my dad. My children have met people who so disliked my dad that they felt compelled to share his faults with them (this happened when my children were eight and six).

When my dad ran for the Republican presidential nomination, my daughter was in sixth grade. One day, I picked her up from school and asked her if she had been experiencing any middle school drama (I had heard that middle school students often experienced social drama). Her reply, "No, we have enough national drama in our family—there is no room for middle school drama."

She was right.

This is also good advice that we should heed as a country. Our challenges are so great that we don't have time for political drama. Enough already. I am no longer afraid to engage in debate; not everyone has to like me, but I have to like myself and stand up for what I believe is right. We have to engage with one another if we are to save our nation from political polarization.

Politics has always been charged, but it seems to have been more highly charged than normal over the past few years. Who's to blame? The media and Democratic Party blame President Trump, while he blames them. Some blame my father and pollster Frank Luntz, who helped craft the language and wording around the 1994 Republican Revolution.

This narrative is laid out in a November 2018 article in *The Atlantic* titled, "The Man Who Broke Politics," by McKay Coppins. The summary? The current nastiness in politics is due to Gingrich's approach to politics, which led to the 1994 Republican Revolution and established a Republican majority in both houses of Congress for the first time in forty years. "He [Gingrich] thought he was enshrining a new era of conservative government," wrote Coppins. "In fact, he was enshrining an attitude—angry, combative, tribal—that would infect politics for decades to come."[3]

As evidence, Coppins cites a June 24, 1978, speech my father made to college Republicans in College Park, Georgia. " 'One of the great problems we have in the Republican Party is that we don't encourage you to be nasty,' he told the group. 'We encourage you to be neat, obedient, and loyal, and faithful, and all those Boy Scout words, which would be great around the campfire but are lousy in politics.' "[4]

What Coppins didn't include from that same speech was Dad's reasoning for these aggressive tactics, to beat the Democrats at their own game. "The great strength of the Democratic Party in my lifetime has been that it has always produced young, nasty people who had no respect for their elders."[5] His call to action in 1978 was for Republicans to beat the Democrats at a game they had been winning his entire life using their same time-worn tactics.

Sixteen years later, in 1994, Republicans regained control of the House. His call to action worked. But it was not a permanent change. Even today we have a political system where power between the parties shifts over time.

Both parties have perfected this approach to power, and with the advent of technology and social media, the result is hyper-speed and hyper-partisanship. Add into that the societal changes and we have the resulting toxic environment. It's not true that he created it, but the approach used by both sides is not working, and it is time for us all to change strategies. That's why I am writing this book.

I am a wife, mother, sister, daughter, friend, and community volunteer, who happens to have grown up in politics. In 1974, I was seven years old when my father first ran for Congress in Georgia's mostly rural Sixth District. It included the Atlanta airport down to Griffin and west to the Alabama state line.

He led the 1994 Republican takeover of the House with the "Contract with America." He then served as speaker of the House from 1995 to 1998. A few years ago, I joined his team's ultimately unsuccessful bid to win the Republican nomination for president in 2012.

I'm going to tell you a good bit about my early life in politics, my community service, and my faith in God, because those experiences are what frame my thinking. I'm explaining my background so that you can see not only how I view the world, but what my potential biases are.

Each of us makes up our mind about matters of import based on the information we consume. As you gather information, whether from news stories, friends, or colleagues—I would urge you to be aware always of the spoken and unspoken biases that inform their views.

My mom knew my father was obsessed with politics when

they first started dating—that was part of the attraction for her. They were both smart and interested in how politics could make a difference and focused on how they could make a difference in politics together.

The question was a matter of when would he run and for what political office, not if he would run. They knew that he would. Dad had taken a year off during his undergraduate career at Emory University to run Jack Prince's 1964 congressional campaign in the Ninth District of Georgia. It was, and still is, a largely rural district north of Atlanta. On election night, aware of the possibility that votes were being tampered with, he called a local election official to track down a ballot box when one of the precincts did not deliver theirs to be counted. "Son," he was told when he called, "my people are tired, and I thought they needed a night off before they counted the votes."

Unsure of whether they were taking a rest or using the time to make sure their candidate (the opponent) had enough votes to win, my dad knew that there was nothing he could do. He learned a lot of lessons during that campaign. Regardless of the events of that night, his candidate lost by a pretty large margin.

After my dad finished his doctoral course work at Tulane University, we spent a year in Brussels, Belgium, where he conducted research for his dissertation. In 1970, our family moved to Carrollton, Georgia, where he taught at West Georgia College (now the University of West Georgia). By then, he had a wife (my mother Jackie) and two children (my sister Kathy and me).

Small-Town Georgia

Once we moved to Carrollton, my dad joined the college faculty and the entire family joined the town's First Baptist Church. My maternal grandmother lived in Columbus, two hours away, and we often visited her there. In a small town in rural Georgia in the 1970s, most of our lives revolved around high school football—and church. Our church was the center of our social life. We attended not only Sunday school, but also choir, Sunday night service, Wednesday night dinner, and Bible study.

In 1974, my dad first ran for office in the Sixth Congressional District race against the incumbent, John J. Flynt, Jr., the dean of the Georgia delegation. If you remember 1974, or if you have read about it, you'll recall the impact that Watergate was having on the nation as a whole. My dad's campaign also felt it. Bear in mind that, at that time, Georgia was a mostly Democratic state. About midsummer, Dad realized that he would probably lose—but we kept campaigning. He lost that election, even though he earned 48.6 percent of the vote. But we were not defeated; we got up the next morning and went to the Ford Atlanta Assembly Plant across from the Chick-fil-A Dwarf House (the first restaurant in the now national chain), shook hands with constituents, thanked them for their votes, and asked them to support him again next time, because we were certain there would be a next time.

Two years later, he ran again. This time, he thought he had a real chance, until the spring of 1976, when Georgia Governor Jimmy Carter began picking up the Democratic presidential primaries in the early states. Carter was very personable and incredibly hardworking, an absolutely fantastic candidate. He inspired hundreds of volunteers (the Peanut Brigade) to pay their own way to travel from Georgia to the primary states to help his campaign (my mother-in-law was one of them). They ran a strong ground game, going door-to-door during the days, then staying up at night to write (by hand) notes thanking each of the men and women they had talked to that day for their time, and asking them to vote for their candidate, a peanut farmer from Georgia.

My dad continued to believe he had a good chance at winning that year, until Election Day, when he went to the public library in Carrollton that was his polling place and saw caravans of buses pull up, and people file out to cast their ballots. There was no real Republican organization in the state. He knew that the bus program was being run by Democrats to get out the vote for Carter and that the people on the buses were not there to vote for some Army brat history professor with a funny name, Newt Gingrich. He was right.

Once again, he lost, securing 48.3 percent of the vote. But once more, we got up the next morning, drove to the Ford factory, and shook hands with workers there during shift change, stopping across the street between shift changes for coffee and food. Visiting the original Dwarf House in College Park reminds me of my childhood, the time we spent campaigning as a family, and our belief that hard work and perseverance would pay off.

Fake News—Back in the 1970s

It was never fun to lose, but we knew it was part of the process. I remember, after Dad's first loss, going to school soon after and having an administrator tell me that he was glad that my father had lost the election. Yes, even in the 1970s, there were plenty of mean-spirited people who felt free to share their opinions—even if that meant they hurt the feelings of an elementary school student. I can also remember reading in the press about my father being chauffeured around in a limousine. I knew it wasn't true. That was my introduction to fake news.

My father mounted his third campaign in 1978. This time, he and my mom both took the year off from work, and my maternal grandmother moved in with my sister and me so my parents could travel and campaign. My dad took out a personal loan to cover expenses (which he paid back many years later), and they worked nonstop. It was during this time that our family "rescued" a Christmas tree from the elementary school trash bin and adopted it as our own. Money was tight. I wore my sister's hand-me-down clothes; we used cinder blocks and wood planks for bookcases; dinners at home often included Spam; and we almost never ate out.

Finally, in Dad's third race, there was no incumbent. Flynt had decided to retire, so my dad ran against the winner of the Democratic primary, Virginia Shapard.

There were a few other changes, too. Dad changed his campaign colors from green and white to blue and white. While that might not seem to be a big shift, it had a big significance. Green was the color of environmental conservation, a traditionally liberal cause, while blue and white were being used by the Tory Party, the conservative party, in Britain. The campaign also rented a Winnebago, which they covered with "Gingrich for Congress" signs. My mom often drove it for the campaign.

Although my dad was the policy wonk and speechmaker, my mom was the one with a natural love of meeting and talking with people. She could strike up a conversation with a telephone pole.

In addition to campaigning in strip malls and by knocking on doors, we walked in parades and attended Rotary and Kiwanis Club cookouts. My father preached in dozens of churches throughout the district (he was a Baptist deacon), and the rest of us would often show up and listen. Small country stores at four-way stops were not too small to stop in to see if we could perhaps find a voter or two. I loved traveling with my dad, campaigning, and spending time with him.

There was no social media, Facebook, or YouTube in 1978. Atlanta, which was an hour away from our home in Carroll-ton, was the nearest big media market. It covered much more than the Sixth District of Georgia, but was just too expensive for our tiny campaign budget. Ours was a real grassroots campaign, including the "Newt for Congress" sign that we attached to the roof of our light blue Chevrolet Impala. While the sign attracted the attention of voters, it also attracted the attention of sheriffs in the small towns where my dad campaigned. I can remember sitting in the backseat of the Impala while sheriffs wrote speeding tickets for my mom or dad. We eventually learned to make sure we adhered to in-town speed limits, often spying the signs behind trees.

Lesson from Dad: Try, Try, Try Again

It all paid off that November, when Dad finally won an election and began his congressional career. Dad won the next several campaigns with ease. But that changed when Georgia's growing population led it to be awarded an eleventh congressional seat, and the state was redistricted for the 1992 races.

In 1990, my dad was the only Republican congressman from Georgia, but his district included Bremen, the hometown of Georgia Speaker of the House Tom Murphy. During the redistricting process, Murphy, who had made no secret of his dislike for my dad, tried to get rid of him as his congressman. Murphy cut the Sixth District, which my dad was representing, into three then-Democratic districts. The new Sixth District was formed in Atlanta's northern suburbs. Murphy had hoped that my dad would be voted out of office. Instead, my father moved to the new Sixth District, and was introduced around by Matt Towery, who had recently won the Republican nomination for lieutenant governor of Georgia.

After I graduated from Presbyterian College in 1988, there were few jobs available due to a recession, so I went back to graduate school full-time and worked thirty hours a week in business valuation at BDO Seidman, an accounting and consulting firm, in Atlanta. After I graduated with my MBA in 1990, I earned my Chartered Financial Analyst designation. My next step was to work for a startup wireless company. I worked in finance, marketing, management, and eventually helped sell off the various parts to bigger players in the industry. It was a wonderful experience. There were weeks when we had to decide which vendors to pay, and which not to pay due to cash flow constraints. In a small company you get experience in every area.

It was during this 1992 race that my dad's opponent in the primary ran a nasty personal attack ad that was untrue. The opponent falsely claimed that my father had abandoned his wife and children. After hearing the untrue allegations, I called my dad and offered to appear in a commercial for his campaign. He took me up on my offer.

I addressed the outrageous personal attacks directly, and noted that they just weren't true. James Farwell, a political and communications expert, oversaw the production. The commercial was successful, and my dad won the primary by 980 votes.

He won the general election easily. After the 1992 elections, the Georgia delegation comprised of seven Democrats and four Republicans—including my dad. Murphy's plan had backfired; he now had three more Republican congressmen than he had had the year before.

After my brief foray back into politics, I focused on my work. As we sold parts of the company to strategic partners, we downsized, meeting often to determine who would be let go in the next round. Eventually, I volunteered to be next and suggested they keep the person with accounting experience. I moved on to BellSouth Mobility, a much bigger player in the industry.

It was a fabulous experience, moving from a 25-million-dollar

company to a several-billion-dollar company. I started in financial reporting, moved to mergers and acquisitions, partner rela-
tions, back to financial planning (managing the budgeting
process for a $3 billion division), and finally landed in strategy.
My entire experience at BellSouth was great.

During this time at BellSouth, my husband Jimmy and I were
married. Our union, built on our love, was also the union of two
families with different political backgrounds. Jimmy's grand-
parents and parents were early supporters of Jimmy Carter. They
helped him run first for governor of Georgia, then for president.
Jimmy's grandfather Philip Alston, Jr., served as ambassador to
Australia under President Jimmy Carter. The family has a long
history of community service and civic support in Atlanta. The
appointment of Callista Gingrich by President Donald J. Trump
as the United States Ambassador to the Holy See has strengthened our families' history of service to our country.

My husband and I were a little nervous when the families
met, but we soon found out we were nervous for no reason. The
simple fact that our two very political families get along while
focusing on family first provides an example of how families can
bridge divisive politics. After Jimmy and I were married, I continued working throughout my first and second pregnancies, but
then took a step back from corporate life to focus on our family.

Moving into the World of Writing

You may be wondering when writing entered the picture. After
all, here I am, writing a book, and here you are, reading it. It
started when I began writing for an Atlanta neighborhood newspaper. My first piece was written spur of the moment, the night
of President George W. Bush's reelection in 2004. My thoughts
about the election spilled onto the computer screen and I e-mailed

the article to a friend (Thornton Kennedy), who was the editor of the *Neighbor Newspaper*. To my surprise, he ran it and asked for more. I wrote for him off and on for a while and eventually became a weekly columnist. After several years, and quite a few rejections, I became a syndicated columnist for Creators Syndicate.

Since then, I have written three books. I co-authored the first one with my father, *5 Principles for a Successful Life: From Our Family to Yours* (Crown Forum, 2009). At the time, I was involved with "Learn, Earn and Achieve," a program for middle and high school students who needed academic help. The program provided them with after-school tutors and paid them to attend tutoring sessions. The students learned that they were capable of learning and improved academically. It was truly inspirational to be part of the academic and personal growth of those students, and they inspired me to write the book.

It included interviews with over thirty people from various backgrounds, as well as stories from my dad and myself. The principles include Dream Big, Work Hard, Learn Every Day, Enjoy Life, and Be True to Yourself. Although the principles are timeless, they require ongoing recall and activation. The book is as applicable today as it was when it was written.

My second book, *The Essential American: 25 Documents and Speeches Every American Should Own* (Regnery, 2010), provides a foundation of our shared American history. It begins with Patrick Henry's speech "Give Me Liberty or Give Me Death" and ends with President George W. Bush's speech the evening of September 20, 2001, as he stood in the well of the House of Representatives after the terrorist attacks on our country. I wrote it because the stories we tell ourselves about our country and its past influence our future.

It was, and still is, clear to me that all Americans need to read and understand the basic foundational documents and speeches that helped shape our country. The book includes the documents and speeches as well as commentary on their historical importance and why they remain relevant today.

Before he entered politics, my dad was an environmental studies professor at West Georgia College, where he extended his work outside the classroom. (He also taught a course titled "The Year 2000.") I remember our family picking up trash next to a highway in 1971, on the second Earth Day. I grew up camping, canoeing, and hiking and learned to appreciate the outdoors. My love of nature explains my service on the advisory council of the Trust for Public Land. This organization saved the birthplace of Martin Luther King, Jr., from being torn down and protected the headwaters and other key river tracts of the Chattahoochee River in north Georgia. (My father helped secure the federal funding for this work decades ago.)

While I have been a council member, we supported and paid for the first study of Atlanta's Beltline, a 22-mile loop of abandoned railroad corridor that connects 45 neighborhoods in downtown and midtown. The Trust for Public Land is working toward ensuring there are parks within a ten-minute walk for people living in urban areas and making the Chattahoochee River more accessible for people to use and enjoy.

I'm passionate about the environment.

Education is also incredibly important to me. My mother, who was the first in her family to go to college, went on to work as a high school math teacher. She was selected as a Student Teacher Achievement Recognition (STAR) teacher several times (by her high school students who had earned the STAR designation). Many of her students have told me that her belief in them and their ability to learn changed their lives. My appreciation of education and my love of learning led me to serve on the board of the Georgia Early Education Alliance for Ready Students, which focuses on quality, early learning, and healthy development for all children, from birth to five years of age. I also serve on the board of the CFA Society Atlanta Foundation, which focuses on improving financial literacy.

Helping to Secure a Home for a Homeless Shelter

For over seventeen years, I've served on the board of directors or the advisory council, and volunteered at Our House, a homeless shelter for newborns and their families. This life-changing organization provides shelter to live and education to thrive. When families arrive at Our House, staff members assess them to determine what led them to become homeless. The next steps are to focus on the health of the mother and baby, then job training and placement, and finally the organization works to find a place for them to live permanently. Our House continues to follow up with the families for five years. When Our House had to leave its former location, I joined with others on the board and signed a loan for the shelter to ensure they could renovate new space and move in before the deadline. We couldn't have a homeless, homeless shelter. We were successful.

As I have stated, my experiences have shaped my world outlook and my biases. Growing up in the place and time I did, my career experiences, and the ways I've been blessed to serve my community, have all shaped my understanding of the world. It is my involvement with community groups that has framed my belief that limited government is most effective and that solutions emerge when people, communities, corporations, and foundations come together and work together.

Choosing Community Empowerment over Government Control

I understand the intellectual appeal of government control but recognize that it contains two key flaws: (1) Government is neither efficient nor effective; and (2) When government attempts to overcome its inefficiencies, it does so by taking away people's freedoms. It's a trade not worth making. Give me my freedom and a relatively inefficient government. With the help of involved citizens, we can make anything happen, but it has to happen at the community level—not through government control.

National governments can't solve problems through top-down approaches—just look at the failures of communism in Russia and Cuba. For us to leave the world a better place for our children, we all need to pitch in and help. And part of being a good American is committing oneself to working with others in our communities.

Socially, I am pretty libertarian. For example, I believe Republicans totally missed the boat on the topic of civil unions. They should have said "Yes." *Yes,* the government should recognize civil unions and provide the same benefits to single-sex and opposite-sex couples. And *yes,* the government also should have let religious organizations decide whom to marry or not.

This would have allowed those couples who want to go beyond creating a legal relationship through a civil union where to go for a church wedding. It would have been a perfect separation of church and state.

When my father ran in the Republican presidential primary for the 2012 election, I served as his campaign's senior adviser and national media surrogate. Focusing on strategy, messaging, and media work, I handled countless news interviews: CNN, Fox, MSNBC, etc. I was the one they often sent in to the adversarial media outlets (MSNBC)—and I enjoyed the challenge. I've had decades of experience dealing with nasty comments.

Fake News in an Irish Bar

For example, the first meeting between my dad and my husband-to-be took place at an Irish bar in Atlanta, when my dad was speaker of the House. The bar was crowded, and I stayed back a bit to give Jimmy and my dad a chance to talk. Two guys were seated near me at the bar, and I could hear one tell the other, "That's Newt Gingrich. He abandoned his wife and children."

Well, this repetition of a fake news story infuriated me. I went over and corrected him, nicely, I think. Their faces initially showed disbelief that I was Newt's daughter, but soon their expressions transitioned to embarrassment. They confessed that they had just said what they had heard from news sources and apologized to me.

Unfortunately, I cannot correct everyone who has mistaken ideas about our family. Fortunately, my dad and my boyfriend (now husband) Jimmy got along famously—and still do today.

The 2012 campaign was challenging. I can remember the week after my dad won the South Carolina primary election and we traveled to Florida to campaign. The song "Strong Enough" by Matthew West gave me strength during that week; I played it often while taking a break from campaigning and running outside.

I can remember standing backstage before we walked out as a family the night of the Florida primary, my dad with his head bowed in prayer. I placed my hand on his back—praying for strength from God for him, and for our family.

God gave me strength that night, and still does.

A few months after the campaign ended, my mother suffered

a debilitating stroke. I spent the majority of the next year helping her through various hospitalizations and moving her into a nursing home. Luckily, the home was close to my family, and we could spend time with her. She passed away in 2013, a year after her stroke.

Since then, I have continued writing my syndicated column, working with my husband to raise our two children, serving on boards, and working in strategy and media consulting, while still making the occasional media appearance. In 2016, I joined the National Association of Corporate Directors and have since earned the NACD Board Leadership Fellow designation.

My decades-long immersion in campaigning, writing, news appearances, and watching as national views have become more and more polarized has led me to write this book. I've seen how the media can make things worse and how local communities can make great strides when people work together. I truly believe that, together, we can do better—for ourselves and for our country. But the people need to lead the charge, not rely on government.

By nature, I am an introvert. It's tempting to remain that way. I love to read, to write, to think. But I also know that if I were to spend all my time alone, I would not grow; I would not change; I would not see glimpses of God in other people.

We cannot be in community by ourselves; we must join in community with other people. I grew up Southern Baptist. As a child, I spent the bulk of my free time singing in church choir or attending youth group functions. My Southern Baptist upbringing provided me with a strong, Bible-based foundation for my faith.

So even now, when relationships get messy and hard, I try to remind myself that the solution is not to withdraw into myself, to protect myself, to make my life easier, but to simply be in relationship, to be there, to listen when I don't agree. To be present. This change in stance is a reflection of my conversion, to the Episcopalian faith, where community is at the heart of knowing and understanding God. My hope is that this book might inspire you, too, to allow yourself to be in relationship with others, even when you don't agree with them, perhaps especially when you don't agree with them.

Jimmy and I had both of our children baptized at St. Luke's Episcopal Church in Atlanta. My transition to a religion that focuses on worshiping in community, rather than by oneself, has reframed my thinking in numerous ways. I used to believe that individuals or an individual could solve political problems. Now I believe that politics can make progress only if we become less polarized. If we solve political problems in community, among people not only from our own party, but among people from both parties.

Finding God in Others

I gain great strength and perspective from my faith. I deeply believe that God made all people in His image and that we all have the spark of the divine within us. I believe that we can often see God in other people, if we just slow down and look. He may not be all of the person, but He is always part of each person.

Just this morning, I heard a sermon that broadened my thoughts about this book and my work. Our preacher talked about what happens when we are bullied and we accept the bully's perspective. He noted that this moment of perspective shift is life-changing—in a negative way. Our acceptance of condemnation and criticism of who we are can threaten our very foundation and sense of self and who God wants us to become. As the preacher said today, it can leave us "barren in spirit" and unable to make sure we brighten the world with our God-given gifts.

I have felt this way at various times in my life, as no doubt others have, too. I had a period of being barren of the spirit after my dad's presidential campaign failed and my mother died. She had been my constant cheerleader, the person who always had faith in me. Her stroke, then death so soon after the presidential campaign, left me exhausted, unsure, and at times almost unable to get out of bed.

It's easy to judge others in order to make ourselves feel worthier. We have all done this at some point—after all, we are all human. We may tear others down or allow others to tear us down—but neither is acceptable. That's because in either case the result is that we don't live up to our potential; we don't use all the gifts that God has given us to make the world a better place.

This is the human condition, the condition of suffering, the condition of being uncertain and feeling unworthy. The answer is not to push others down to signal our own virtue but instead to allow God's blessing to work through us with the knowledge that, by flowing through us, God's blessing will become less than perfect. But that should not stop us from asking God to help us anyway.

I have prayed often for God's guidance through this project, and my prayer is that you see more of Him than of me in the final product. My intent is that you will see the spark of God in yourself, but also in others—especially those with whom you disagree—and that together we can help each other and save our broken nation.

Why I Care

I hope it's clear to you by now that I love my country. I feel blessed to have been born an American. My children were born in this country. I believe that ours is the best country in the world.

While we are not a perfect country, and we can improve, I love America.

That's why I care about people around the country ranting and raving at one another, and the potential danger that this moment of political polarization presents. A great divide that could lead to disastrous events. It would be easier to close myself off, to ignore the signs of danger, to not listen to others, but that doesn't solve the problem—it just pushes it out of my mind.

Different regions have different terrains, weather patterns, and history. We are a complex country, with a history of leading the world, providing an example for other countries, especially in the areas of individual rights and economic activity. Currently, we are not the shining city on the hill that the world needs to inspire other countries. Instead, we have become a conglomeration of bickering, resentful family members, more focused on tearing down other individuals than in building up our nation. In many cases, we have withdrawn to our own corners and refuse to engage. We are greatly divided. We must do better. The world needs our nation to be a shining example of economic activity and citizen engagement—and it's up to us to make this change.

I am grateful to live in a country where we can disagree, both with the political power structure and with one another. If we can remember how unique this is—possibly we can all be grateful for our ability to participate and approach the political process with more gratitude than grievance.

I also love Americans. I love the people who live in our country, even when I don't agree with them. I love our passion, our fight, and our willingness to jaywalk—even when the red hand is flashing "Don't Walk." I didn't realize that such behavior was unusual until I visited Finland and watched people stand, waiting for the light to change, even when there were no cars in sight.

I Need Your Help

But the bickering that permeates nearly all of the news media has become louder, shriller, and more personal. I don't want the next generation to have to settle for ranting and raving at one another, or to shrink from public discourse altogether because they are afraid of the possible repercussions. I want to set a good example, but I can't do it alone. I need your help. We need to set a good example—together.

Just as my husband, Jimmy, and I model being active community members for our children, I feel compelled to write this book to challenge you to step up and be a good example of how to engage in politics with those with whom we disagree.

It's too easy to point a finger and blame the people in national politics for the polarization we experience every day. For instance, President Donald Trump for his outrageous and often bullying tweets or comments. But remember, he is a New York developer who became a reality TV star, and then president of the United States. If I could change it, I would—but his actions are not going to change, nor should we expect them to.

Nor are those leaders on the left going to change their actions. For instance, Senator Bernie Sanders of Vermont is going to continue to offer free anything to anyone in an attempt to win votes to secure the Democratic presidential nomination. He is a socialist who has made millions in our capitalist society and owns three houses.

The only people who can solve this problem are you and me. Every day, we get to decide how we will act, how we will engage, and whether we can create solutions for the real problems in our country.

For decades, many of us have been focusing on creating careers, raising children, and making money. It's time we take the lead in changing the national narrative. I need your help. Together, we can effect change simply by reaching out, meeting and talking, and joining together in community with one another. We have to be able to disagree without dissolving into factions and insular tribes. It's worth the work and the discomfort.

Should You Care?

I think you should, or I wouldn't have written this book. However, no matter how much I may care, and how much I may urge you to care, at the end of the day, your actions are up to you. Do you love our country enough to change the trajectory we are on? Do you love our nation enough to truly engage in being a citizen? My hope and prayer is that you do, but it's up to you. My task in writing this book is not to coerce or scare you into taking some drastic action; it's to remind you that our country is great, not perfect, and that we can improve it, but we can do so only by working together.

CHAPTER 1

The Proposition

The current environment of ranting and raving and the resulting political polarization is dangerous, and I believe that our nation is in crisis. I also believe that our nation is exceptional and therefore worth saving.

My goal with this book is to clarify, not complicate, and to inspire you to join me and make the changes and take the actions we need to save our country.

First, we must answer three questions:

1. Are we experiencing political polarization?
2. If so, is it dangerous to our country?
3. Is our nation exceptional and worth saving?

The answer to all three of these questions is a resounding YES!

Our nation is deeply divided—by geography, race, age, income, gender, education, and politics, to name a few. It's not just that people identify with separate subgroups, but that we often identify more with these respective subgroups than with America in general. It's human nature to want to belong to a group; at the most basic level, belonging to a group provides safety. The challenge is, when we lose ourselves in service to a group, we risk losing our identity—the core of who we are as people. Remember, God made each of us in His image, and each of us has a spark of the divine in us. To continually group and divide one another by attributes ignores our individuality—and our God-given uniqueness.

It's simply wrong. We are each different, and we each have talents that the world needs.

Watch Out for Opinion Masquerading as News

These days, it's almost impossible to carry on a civil discussion about politics and political issues without emotions overflowing and people erupting in anger—or worse. It happens in our daily interactions with friends and family, and everyone can watch it happen on the news any time of day. Networks and papers are labeled "liberal media" or "right-wing thinking." Gone are the days of real, unbiased, fact-based news—now our airwaves and device screens are dominated by opinion labeled as news.

It's sad that people often truly don't know the difference between news and opinion. The media are partly to blame for the devolution of news into infotainment. Opinion-based news has a place in our world, but we need to be able to understand the difference between fact and opinion. Real decisions require real information. Compromise is possible only after you take the time to understand the difference between opinion and reporting, and to learn the applicable facts regarding the issue at hand.

When this is taken to the extreme and "news" becomes pure opinion, opinion becomes propaganda, propaganda changes our society, and the meaning of reality is lost. Currently, emotions and opinions are escalating and tensions are on the brink of eruption. You can watch MSNBC one minute and Fox News the next and think you're on two different planets. But you are not—it's just that their perspectives are so different. The sheer vitriol that pours forth from these networks reflects the same caustic feelings that many Democrats and Republicans—and everyone in between—are experiencing throughout this country.

I grew up believing that the presentation of "news" was supposed to be done in an unbiased fashion; that facts are facts; that people form their individual opinions based on how they interpret those facts; and that those interpretations are based on their perspectives and experiences.

Not anymore. Now, each member of the news media has an opinion and wants you to hear it, and each member of the news media presents opinions as facts, even if they are not.

On the left, if you don't agree with their opinions—then they call you names and attach labels in an effort to put you into the "bad" category. This allows them to dismiss your argument. Under their approach, if they don't agree with your perspective, you're a bad person. If you're a bad person, your argument is not valid. Unfortunately, this happens on the right, too.

The Tale of Two Marches

Let's take the video shot in January 2019 after two marches near the Lincoln Memorial in Washington: the Indigenous Peoples March and the March for Life. The initial posting, which went viral, showed an indigenous man beating a drum and chanting in front of a group of mostly white male teenagers, with sixteen-year-old Nick Sandmann in front, saying nothing as he stood, smiling, just a few inches from the drummer. The teenagers were wearing red Make America Great Again (MAGA) hats. The media decided that the teenagers were mocking the drummer. It didn't take long for Twitter to take off—assuming the worst about the white, Catholic school boys who had attended a pro-life rally nearby. Evidently these descriptors sufficed for many to assume the worst about the boys.

The students were vilified online. Twitter users assumed they were the instigators, that they were racist, that they were evil. Some called for the students' private information to be made public so they could be tormented in real life, too; others called for them to be attacked physically.

"#MAGA kids go screaming, hats first, into the woodchipper,"[1] tweeted Jack Morrissey, who produced Disney's *Beauty and the Beast* and the *Twilight* series.

Doesn't sound very family friendly to me.

After seeing the initial video, neoconservative political analyst Bill Kristol tweeted, "The contrast between the calm dignity and quiet strength of Mr. Phillips [the drummer] and the behavior of #MAGA brats who have absorbed the spirit of Trumpism—this spectacle is a lesson which all Americans can learn."[2]

But the release later of a second, longer video told a different story. It showed a group of black men shouting abuse at the boys. According to an article by Mark Curnutte, published the Monday after the event in the *Cincinnati Enquirer*, "The four African-American protesters near the Lincoln Memorial have been identified as members of the Black Hebrew Israelites."[3] The Southern Poverty Law Center, in its magazine *Intelligence Report*, noted the group is "obsessed with hatred for whites and Jews" and is becoming "more militant."[4]

Nathan Phillips, the Omaha tribal elder who was seen on the first viral video beating his drum as the teenagers in MAGA hats watched, told reporters that he had felt threatened and heard the chant, "Build the wall, build the wall." According to the *Washington Post*, the chanting could not be heard on the video.[5]

After the longer video's release, tweets were deleted, apologies made—by some. Kristol and Morrissey deleted their tweets.

Savannah Guthrie of NBC's *Today Show* interviewed both

Sandmann and Phillips in the week following the incident. "People have judged me based off one expression, which I wasn't smirking, but people have assumed that's what I have," Sandmann said. "And they've gone from there to titling me and labeling me as a racist person, someone that's disrespectful to adults, which they've had to assume so many things to get there without consulting anyone that can give them the opposite story."[6]

Phillips told Guthrie, in a separate interview, that he forgave the students.

Why? The boys had done nothing wrong. Why Phillips thought the boys should be forgiven, I have no idea.

But much of the media and social media coverage still focused on the original video. What about the new material, the new group in the longer video? Where was the outrage and hate toward them, and who were they?

Why did much of the focus stay on the teenage boys, even after the longer video came to light in which the Black Hebrew Israelites were yelling at the Catholic students? Because they go to a Catholic high school? Because they had attended a pro-life rally? Because they are white? Because they are boys? Or because the first video left the deeper impression?

Whatever the initial reason, a $250 million lawsuit was filed on behalf of Sandmann against the *Washington Post* for "compensatory and punitive damages," in February 2019, according to a CNN news story by An Phung.[7]

Whatever the outcome of the legal wrangling may be, one lesson is clear: People are all too fast to jump to a conclusion that might be wrong.

It's really no wonder there's a lack of listening on all sides. People on both ends of the political spectrum are often unwilling and/or unable to listen to one another. How can you listen when you are busy screaming or when someone is screaming at you? The result? We are unable to come up with solutions that draw us together. Instead, we are continually being ripped apart. Instead of listening, people too often jump to conclusions and assume the worst, as they did with the teenagers.

Sadly, the one thing that most of us can probably agree on is that we are a nation greatly divided, in so many ways. We are divided by geography, by religion, by race, by wealth, by politics, by words, by actions, and by outrage, to name just a few.

Many of us might also agree that, despite these divisions, we should find ways to work together, to find common ground and to thereby make our nation better. The challenge is the world in which we now live. A world of interconnectedness, instant notifications, social media, infotainment instead of information, opinion instead of news, political correctness, and information overload. This environment is perfectly suited to creating and nurturing a culture of outrage.

More often than not, it's people raging *against* something, rather than *for* something. And there is a lot of negativity. This ranting and raving is largely the result of the desire by news media executives to drive ratings and by politicians to use the media as a tool to reach the public. The result is political polarization in our country.

The danger posed by this political polarization is real, and I am concerned about the potential consequences: a population divided, filled with hatred and disgust for one another. A country so filled with hate cannot be sustained long term.

The Curated Lives You See on Social Media Are Not the Real Thing

As our nation grows more racially and ethnically diverse, and as technological innovations lead us to become more interconnected than ever, we are becoming increasingly aware of our differences. Social media allows us to see what everyone is doing, near and far, in real time. However, the posts that we see show only a tiny slice of others' lives. We all pick and choose what we share on social media. The images we create on Facebook and Instagram and Twitter do not reflect our full lives; they are our curated lives, made visible in the way we choose, filters and all. We can't help but compare the filtered versions we present to our friends and to the public with the messy, real lives that we experience. No wonder so many of us feel as if we are constantly falling short.

Social media can give us a sense of interconnectedness and relationship; but it's not the same as a real in-person connection.

Fashion shoots are staged to make all moments seem beautiful and effortless, even when they are not. No one lives in a perfect world or looks perfect all the time, but with the rise of influencers, filters, and selfies, social media can make everyone appear to be living great lives.

We used to be able to escape the world's scrutiny by going into our homes and shutting the door. No longer. Now, when we go home and shut the door, we all too often invite others to join us there by staying connected to social media. Now we are always on stage, our every movement monitored by the technology that surrounds us.

Be honest, how often do you power off your phone and disconnect? Your kids might call, the school might need something, that important e-mail might finally show up. So, for most of us, the world stays with us, 24/7, everywhere we go.

Twenty years ago, teenagers who were bullied at school could regroup and find peace by going home and spending time with their families. Now, the bullies can extend their toxic influence into their victims' homes through social media, texts, e-mails.

The bullies are ever present on the very devices their victims need to do their homework.

Another thing driving us farther apart is our innate sense of what our culture has recently termed "tribalism"—an "us-versus-them" mentality. As things have changed, we've found comfort by allying ourselves with like-minded people. In doing so, we have isolated ourselves from those who don't share our beliefs and opinions. We back ourselves into a corner and rant and rave at the people on the other side, and vent to those who share our views, our "tribe." While this drives up the attention given, it does not lead to solutions.

As debate heats up, everyone feels the need to be heard—and to be right. Instead of seeking space for questioning and learning, people seek to stand their ground, no matter the cost, even if they are wrong. But there's little chance that we will acknowledge being wrong. In this age of instant access to information, everyone thinks they know everything, and therefore, we all believe that we are right. We no longer leave complex issues to the experts. Instead, we all too often assume we know more than the experts.

Finding Our Comfort Zone

As many of us have found comfort zones among like-minded allies at the extremes of life's spectrums, so, too, have politicians, who have also moved farther to each side to attract the votes they need to win their party's nominations. Instead of running on policies, many candidates run on personality, or on identity.

Instead of creating a political climate marked by receptiveness to others' ideas, we have created a political climate that is often hostile and dismissive to anyone who does not share the majority view.

For example, in March 2019, tennis great and human rights champion Martina Navratilova, one of the first openly gay athletes and a tireless champion of LGBTQ rights, publicly raised concerns about how to ensure fair competition for women in sports on her Facebook page. She questioned whether it was fair for transgender women to compete against women who were born female since the former tend to be taller, stronger, and endowed with greater lung capacity—due to the impact of greater levels of testosterone during adolescence on their body's development. The low-end testosterone measurement for men is four times the high-end measurement for women.

After raising those concerns, Navratilova was vilified on social media and was dropped as an ambassador for Athlete Ally, a nonprofit focused on LGBTQ rights and sports.[8]

Displays of incivility and vitriol seem to be increasing every day, and these displays are hastened by the proliferation of social media. Everyone can have an audience, and everyone can find people with whom they agree and egg each other on to more and more dramatic behavior, and they can do it from the comfort of their homes. Additionally, vitriol from bot accounts—not even real people—adds to the noise and confusion.

In 2018, we saw attacks on politicians, people screaming at administration officials in public places, and suspicious packages mailed to well-known politicians just weeks before the midterm elections.

In June, the owner of a restaurant in Virginia decided that White House spokeswoman Sarah Sanders should leave the restaurant because she works for the Trump administration.

That month, Democratic activists screamed at Florida Republican Attorney General Pam Bondi as she was attempting to attend a screening of a documentary about Mister Rogers.

Doesn't sound very neighborly, does it?[9]

"We were in a movie about anti-bullying and practicing peace and love and tolerance and accepting of people for their differences," Bondi told the *Tampa Bay Times*. "That's what Mister Rogers is all about. We all believe in free speech, but there's a big difference there."[10]

In July, the Nebraska Republican Party office in Lincoln had its windows broken by a brick bearing the words "ABOLISH ICE."[11]

Republican Sen. Ted Cruz of Texas, who was with his wife at a restaurant, was harassed by protesters who denounced his support for Kavanaugh during the confirmation hearings. "We believe survivors!" they shouted.

Republican Sens. Lindsey Graham of South Carolina and Mike Lee and Orrin Hatch of Utah had their personal information posted on *Wikipedia*.[12,13]

That same month, Republican congressional candidate Rudy Peters was allegedly attacked in California by a man who was wielding a knife, while yelling derogatory remarks about Republicans.

Also in September, in Laramie, Wyoming, an office of the Republican Party was set on fire. Kellen Sorber pled guilty and was sentenced to three years in prison.[14]

In October, a New York City Republican Party office was vandalized with the words "Our attack is merely a beginning" written on the walls.[15]

The day after the midterm elections, while Fox News commentator Tucker Carlson was at work, members of an antifa (anti-fascism) group calling themselves Smash Racism DC attacked his house in Washington.[16] "I called my wife," he told the *Washington Post*. "She had been in the kitchen alone getting ready to go to dinner and she heard pounding on the front door and screaming. . . .

Someone started throwing himself against the front door and actually cracked the front door."[17]

His wife locked herself in the pantry and called the police; she thought their home was being invaded.[18] The *Washington Post* called the incident a protest, but if a person throws himself against the front door of a person's home with such force that it cracks, doesn't that seem like an attempted home invasion? Many on both sides of the aisle condemned the attack, but not all.

In response to my e-mail expressing sorrow over the attack, Carlson told me that, as a result of what had happened, he had taken a sabbatical from Twitter and was getting off e-mail. He has since rejoined Twitter.

Most of the personal threats come from the left against the right. The attacks are not about policy or about position, but an attack on individuals themselves. Democratic leaders have publicly called for public harassment.

"Tell Them They're Not Welcome Anymore, Anywhere!"

In June 2018, on MSNBC, Rep. Maxine Waters, D-CA, commented about administration officials who were being personally targeted. "I have no sympathy for these people that are in this administration who know it's wrong for what they're doing on so many fronts," she said. "They tend to not want to confront this president or even leave, but they know what they're doing is wrong. I want to tell you, these members of his cabinet who remain and try to defend him, they won't be able to go to a restaurant, they won't be able to stop at a gas station, they're not going to be able to shop at a department store. The people are going to turn on them. They're going to protest. They're absolutely going to harass them until they decide that they're going to tell the president, 'No, I can't hang with you.'"[19]

Waters challenged her supporters to be aggressive: "If you see anybody from that cabinet in a restaurant, in a department store, at a gasoline station, you get out and you create a crowd. You push back on them. Tell them they're not welcome anymore, anywhere!"[20]

Soon afterward, Waters canceled an event after receiving a death threat,[21] and then pushed back that she was calling only for "peaceful protests," not violence, according to the *Huffington Post*.[22]

In September 2018, Democrat Kiah Morris ended her reelection bid and resigned her seat in the Vermont House of Representatives, according to a *New York Times* story by Liam Stack, after "what she described as a yearlong campaign of racially motivated harassment and threats."[23] In today's environment it's a miracle that anyone runs for office. Would you want to?

"When They Go Low, We Kick Them"

In late October 2018, an outspoken conservative, Cesar Altieri Sayoc, Jr., was arrested in connection with pipe bombs that were sent to Democratic leaders and supporters, including former President Barack Obama, 2016 Democratic presidential candidate Hillary Clinton, former Attorney General Eric Holder, Sen. Cory Booker, D-NJ, Sen. Kamala Harris, D-CA, and former CIA Director John Brennan.[24]

They were "not hoax devices," FBI Director Christopher Wray said, according to the *New York Times*.[25] Sayoc pled guilty.[26]

In October, former U.S. Attorney General Eric Holder joined the fray while campaigning in Georgia for Democratic gubernatorial nominee Stacey Abrams. "Michelle [Obama] always says 'When they go low, we go high,'" he told Abrams's supporters, according to the *Washington Times.* "No. No. When they go low, we kick them."[27]

These horrible examples illustrate the essential point—that we are losing our civility. It's okay to have a difference of opinion, and it's fine to argue your perspective with passion, but it's not acceptable to physically attack those who do not agree with you, no matter how outrageous their perspectives might seem, nor to incite others to attack. Violence toward those with whom you disagree is not part of the social contract of a civil society. Nor is it helpful to label anyone who disagrees with you as a bad person for having a different opinion.

So what, exactly, is driving the division? Why now? And why at such a heated pitch? In part, because both parties have moved away from the center of political ideology, and there exists a wider gap in their beliefs. According to the Pew Research Center, "In 1994, fewer than twenty percent in both parties viewed the opposing party very unfavorably."

That has changed dramatically. In 2017, Pew found that this number had more than doubled for both sides, with 44 percent on the Democratic side and 45 percent on the Republican side viewing the other as very unfavorably.[28] Think about the result of this drastic change. In 1994, if you walked into a room filled with ten people from the other political party, only two would dislike you instantly for belonging to another party. This is a relatively small minority. Today, if you walked into the same room, almost half would instantly view you unfavorably—just because you belonged to the opposite political party—even though you had never met!

But we can't blame just the greater gaps between our political beliefs for the increasing dislike we feel. The dramatic change in the way we get our news also bears some responsibility. The news media have transitioned from delivering news through relatively dry, nightly, half-hour programs to delivering it in unending fashion through 24-hour channels that focus more on opinion than on news.

At the same time, technology has increased the ways we can consume information. Gone are the days when our choices were limited to radio, TV, or newspapers, and here to stay are the days of radio, TV, newspapers, tablets, computers, phones, apps, websites, social media, push notifications, blogs, vlogs, livestreams, and more. You get my point.

We've also significantly broadened the physical areas where news and opinion can be consumed. We now find screens in elevators, airports, cabs, and even gas stations. Meanwhile, phones, tablets, and computers can connect in most places with Wi-Fi or cellular technology. Add to that the rise in popularity of smart watches, and news stories are just a glance away at any given moment, even while watching a movie or talking with your doctor. On top of these changes, the creation and rapid spread of social media have changed the ways in which we receive and respond to information.

Much else has also changed in the last thirty years. We have moved from being a society that embraced immigrants as a valued and essential part of the fabric of our nation to one that is wrestling with immigration and assimilation. Most Americans favor legal immigration. While most Republicans are for border security and legal immigration, many on the left have twisted this stance to be anti-immigrant, or racist—which for the majority of Republicans, it is not. On the far left are those like Stacey Abrams who want illegal immigrants to be treated the same as citizens. During her unsuccessful gubernatorial campaign, Abrams's website reflected her desire to represent everyone in her state, not just those who were there legally.

"I want to be clear: I do mean everyone who resides in our

state . . . new Americans, naturalized citizens, and all those on the long, arduous path toward citizenship,"[29] she wrote on her campaign website in 2018. In other words, Abrams—who narrowly lost her bid for the job—wanted to represent everyone living in Georgia—even those who broke the law to get there.

This is a long, long way from the American tradition of welcoming legal immigrants who then became part of our "melting pot" society.

The idea of America as a melting pot was once central to our cultural identity. Since the early days of America, when New York City was founded by people from multiple backgrounds focused on commerce and not a specific heritage, the idea of multiculturalism—which celebrates the simultaneous coexistence of multiple cultures within a society—has spread throughout our nation. The initial concept of celebrating a culture has sometimes morphed into identifying with the culture above all else.

Looking for a Common, Shared Culture

But that identification with a particular culture has drawbacks: It often creates an environment where there is no common, shared culture. And it is not easy to create an environment that promotes a shared culture, now that town squares across the nation have been replaced by Amazon and Walmart and religion is declining.[30] As people identify with groups that decry their "victimization," and as those groups segment and multiply, individuals can wind up belonging to multiple groups that perceive themselves to be victims. Once established, they may continue to identify themselves as victims permanently. Everything is seen as oppression, regardless of whether that was the intention.

For decades, our country has provided a safety net to help those who need assistance. Initially, it was for a very limited

percent of the population. But government spending on welfare for our citizens has grown dramatically during the last fifty
years. A report released by the Congressional Budget Office in
March 2018 found that the bottom 40 percent of the nation's
households in terms of income received some type of tax benefit
or income transfer payment from the government.[31]

Taxpayers foot the bill for all the payments, in some way,
shape, or form, either through taxes paid or money borrowed by
the government to fund the transfers. These payments include
unemployment benefits, money for food (through programs
such as SNAP, the Supplemental Nutrition Assistance Program),
money for medical care (through programs such as Medicaid),
and many other programs.

According to John F. Cogan, author of *The High Cost of Good
Intentions*, roughly 180 million people (55 percent) of the U.S.
population receives government assistance of some sort (not
including tax breaks).[32] In total, "the $2.4 trillion the federal
government currently spends on entitlements equals $7,500 for
every man, woman, and child living in the United States, an
amount that is five times the money necessary to lift every poor
person out of poverty."[33]

We are no longer helping people, giving them a hand up. We
are providing a way to live, a way of life. What's worse is that for
decades we've been spending trillions of dollars without a positive outcome.

Instead of praising the process of providing cash assistance,
we need to look at whether we are achieving our goals. What do
we want? How about we work toward creating a country where
fewer Americans are living in poverty, where we have greater
income mobility and greater opportunity so that fewer children
are born into poverty? Just look around and ask yourself if what

we have been doing is working. If your answer is no, then why would we think that doing more of the same will yield different results?

Historically, we have been a society that reflected our faith through acts of good works. Even in American movies, charity work has often been depicted as a part of civic duty.

But acts of hard work, charity, helping family and community have waned as we have moved from being personally virtuous to being people who signal their virtue through postings on social media. This shift makes good works no longer about those in need, but about those who need to be recognized as doing "good."

Tribalization Is Growing

As our news, technology, and society have changed, we have become more segmented and tribal, less willing to reach out to others who might be different, and more likely to instead label an entire group as "bad" or "evil" in an effort to make ourselves feel more virtuous. This is anti-individual and is anathema to our foundational values as a nation. Since the passage of the Civil Rights Act of 1964, discrimination on the basis of race, color, religion, or national origin has been illegal. It is also incorrect to prejudge another group, any group, even if they do not have a history of being discriminated against.

In their attempt to end discrimination, the political left has embraced political correctness and victimization. This has led to a culture that has no patience for differing opinions. Instead, if you disagree, then you are labeled as wrong and bad. This extreme form of political correctness has led to expressions of outrage against people with opinions that are different. Regardless of our Constitution's promise of freedom of speech, many today feel their right to free speech is chilled by the threat that comes with the outrage that they know they will have to endure if they simply express an opinion.

What could happen? If the political polarization and accompanying ranting and raving become all-engrossing, there arises a very real possibility of incivility escalating to violence, and of that violence leading to another civil war.

American Exceptionalism

Our country is exceptional, not because our citizens are exceptional, but because our government was structured in an exceptional way. Our Declaration of Independence states that "We hold these truths to be self-evident, that all men are created equal, that they are endowed by their Creator with certain unalienable rights, that among these are life, liberty and the pursuit of happiness.—That to secure these rights, governments are instituted among men, deriving their just powers from the consent of the governed..."[34]

This is important and unique to our country as it acknowledges that fundamental human rights are granted solely by God.

First, all men are created equal by God. We all have equal value at birth; we are each the same. What it does not promise is that we will live or end up equal, regardless of the decisions we make or the work we undertake. We begin, not end, as equals. We have God-given rights and talents, but we each get to decide how to use them—and whether to use them, or not.

According to the American model, our Creator—not the government—gives rights to people. These rights are life, liberty, and not the guarantee—but the pursuit of happiness. The people receive their power from God and then loan power to the government. This means we have control over how much power the government holds. It holds only as much power as we the people are willing to yield.

This is vastly different from what happens in other forms of government, where the ruler holds the power and loans it to the people. That was the system (monarchy) that held sway in this country prior to the American Revolution. For our Founding Fathers to not only break from the English government but also to create an entirely new structure of government is what makes our country exceptional.

Communist and socialist governments are not based on the belief that their citizens have unalienable rights, given to them by God. Instead, they are based on the belief that the state has all the rights and can control citizens as its leaders wish. For example, China, the largest country in the world with 18 percent of the population, enumerates in its constitution that the government is controlled under the leadership of the Communist Party. This same basic structure was what led us to break off from Britain, because the king held the power, which he then loaned to the people. And we didn't like that.

Finally, our Declaration of Independence specifically states that each person has the right to pursue their happiness—whatever that might mean; they don't have to apply to a Bureau of Happiness or agree with what any given state's definition of happiness might be at any given time. It's the individual's happiness that matters.

Many on the far left reject the notion that we are an exceptional country, asserting instead that we are like all other countries. Perhaps even you may be thinking, "Maybe we were created differently as a country, but that was a long time ago."

But that way of thinking ignores the fact that many millions of people over hundreds of years have left their countries of birth and have made long, often difficult journeys to this country in hopes of finding a better life. They understand what we should appreciate—that our government is structured differently, that it is exceptional, and for this we should be grateful.

Our Constitution is also exceptional. At its core is the belief in the liberty of the individual, reflecting the Declaration of Independence's view that we the people loan our God-given power to the government. It balances the large states against the small states, limits the amount of control given to the federal government, and creates a framework to prevent control by the majority over the minority, all while securing the rights of the citizens.

The United States Constitution begins as a declaration from the nation's citizens, not from the government; the people are the ones in control. "We the People of the United States, in Order to form a more perfect Union, establish Justice, insure domestic Tranquility, provide for the common defense, promote the general Welfare, and secure the Blessings of Liberty to ourselves and our Posterity, do ordain and establish this Constitution for the United States of America."[35]

The Constitution provided the framework of our government, creating the three branches of government, the executive, legislative, and judicial. The legislative branch is then further divided between two chambers, the House of Representatives and the Senate, each with different timing, structure, and powers.

This was done because the Founding Fathers knew that it was one thing to create a new government, but it would be another matter to protect the government. James Madison wrote in Federalist Paper No. 51, "In framing a government which is to be administered by men over men, the great difficulty lies in this: You must first enable the government to control the governed; and in the next place oblige it to control itself. A dependence on the people is, no doubt, the primary control on the government; but experience has taught mankind the necessity of auxiliary precautions."[36]

This structure is not made to be efficient or fast, but to provide checks and balances among the various branches. The ultimate intention is to guard against a single person taking control of the country. It's important to remember that our founders were reacting to, and attempting to prevent, the establishment of a monarchy similar to the one they had escaped in England.

Spending bills start in the House of Representatives, both the House and the Senate have to agree on any given bill before sending it to the president to sign into law, and additionally, provisions were made to ensure that if a bill was vetoed by the president, the legislature could overrule the veto with a two-thirds majority vote.

Also included in the Constitution was the ability of the legislature to remove the president or vice president from office through impeachment proceedings, where the House would pass the charge, and the Senate would try the case. The justices of the U.S. Supreme Court were to be appointed for life—thereby insulating them from day-to-day political winds.

The Constitution was adopted with the understanding that it could be changed through an amendment process; the first ten amendments became the Bill of Rights, which clarified the rights of citizens. After declaring their independence and fighting for their liberty and freedom, the leaders of our young country wanted to guard the rights of future citizens, too. These amendments include freedom of religion and speech, the right to bear arms, freedom from quartering soldiers, protection from unreasonable search and seizure, due process, speedy trial, trial by jury, no cruel or unusual punishment, and for all rights not specifically given to the federal government to reside with the states.[37]

The overall construct of our nation is that of a representative democracy. Citizens vote for their representatives, who then pass legislation that the president signs into law. Historically, our country has been the most innovative and active in the modern world. We helped win both World Wars, and we defeated the Soviet Union in the Cold War without going to war at all. We were the first to put a man on the moon, and we serve as the home base for many of the world's most innovative companies, including Disney, Apple, and Google.

But most telling of all is the undebatable fact that our country is and has long been the world's top destination for immigrants. More people come here than go to any other country in the world.[38] We are truly still an exceptional nation, at least to those people who are looking for a new place to live.

Options

If you've read this chapter and still don't believe that our country is constructed in a way that is better—or at least different—than others, well, that's your prerogative. I suggest that you move to a country that you think is better and reevaluate that belief in a few years.

If you can't move due to family, employment, or financial circumstances, then I challenge you to think of the millions of immigrants who have risked, and often lost, their lives so that they could have the chance to live in this great country. Perhaps they are on to something, and maybe they even know a few things that you don't.

If you agree with me that our country is exceptional and different and believe that it is worth saving, I would like to present you with two options:

1. Sit back and hope that someone else saves America.
2. Decide that our great country is worth the effort and become a more active and engaged citizen—with the intent of making our country better.

As a nation, we are at a crossroads. We have a choice: We can continue on this course of ranting and raving or we can learn how to engage with gratefulness for our incredible country and build on our strengths together, respecting each other—even when our opinions differ.

Members of the far left are willing to let anyone into our country—legally or illegally—and don't understand why assimilation makes sense. Instead, their focus seems to be on diluting and diminishing the very ideas and structures that make our country exceptional.

There is also a core disagreement between the left and the right regarding economics and government control. The left wants to provide economic security for all through government control. The right understands that the only way to control the economy is to control the people who make up the economy and that that has only one outcome—totalitarianism. Instead, the right focuses on ensuring individual freedoms and supporting initiative. That focus has, for generations, helped push our country forward.

The time has come to stop ranting and raving. To decide that the great divide in our nation needs fixing. If we don't, the results will be catastrophic. I know we can do better, and for the sake of our children, we must.

So how can we stop ranting and raving? How can we come together when both sides are poised at every moment to be nasty and polarizing toward one another? I strongly believe that we should be able to have differing opinions, yet still have understanding and respect for one another.

However, when we make it personal, we often lose the ability to argue our points effectively. Worse yet, personal attacks typically lead the person being attacked to shut down—immediately. The same result holds true when those attacks occur outside of the public eye—in private conversation. That's because people are no longer attacking the issue; they're attacking the other's identity.

Championing Free Speech

What's most important is that we hear and truly listen to others—not that we agree with them. It's also important that we speak up—respectfully, but forcefully—when we disagree. If those who disagree are silent, then their perspective cannot be understood. Here's the problem: If one side can silence the other for sharing ideas they disagree with, then it's very possible that, in time, the other side will turn against and silence those with whom they do not agree. Those who suppress free speech risk having their own free speech silenced as well, possibly at a later time.

Things have to change. Together, we can stop ranting and raving and save our nation.

For our democratic system to work, we need two vibrant parties. There are ways for people with differing opinions to govern our country while retaining respect for the rule of law and for one another. This ability to agree to disagree, but to work together civilly, will help us more forward as a country and make changes that benefit our entire nation.

We should be grateful we have a two-party system.

But to make the changes we need, we have to stop living in the cauldron of seething, ongoing outrage in which we currently find ourselves. If we don't, the political polarization that we see around us now will have long-lasting and potentially disastrous results. Instead, let's challenge ourselves to reach out, not over Twitter or Facebook, but in our communities, to one another; not to point fingers and blame, but to join hands and help. If you're active in communities that exist on social media, that's okay, too. But it is not enough. My point is that we need to take those relationships off the screen and into our streets, churches, and homes. Social media can be a great way to connect, but it is essential to remember that those connections must extend beyond the screen to foster true understanding.

Our most inspirational leaders, throughout our history, have believed and communicated that our future was bright, that our foundation was different, and that the American people would rise to whatever challenges we might encounter. I believe that they are right, and I hope you do, too. I just need your help. Together we can stop ranting and raving and save our country from the dangers of political polarization.

CHAPTER 2

The Death of News

Introduction

Let's set the scene. It's a Wednesday night in 1938. You, your parents, and your three siblings sit down together in the dining room and share a home-cooked meal. Afterward, you and your siblings gather the dishes from the table and take them into the kitchen to wash, dry, and put them away. You finish just in time to join your parents in the living room to listen to the eight o'clock radio show, *One Man's Family*. You settle next to your mother's feet as the show begins.

"*One Man's Family* is dedicated to the mothers and fathers of the younger generation and to their bewildering offspring,"[1] the dulcet-toned host proclaims over organ music. You rest your head on your mother's legs as she rubs your hair. Yours is but one of thousands of families who are listening to the NBC program at the exact same time.

The next day, as you go to school and your parents go to work, you run into friends who've had the same experience—at the same time. Those who missed the program will have to talk with others to catch up or try to figure out what they missed by listening to the next episode.

Fast forward to 2019. You and your siblings have after-school sports, attend a tutoring session, and arrive home at 7 p.m. Your mother and father arrive from work around the same time, and you sit down to eat take-out food. Once you're done with your meal, you toss the cartons into the trash and your parents pick up their laptops to get back to work. You go into your bedroom and watch a Netflix show, then take a bath. Later, while you finish your homework, you FaceTime with your best friend on your laptop.

The next morning, you listen to music as you get dressed, check your GroupMe for any updates on your civics project, and get news notifications from your BuzzFeed app. When your parents arrive at work, they avoid political talk. They know from experience that they watch Fox News and their co-workers watch MSNBC or CNN. There are no shared experiences.

How did we get here? How did we go from sharing a limited number of cultural experiences and stories to experiencing life in polarized, isolated media bubbles? When you think about the span of human history, and even the relatively short history of our country, eighty-one years isn't much time, and yet it is long enough to have seen seismic cultural shifts, particularly in the way that we consume news and other forms of media.

News: From Once a Day to All Day

In the early 1900s, daily newspapers were the primary source of news for most Americans. The national and international news was transmitted via telegraph and printed by each local newspaper. The local publisher determined what to print and how to present it. Papers were then distributed each morning to homes and local stores.

Some newspapers published the stories they got from wire services unchanged; others added their editorial viewpoints before distributing them to the end users, aka the American public. This model of news dissemination persisted for decades, until a new technology arrived that changed everything.

The radio revolutionized the relationship between the news and those receiving the news. Information could be broadcast quickly, directly to the listener. However, the broadcaster still had the ability to determine what news to cover and how to cover it. There was still a significant editorial process that determined what news was reported on the air.

The household radio grew rapidly in popularity. By 1930, radios could be found in 40 percent of households; in just ten years, it had doubled to 80 percent of households, while 90 percent of the population had access to a radio, even if they didn't have one at home. Radios tended to be bulky and wooden, more furniture than appliance. Many families took great pride in their radios and made them the center of their living room.[2]

According to the PBS series *History Detectives*, the rapid adoption of radio technology and the resulting ability for the majority of the country to hear the same news, information, and programming, "provided a source of inspiration, with heroes like the Lone Ranger and The Shadow getting embroiled in deadly capers."[3]

But the impact of radio programs went beyond that: "They also promoted old-fashioned American family values and gave people a model to live by."[4]

Most important, radio allowed for rapid dissemination of the news. No longer did the news travel to town by telegraph and get reprinted and reinterpreted by the local newspaper. With the advent of radio, the news was communicated directly to the people by announcers. Reporters could be on the scene of a story, reporting as it occurred. "When the Hindenburg airship exploded in 1937, reporter Herb Morrison was on the scene, recording the events to be broadcast the following day."[5]

The rapid change in radio technology and adoption did not affect just news reports and cultural stories. Political communication also changed rapidly. When President Franklin D. Roosevelt took office in 1933, he reached out directly through radio addresses to the American people through his fireside chats. The first chat was broadcast March 12, 1933, and focused on a banking crisis that had led some banks to close. President Roosevelt used the chat to educate the American people on how our banking system worked, as well as to explain his decision about implementing a nationwide banking "holiday," which gave the Federal Reserve time to issue additional currency "and to enable the government to make common-sense checkups."[6]

Throughout his presidency, President Roosevelt used fireside chats to connect directly with the American people. This allowed him to convey his message directly, untainted by the editorializing of newspaper writers and editors. The fireside chats began as twice-a-year events but became more frequent after 1942, when the United States entered World War II.[7]

President Roosevelt's predecessor, President Herbert Hoover, also used the medium of radio. However, Hoover approached his radio addresses as traditional political speeches. He was much more formal in tone and connected less strongly with his audience.

Fireside "Chats" Were Highly Scripted

Though "chat" implies speaking in a friendly and informal way, President Roosevelt wasn't improvising with his fireside chats. These were highly scripted and the words carefully chosen, produced to convey information in a certain way. However, his delivery made the difference. Roosevelt's warm voice, natural inflection, use of common words, and slow rate of speech made it easy for listeners to connect to him as a person, rather than as a politician.[8]

Many journalists didn't appreciate Roosevelt's use of radio as a direct channel to the people. (Similar to President Trump's use of Twitter.) These journalists preferred to be the public's conduit for information, a role they viewed as both their livelihood and their duty; they wanted to maintain control of the news. After President Roosevelt talked to Prime Minister Winston Churchill, a reporter asked Roosevelt if he would talk about his discussions with Churchill during his fireside chats. "It's up to you fellows," Roosevelt replied. "If you fellows give the country an exceedingly correct picture, I won't go on the radio."[9]

For much of the next two decades, politicians used radio as their primary way of communicating to the nation. However, as television grew in popularity in the 1950s and 1960s, it introduced a new variable into the mix: No longer did it suffice for politicians to speak clearly; now they needed to worry about how they looked, too.

For older, more experienced, established candidates who were accustomed to being heard, but not seen, the results sometimes proved catastrophic.

On June 26, 1960, the first televised presidential debate was held between the Republican nominee, Vice President Richard Nixon, and the Democratic nominee, Sen. John F. Kennedy of Massachusetts.

Before the debate, Nixon was polling slightly ahead of Kennedy, according to Gallup. After the debate, the polls swung 4 points, with Kennedy ahead of Nixon. Kennedy won the election.[10]

Both candidates were accustomed to radio and print media

debate coverage, which summarized and highlighted key elements. That all changed when TV entered the picture. Now candidates had to worry about how they looked as well as what they said and how they sounded.

"I Think My Husband Was Brilliant"

Going forward, the visuals of the two candidates on camera would make a significant difference to the television audience outside the debate hall. Kennedy was forty-three, tan and well-rested, having taken time off from traveling before the debate. Nixon was forty-seven and had just returned from campaigning across the country. He had recently been hospitalized for a knee injury and had lost twenty pounds; he appeared gaunt and weak.[11]

Kennedy's dark suit contrasted with the background, while Nixon's lighter suit blended with the background, so much so that he seemed to fade away. Kennedy looked straight at the camera while answering questions, which made those watching the debate at home feel as if he was talking directly to them. In contrast, Nixon looked back and forth between the reporters—who were often not on camera—which resulted in him looking shifty-eyed to the viewers at home.[12]

The contrast between the two men could not have been more dramatic. In addition, Kennedy's wife, Jacqueline, was pregnant with their second child and was hosting "a debate-watching party at the family's summer home in Hyannis Port, Massachusetts. Newspapers fawned over every last detail, from Jackie's fashionable maternity wear and distinguished guest list, to her living room furnishings and choice of refreshments. When the first debate ended," according to History.com, "the future first lady reportedly concluded, 'I think my husband was brilliant.'

Meanwhile, Nixon's mother immediately called her son to ask if he was ill."[13]

The 1960 race ended with Kennedy elected president of the United States of America and television, for the first time, assuming a major role in campaigns. Since then, that role has grown. It is not only television appearances and debates that make a difference; television commercials have been a key component of campaign strategy for over half a century.

In recent presidential races, after a televised debate, the candidates or their surrogates would enter the "spin room," a large area designated for members of the press corps to ask questions of each of the campaign representatives. Depending on the performance of the candidate, the ranking in the polls, and the subject of the day, reporters would swarm to ask questions, and the responses would be captured for television. The goal of every camp would be to highlight their wins and mitigate their losses. Sometimes the candidates would walk in and participate; at other times that job would be left to staff.

One Debate Slip Can Doom a Campaign

Less than a decade ago, a bad debate performance could sink a candidate. In the 2012 Republican presidential primary, during the November 9, 2011, debate in Michigan, Texas Governor Rick Perry made a mistake that would doom his bid for the nomination. He was asked what three cabinet-level departments he would eliminate. The question should have been a "gimmee," since he had made the pledge earlier.

But Perry stumbled over his answer, saying, "And I will tell you, it is three agencies of government when I get there that are gone. Commerce, Education, and the . . . what's the third one there? Let's see."

Perry paused. Rep. Ron Paul, R-TX, spoke up. "You need five."

Perry responded, "Oh, five, OK. So, Commerce, Education, and the…"[14] His voice trailed off again. His failure to remember the third agency proved to be a moment that the public would not soon forget. That moment became a sound-bite that the news media played on a loop. His campaign never recovered, and he pulled out of the race on January 21, 2012, two days before the South Carolina primary.

The 2016 presidential election included twelve Republican primary presidential debates and nine forums. The Democratic primary included ten debates and thirteen forums. Throughout the primary process, the number of participants in each of the events dwindled. The candidates were given podium placement based on their ranking in the polls, and the front runners normally received the most questions and airtime. The public watched, tweeted, and then stayed tuned for pundits on various channels to weigh in after the event.

Republican candidate Donald Trump used his media training as a reality TV star to his advantage, holding hundreds of rallies during his campaign as a way to connect with voters, draw attention, and get out his message directly to the people. These rallies were given wall-to-wall coverage from television, especially CNN. From Trump's perspective, it was free nationwide advertising.

President Trump also uses Twitter as a way to make breaking news announcements and connect directly with the American people. Instead of newspapers receiving his administration's press releases and then determining which to print and within what context, we now have a system where the president, and anyone else with access to a smartphone, can tweet to the entire world, 24 hours a day. We live in a never-ending cycle of information, some of it news, some of it not.

In the middle of the twentieth century, American families moved their wood-cabinet radios out of the center of their living rooms and replaced them with wood-cabinet televisions. In the beginning of the era of television dominance, broadcast channels reigned. The programming you received was determined by the airwaves that your television could pick up on your rabbit-eared antennae. Just imagine, instead of a 24-hour news world, you had a television that stopped broadcasting programs altogether at the end of the day (a few of you reading this may even remember that era, probably fondly). With nothing else to do but read, or listen to the radio, you had little to get in the way of real sleep.

The daytime shows on early broadcast television included soap operas (sponsored by soap companies that were targeting the largely female audiences, hence the name), entertainment shows, and fifteen-minute nightly news programs at dinnertime. The news shows were predominantly delivered straight-to-camera by a white male anchor with little commentary.

After the broadcast of *The Tonight Show Starring Johnny Carson*, or a late-night movie, the station would broadcast a short announcement, often a patriotic song, signaling the end of its broadcast day. As a child living in rural Georgia, I can remember seeing a picture of a United States flag waving before the station signed off. Afterward, it would show a static picture, a test pattern.

When the transmission signal ended, viewers were left with a random dot pixel pattern of static called "snow."

For many years, television news was not expected to make a profit, and it didn't. That all changed in 1968, when CBS launched *60 Minutes*, which became tremendously popular and tremendously profitable.

While it was good for shareholders that the news programming was profitable, it also meant that the owners now faced a new challenge—increasing profit. And what drove profit? Programming that grabbed viewers' attention.

Twenty years later, CBS News launched *48 Hours*, another newsmagazine that was briefly renamed *48 Hours Investigates* and is now called *48 Hours Mystery*. Given a chance in a new time slot, the producer ran a story about spring break. It used sex, beer, and bikinis to draw viewers and, by extension, advertising dollars.[15] By this time, due to the pressure of ratings and making money, news shows were being driven more by opinion and sensation than by facts.

CNN First in 24-Hour News

The next phase of television was 24-hour cable news. CNN began airing on June 1, 1980. Led by media mogul Ted Turner, it changed the world of televised news from a 30-minute, once-a-day program into a 24-hour news cycle. Televisions no longer went dark overnight, since there was money to be made then, too. With extra time to fill, producers needed more content. Programs were recycled and replayed, but even that did not fill the vast void posed by a 24-hour commitment.

And news was about to expand beyond fixed televisions. Just three years after the start of CNN, the first commercial cellular call was made, from Soldier Field in Chicago. Although it would take decades to build out the now-ubiquitous, nationwide network we know today, one that can also handle data, this initial call provided a glimpse of the future. This innovation would lead to great convenience, but would also result in our current culture of constant connectivity. Luckily, we had a few decades before it came to fruition. In the meantime, television was rapidly changing.

I remember traveling to Helsinki, Finland, during the summer of 1989 to meet with a client. When I got to my hotel room,

I turned on the television and was thrilled to see CNN Headline News. No matter where I was, I could get news 24 hours a day. At this point, I still needed a television set to receive the program—but that was soon to change as well.

In 1984, when the Federal Communications Commission (FCC) relaxed rules regarding product commercials, infomercials began to fill the overnight airtime slots, with some channels being dedicated solely to infomercials. One of them, the QVC (Quality, Value, Convenience) Channel, was founded in 1986 and now reaches 350 million households nationwide.

By 1995, fifteen years after the founding of CNN, "there were 139 cable programming services available nationwide, in addition to many regional programming networks. By the spring of 1998, the number of national cable video networks had grown to 171."[16] Shows were often repeated multiple times during the day and overnight in an effort to fill time and save the money it would have cost to produce fresh stories.

I began working for Sterling Cellular in 1993. It was a startup wireless company that focused on rural service areas. The phones we sold were often installed or mounted in a car by a technician. There were also bag phones, which fitted into a briefcase. They were heavy and clunky. Relatively simple, hand-held phones were available, but they were not particularly useful in rural areas, where coverage tended to be sparse.

During the early to mid-1990s, cellular coverage was not ubiquitous and not all carriers allowed other carriers' customers to use their network when traveling. If they did allow them to "roam" on their network, the cost was high. There were no smartphones, and most businesspeople (including me) wore pagers in addition to carrying cell phones. Cell phones then could not receive news or information via data but were used instead simply to connect to others through voice communications.

The data wireless world in the mid 1990s was dominated by BlackBerry. During the 1990s, wireless networks transitioned from analog technology to digital technology, which paved the way for more and more data to be transmitted at lower and lower costs. As the networks grew and became faster, the transition from the cumbersome car phone to the sleek iPhone and its ilk became only a matter of time.

In 2007, Apple introduced the first iPhone, announcing it in January and beginning sales in June in the United States. This new technology quickly revolutionized the way people interacted with their communication devices. I still ask my husband if he knows where I left my "phone," but the device I can't find can do so much more than make a call.

Always-Connected Culture Has Given Rise to More Ranting and Raving

As mobile devices became easier to use, and the wireless networks expanded both their coverage and data capacity, the potential applications of this technology grew exponentially. Today, smartphones include calendars, e-mails, text, applications, and streaming video and video calls. It's the dramatic innovation and adoption of the mobile phone and the network that has created the connected culture that has given rise to the phenomenon of ranting and raving that threatens us today.

It's no longer communication that drives mobile traffic; it's real-time entertainment. We don't merely have mobile telephones in our hands; we have miniature computers that connect wirelessly to the Internet almost everywhere we go. This always-on, always-connected mobile device provides the platform that social media networks use today. With 98 percent of the United States population covered by a wireless network, according to Verizon,[17] and 95 percent of the population owning a wireless phone, according to Pew Research (77 percent using a smartphone),[18] the result is almost total, immediate connection constantly.

Children have also been affected by the communications revolution—they are getting access to cell phone technology earlier and earlier. According to Nielsen, 45 percent of the ten-to twelve-year-olds[19] in the United States have a smartphone, and all the information and constant connection that come with it. It's not unusual to see a child in a stroller using an iPad or a smartphone.

It seems clear that mobile technology is here to stay and will become more and more integrated into our lives and the lives of our children. This is important to remember as we consider how news is disseminated, who controls that dissemination, and how we connect with those who share, or disagree with, our beliefs. The ubiquity of mobile access cannot be ignored when discussing the proliferation of sources of news and how we distinguish fact from fiction.

With the proliferation of distribution channels of news and information, from print to radio to broadcast television to cable, and the rapid adoption of the Internet and social media around the world, there is now a multitude of ways to get news and information. Some Americans still tune in to local or national radio stations while driving, others watch TV, while some now rely on friends to share information about world events with them via social media.

Ratings Matter

With a greater number of distribution channels for news, the battle for viewers has grown among the channels of distribution. Ratings matter, because ratings drive advertising revenue, and advertising revenue drives overall revenue and profit. As competition for viewers increases, the incentive for news channels is to focus more on grabbing attention (and the advertising dollars that come with that attention) than on delivering hard, accurate news.

As a result, TV news has become more personality based, relying for ratings as much, if not more, on the "talent" who is delivering the news, and less on the facts that are being presented. Imagine the contrast between a 1940s-era, 15-minute radio news program on CBS anchored by Douglas Edwards and broadcast at 7:30 p.m. ET and the sometimes hours-long presentations at any time on any of the 24-hour cable news channels.

Most listeners in the forties had no idea what Edwards looked like, and I would guess they couldn't imagine that his appearance would have any bearing on his ability to deliver the news clearly each evening.

Contrast that with the 24-hour news cycle of the twenty-first century and the elaborate hair, wardrobe, and makeup required of every on-air TV news personality, regardless of gender.

Despite the drive toward infotainment and the never-ending ratings battles, traditional media is trusted twice as much as social media. According to the Knight Foundation, "Americans believe that 39 percent of the news they see on television, read in newspapers or hear on the radio is misinformation. They estimate that nearly two-thirds of the news they get from social media is misinformation."[20]

Then there is the challenge of getting the facts right, which is not to be underestimated. For example, in June 2018, *Time* magazine depicted President Trump on its cover next to a little girl crying. The title: "Welcome to America." This was an attempt to highlight immigrants being detained away from their families.[21]

On June 16, 2018, the New York *Daily News* ran the same picture and the title "Callous. Soulless. Craven. Trump."[22]

But when reporters dug into the story behind the image, they discovered that the girl, Yanela, was with her mother. Both had been detained in Texas. They had not been separated.[23]

"The *Washington Post* reported that the mother, Sandra Sanchez, had been deported in 2013 to Honduras," wrote Daniel Bates and Karen Ruiz for the *Daily Mail*. "Her husband told the Post that she left without telling him she was taking Yanela with her and he couldn't contact her. But then he saw the picture on the news."[24]

The damage was done. "Callous. Soulless. Craven. Trump."[25] The *Time* magazine cover could have been titled "Mother kidnaps child and flees to foreign country without telling husband." At least that headline would have been accurate.

A month before this story ran, social media blew up over a picture of a child in a cage. The implication was that the child was caged in a detention center. It turned out the child was the son of a protester and had been put in the cage as part of a demonstration; he was not being held in a cage against his will—he was put there by his father for a photo-op.[26]

Jose Antonio Vargas, a writer and illegal immigrant who lives in California, shared the picture on Twitter with the note, "This is what happens when a government believes people are 'illegal.'"[27] The tweet has garnered tens of thousands of retweets and likes.

Other stories shared on social media included pictures of a bus with child safety seats in place of adult seats. Supposedly the bus had been used by the Trump administration. Not true—the picture was originally from April 2016, during Obama's administration. According to the Geo Group, the company that made the buses, they were delivered in early 2016 and were outfitted with child safety seats "equipped with a DVD system with four drop down screens to provide entertainment to the children with onboard movies during transport missions."[28]

The reason that the false news and inflammatory images work is that confirmation bias is natural to humans. We take in information and then attempt to make it fit something we already believe and understand; we search for facts to support what we already believe to be true.

Don't like Trump; see a picture of a child crying behind her mother; assume it's Trump's fault. Don't like Trump; see a picture of a child who appears to be in a cage; assume it's Trump's fault.

Don't like Trump; see a picture of a bus outfitted with children's seats; assume it's the handiwork of Trump's administration.

All three assumptions are wrong.

Trust in the Media Has Eroded

Trust in U.S. news media reached a high point in 1976, after Watergate. According to a Gallup poll, 72 percent of U.S. adults said then that they had a great deal or fair amount of trust in the media.[29] In 2016, Gallup reported the lowest confidence in the media ever, with only 32 percent of adults saying they had a great deal or fair amount of trust in the media. The trust level moved up to 45 percent in September 2018. Of the remaining 55 percent, 30 percent said they did not have very much trust and 24 percent said they had no trust at all in the media.[30]

Trust in media has fallen by half since 1979, with less than a quarter in 2018 reporting they have a great deal or quite a lot of trust in newspapers.[31]

Trust in television news was even lower, according to Gallup research, with 23 percent saying they trust television a great deal or quite a lot and 45 percent saying they have no or very little trust in television. News from the Internet is trusted the least, with 16 percent of adults saying they had a great deal or quite a lot of trust in its accuracy and 47 percent saying that they had no trust or very little trust in its accuracy.[32]

More than half, 60 percent, said news organizations are often inaccurate. And overall, people believed that news organizations are biased. Forty-three percent of respondents believed they were biased toward Democrats, and 13 percent believed they were biased toward Republicans.[33]

While most adults in the United States appear to have lost trust in the news media, most of those same individuals said that that trust can be regained. The lack of trust was due to a lack of accuracy in reporting and bias, they said.[34]

If you're an average American, you're probably focused on your job, your family, your friends, and your community. You have bills to pay, clothes to wash, and groceries to buy. When you get home from work, you're tired and want to relax. Maybe you have a spouse, children, and are taking care of aging parents. You are overwhelmed and the last thing you have the time and energy to do after getting home, grocery shopping, and making dinner is to sort through all of the different channels of information and try to discern which one is correct.

Instead, you may turn the television on to watch a reality show or some other form of entertainment, or maybe you choose the news. When you do catch the news, it's one side blaming and vilifying the other. You don't know whom to trust, so you trust no one. When you go on Facebook to catch up with your friends, you often see reposts of stories or videos, maybe you read or watch them, or maybe you just ignore them.

Whom to Trust?

It's not just the accuracy and trust that is an issue. According to different Gallup research, most people (58 percent) believe that the increase in information channels makes it more difficult to be well-informed.[35] There are more channels to sort through, and you're now tasked with having to weed through bias as well. However, this varies by political ideology. "Less than half of Democrats (47 percent) say the increase in available information makes staying well-informed harder, whereas clear majorities of Republicans (69 percent) and independents (61 percent) believe it does."[36]

The media landscape is more confusing than it used to be. A little over a quarter of adults are "very confident" about sorting through media bias and almost half are "somewhat confident."[37]

It is clear that the evolution of television news from a source or two on broadcast TV with relatively unified stories and voices to a number of cable channels to a plethora of Internet shows, podcasts, and livestreams has had a profound and irrevocable effect on the way we receive, process, and further disseminate information. The proliferation of news sources has been exponential, from a few sources and one primary medium to a seemingly infinite number of voices on ever-changing platforms that multiply faster than we can comprehend.

As this shift has occurred, news programs have become more opinion-based and viewers have begun to sort themselves, watching the programs that confirm their beliefs. According to the Pew Research Center, almost a majority of consistent conservatives (the 20 percent on the right "end of the spectrum") watch Fox News, and 88 percent say they trust Fox News. Almost two-thirds of this group "say most of their close friends share their views on government and politics."[38]

On the opposite side of the political spectrum, liberals consume and trust a wider variety of news sources, according to Pew. CNN was their top source, at 15 percent, followed closely by NPR, MSNBC, and the *New York Times*. They are the group most likely "to block or 'unfriend' someone on a social network—as well as to end a personal friendship—because of politics."[39]

The Front Line of Breaking News

Social media has also become the front line of breaking news. As cable news is becoming more about entertainment, social media is stepping in to fill the gap. A movement to Twitter for breaking news is new and filled with challenges, as Twitter is full of anonymous accounts and bots. Anyone can open a Twitter account while masking his or her identity, and that can increase the difficulty of determining what information is accurate.

Information is no longer delivered in the dry, straight-to-camera style of the mid-twentieth-century newscast from a broadcast station. Instead, we get personalities providing their opinions about the news while often attacking the opposite perspectives. While it might make for entertaining television, it does not make for a good way to distribute facts. With a multitude of channels and hosts screaming at guests, and guests dramatically walking off set, it's easy to understand why people might disengage from media, particularly as a source of relevant political information. For example, Glenn Beck walked off the set of CNN's *Reliable Sources* while being interviewed by host Brian Stelter.[40]

Stelter said this to Beck: "I have to ask you, there's this new headline on the Daily Beast saying your company's in trouble. Is this related to [your] point about people not talking to each other? That you want to create a media company, and there's not interest?"[41] After pushing back on the question as being ridiculous and a waste of time, Beck got up and walked off.[42]

The process of determining what news to trust has become a burden and is emotionally draining, at least for me.

Nightly news shows on broadcast TV have seen their viewership totals eroded by the incursion of cable TV. In 1980, 23 percent of Americans watched network news; by 2014, that percentage had dropped to 8. While the networks continue to deliver their news in a relatively dry style compared to that used by their cable counterparts, their definition of what merits coverage has changed.

For example, the ongoing negative focus on President Trump and his administration is breathtaking. A report from Media Research Center (MRC) before the 2018 mid-terms "found the ABC, CBS and NBC evening newscasts spent a paltry 157 minutes on all developments in the war against ISIS," while "those same newscasts devoted more than 33 hours of airtime to the ongoing Russia investigation."[43]

"From June 1 to September 30, [2018], the MRC found the Trump administration's successful economic policies drew only 14 minutes out of 1,960 minutes of overall coverage, or a measly 0.71 percent," wrote Bill D'Agostino for NewsBusters.[44]

On Cable News, Outrage and Offense Rule

If you turn on cable news opinion shows, you will soon notice that outrage and offense rule the day. There is no happy medium. There is no clear flow of information. Instead, there is a narrative that needs to be reinforced and regurgitated. It's only worse when you spend a bit of time on Twitter and other social media channels. Without any immediate human connection, it's increasingly easy to be nasty, hateful, and dismissive to others, especially when you disagree with them—or possibly their entire perspective or ideology.

However, Twitter does allow for direct connection to an audience. The recent addition of the "Retweet with comment" functionality has shifted this dynamic slightly, but the original message remains unfiltered, particularly when compared with communications styles of the twentieth century. Some might say that it's occasionally a little too unfiltered. This ability to communicate directly to the public, without a filter, is what drives President Trump to tweet today. He also uses it to correct filtering by media outlets, similar to the way President Roosevelt used his fireside chats. The difference is that Trump's tweets are not scripted, and he can—and does—react almost instantaneously to the news and developments of the day.

Social media, mainstream media, and the resulting personal interaction are all interwoven. The instantly created, opinion-filled, rapidly delivered content that is churned out ceaselessly by the cable networks takes sides. Based on a report by Media Research Center, the "network coverage of Republicans is far more hostile (88 percent negative) than that meted out to Democrats (53 percent negative), but we found nearly ten times more negative statements about Republicans and President Trump (97 percent) than all of the Democratic candidates combined (10 percent)." Comparatively, during the 2016 presidential race, the coverage of the then Republican candidate Donald Trump was 91 percent negative."[45]

No wonder so many Americans don't trust news sources.

So what does this all mean? It means that there are opinions available from every angle, but very little news. Real news programming requires hiring reporters, producers, and sound techs, giving them the time and resources they need to hunt down all the various points of view that reflect the complexities of any given story, and then presenting that story in a coherent, compelling way.

Turn on a cable news program today and you're more likely to see a host chitchatting with a lineup of "experts" about the events of the day. They tend to pluck the information they use from the pages of newspapers and wire service stories rather than find it themselves.

When receiving information, always consider the source and their biases. Get additional information from other outlets, with opposite biases, and then weigh all of the data to come to your own conclusion—and don't feel pressured to jump on someone else's bandwagon just to fit in.

CHAPTER 3

Media/Technology and Interconnectedness

The first movement toward transforming the way we get news came in 1980, when CNN launched a 24-hour-per-day news network. No more need for planning on watching the evening news when CNN made news about the day's events available 24/7.

Newspapers, which used to be printed and then distributed once or twice a day, now use the Internet to update their stories as many times per day as events warrant. No more need to walk to the corner to pick up the latest edition of the local paper when it is instantly available on your home computer and your phone.

As news for many of us has changed from a once-a-day, fact-based delivery to an unceasing flow of opinions, technology has changed, too. These two developments have transformed the way we consume news and integrate its content into our daily lives. There is no sign that the speed of the technological innovations and interactions is slowing, or ever will.

My grandmother, who was born in 1915 and died in 1988, would not recognize the technology and media that we now accept as routine. The volume of available information has expanded exponentially as have the ways we can download and listen to, watch, or read it.

In the 1930s, families gathered around the radio to hear the news of the day or listen to serial programs like *The Shadow* or President Franklin D. Roosevelt's fireside chats. Decades later, long after most families had replaced their radios with televisions, we still gathered once a day to learn about the news, which was typically delivered concisely and dryly. In our house, this occasionally meant using TV trays to hold our dinner plates while we watched the news shows together.

No longer. Over the years, the cost of a television has plummeted and their numbers have proliferated. They no longer contain vacuum tubes, and they are no longer found just in the living room. In many homes, they can be found in bedrooms, kitchens, bathrooms, and outdoor living areas.

At work, they can be found in lobbies, elevators, break rooms, and kitchens—in addition to offices.

And that's not all. While dining out used to be solely about quiet ambience, service, and good food, it is now about entertainment, too. To meet that perceived demand, many restaurants have installed televisions.

Numbers of TVs don't tell the whole story. One must also consider the increase in the types of devices, their portability, and their connectivity.

Computers have been similarly transformed. When I was in high school in the early 1980s, they ran on punch cards. By the time I got to college, I was using a personal computer, and by the time I reached graduate school, I was using a desktop. Now, the smartphone I carry has more computing power than my desktop did, and it is almost always connected either through Wi-Fi or wireless networks.

This unbounded, always-on, always-connected environment means that users have changed the way they interact with media through their devices. Remember, news and information used to be primarily one-way conduits carrying information from a central source to individuals. Now not only can we share news through social media, but we can also communicate to the news organizations and their lead personalities directly. It's a never-ending, simultaneous exchange of information.

We are a society constantly connected to entertainment and news. Radio reaches almost all Americans (92 percent) according to Nielsen, with television not far behind (88 percent). In the first quarter of 2018, television (both live and time shifted) accounted for "four hours and 46 minutes" per adult per day.[1]

While traditional media consumption has remained relatively constant, newer platforms have driven up consumption, as has the ability of just about everyone to take a device (smartphone, tablet) anywhere and consume content anytime. This has driven average time per person per day on digital devices to three hours and 48 minutes in the first quarter of 2018, according to Nielsen.[2]

American adults spend almost half their day, 11 hours, "listening to, watching, reading or generally interacting with media," according to a recent Nielsen survey. Since a person can both watch TV and interact with Facebook at the same time, some of these hours are overlapping.[3]

While the recent pace of innovation and proliferation of connection and content is mind-boggling, it's not decelerating. The pace of technological innovation is accelerating, integrating into all aspects of our lives.

At the same time, the social construct around work has also changed. That's because many workers no longer have to show up at a certain time and place to work at a certain desktop computer. Instead, they can work at any time, in any location, and on any platform. This leads some people to wake up in the middle of the night for conference calls to India, others to become professional nomads of sorts, working weeks at home followed by weeks overseas. One of our friends has worked in Europe for years, commuting back and forth to Atlanta. Another lives in Atlanta, but works as a CEO of a company located in Europe and India.

It's not just our work lives that have changed; our private lives are also more connected. You can use your phone to change the temperature in your home, turn on lights, and see who is ringing your doorbell. You can use it to stream music, order food or equipment, call people from your contact list, and ask your digital assistant to read text or tell you the news or the weather forecast.

"Hey, Siri, Order Me a Dozen Pizzas"

The use of digital assistants is exploding. "Smartphones and smart speakers that use digital assistants like Amazon's Alexa or Apple's Siri are set to outnumber people by 2021,"[4] according to Ovum, a research group.

Unfortunately, advances in technology have been paralleled by advances in hacking and the implications are hair-raising. In 2018, a "group of Chinese and American researchers from China's Academy of Sciences and other institutions, demonstrated they could control voice-activated devices with commands embedded in songs," wrote Craig Smith for the *New York Times*, "that can be broadcast over the radio or played on services like YouTube."[5] These commands were not noticed by the people who were using the devices.

The result: Someone you do not know can command your digital assistants—to order pizzas or taxis or make phone calls or send e-mails—without your knowledge.

It's not just digital assistants that are being hacked; it's also the federal government. In 2014, the U.S. Office of Personnel

Management was breached by hackers backed by the Chinese government. They also breached several health insurance companies, a federal contractor, and the Department of Homeland Security, according to U.S. officials.[6] China denied being behind the attack. In March 2019, an internal review by the Navy found that they had been under attack, along with several universities and research institutions that work with them, according to the *Washington Post*. They were attacked by hackers working for the Chinese government, and the attack had started by April 2017.[7]

As the number and complexity of smartphones have increased and their cost has dropped, the use of social networking apps has proliferated, rapidly changing the way we have integrated these devices into our daily lives. According to the Pew Research Center, only 5 percent of American adults were using social media in 2005. By 2011, 50 percent of Americans were using social media—a tenfold increase in six years.[8]

In 2018, over two thirds of American adults (69 percent) were using some type of social media.[9] As I write this in 2019, Facebook is the dominant social media platform in the United States, according to Pew Research, both in number of users (69 percent) and frequency of use (about three quarters of Facebook users access it daily).[10]

But the behemoth had humble beginnings. The social media pioneer was created as a way for Harvard students to connect to one another. It was later opened to students from other colleges and, eventually, to the general public. It was a way for people to connect electronically with those they already knew or those who were in similar communities.

What started as a social tool has also become a business tool, one that connects people and companies to customers. Organizations use Facebook to post events and host online communities. As its users and usage have morphed, so, too, has Facebook. You can now raise funds on Facebook, host a Facebook live event, or create a private group page.

Facebook, too, has been hacked, with over 50 million accounts affected in the fall of 2018.[11] There are constant e-mail phishing scams that people fall for.

The social media companies and their offerings have changed over the years. Many people use more than one platform. Pew found that "90 percent of LinkedIn users also use Facebook." Additionally, nearly "three-quarters of the public (73 percent) uses more than one of the eight platforms measured in this survey, and the typical (median) American uses three of these sites."

As a result of their growth in popularity, our interconnectedness is also growing—exponentially.

Video Growth Explodes

That growth in interconnectedness has been hastened by the simultaneous proliferation of video platforms. Video can be more engaging and entertaining, and with the widespread adoption of closed-circuit TV cameras and smartphones, it is nearly ubiquitous. YouTube "is now used by nearly three-quarters of U.S. adults and 94 percent of 18- to 24-year-olds."[12]

Not only do nearly all of us carry smartphones, but most of us are connected via social media apps to our friends, colleagues, and millions of people we don't even know.

Where there is a web of connectivity and information, political action is sure to follow. Social media's ability to connect people and amplify their messages has made it a perfect medium for political action and messaging. Since anyone can create a social media account, everyone has access.

Barack Obama was the first president to use social media. In May 2015, he introduced the @POTUS handle for Twitter.

By that same time, the White House Office of Digital Strategy included fourteen staff people, more than the two previous presidents had in their entire press operation. In anticipation of Obama's 2015 State of the Union Address, the White House produced and released eighteen videos. Think of them as teasers or trailers for a traditional production. The speech was livestreamed and included 127 slides released online, bypassing traditional news outlets to go directly to the viewer.[13]

For the Obama presidency, social media provided another advantage. According to Juliet Eilperin of the *Washington Post*, "The success, and the reach, of the White House new-media strategy is due in part to a series of close relationships between the White House and people in the new-media business, many of whom support the president politically."[14] West Coast techies would often fly to Washington on their own dime to collaborate with the White House on how to use their newest technology. These relationships provided "access to both power and content" for the social media companies. The White House was able to "use cutting-edge technology to advance the president's agenda."[15]

The real challenge is the political bias against conservatives from technology and social media companies. For example, the employees of Alphabet, the parent company of Google, have vastly skewed political donations with over "90 percent of their political donations to Democrats," wrote Jake Kanter in *Investor's Business Daily*, with a measly 10 percent going to Republicans from 2014 to 2018.[16] This liberal bias comes out not only in the way their employees fund candidates, but also in the way the companies treat conservative voices on their platforms.

Google's algorithm prevented "people from searching for guns online in shopping; temporarily attached fact-checks from leftist sites like Snopes and PolitiFact to conservative websites but not leftist ones," wrote Ben Shapiro for *National Review*, "[and] showed more pro-Clinton results than pro-Trump results in news searches. This was confirmed by Paula Bolyard's google search."[17] Clear bias.

In August 2017, Google employee James Damore's memo titled "Google's Ideological Echo Chamber, How Bias Clouds Our Thinking About Diversity and Inclusion"[18] was made public via the Gizmodo website and drove a discussion about bias in Google.

"At Google," Damore wrote, "we talk so much about unconscious bias as it applies to race and gender, but we rarely discuss our moral biases. Political orientation is actually a result of deep moral preferences and thus biases. Considering that the overwhelming majority of the social sciences, media, and Google lean left, we should critically examine these prejudices."[19]

Regarding political bias, "Neither side is 100% correct," wrote Damore, "and both viewpoints are necessary for a functioning society or, in this case, company.... Google's left bias has created a politically correct monoculture that maintains its hold by shaming dissenters into silence."[20]

Damore subsequently was fired by Google.[21]

Controversy Sells

Those who get noticed on social media are often those who draw attention to their postings by making shocking statements or highlighting or intentionally creating controversy.

Years ago, when my dad and I were being interviewed by then–Fox News host Bill O'Reilly about our book, *5 Principles for a Successful Life: From Our Family to Yours*, the three of us spent a few minutes chatting before the show began. "So, what's the controversy?" O'Reilly asked. I responded that there wasn't any. He replied, "Controversy sells."

We had included our personal perspectives, as well as those from thirty-four other people, about how to live successfully, but we were offering nothing controversial. Any consumer of media today knows that controversy does sell, and not just on cable TV, but even more on social media sites where there is a lot of content competing for eyeballs.

Passion and excitement also sell. Due to the widespread access people have to social media, nearly anyone can share his or her opinion—without spending a dime. The result is that social media is teeming with opinions that never make it to the mainstream media.

But the role of the mainstream media as gatekeeper to information is diminishing. President Trump has endured almost constant negative mainstream press coverage. But he has been able to shrug much of it off simply by using social media to talk directly to the American people without waiting for broadcast news or cable news to cover him. With almost 60 million followers on Twitter, over 11 million on Instagram, and over 24 million followers on his Facebook personal page, the president can use those sites to talk directly to the American people, circumventing the traditional media. During the government shutdown in January 2019, Trump tweeted, "Without a Wall there cannot be safety and security at the Border or for the U.S.A. BUILD THE WALL AND CRIME WILL FALL!"[22] as he pushed toward a resolution for funding a wall on our country's southern border.

Freshman Rep. Alexandria Ocasio-Cortez, D-NY, has used social media to build a following and push her far-left ideas, which include calling for a 70 percent tax rate on income above $10 million.[23]

According to Pew, nearly two-thirds of Americans (65 percent) agree that "social media highlight important issues that might not get a lot of attention otherwise."[24]

A similar share, according to Pew, believes that these platforms help give a voice to underrepresented groups. In addition to providing access for those in minority groups, over half (56 percent) agree that "social media make it easier to hold powerful people accountable for their actions."[25]

Let's take a recent example of a social media firestorm that provided people with a way to spread their message that might not have been available previously. In October 2017, actress Alyssa Milano tweeted, "If you've been sexually harassed or assaulted write 'me too' as a reply to this tweet."[26] The response was enormous: Some women shared stories ranging from harassment to assault, many men provided their support, and others simply listed the hashtag #metoo.

The "@MeToo" movement was launched by activist Tarana Burke, who had been a victim of sexual abuse. While Burke was a director at a youth camp, a child confided to Burke that she had experienced sexual abuse. Burke sent the child to an adult for help. Even though Burke was also a victim of sexual abuse, she was unable to verbalize the words "me too" to the child.

The trigger for Milano's tweet exposed film mogul Harvey Weinstein's allegedly decades-long practice of sexual abuse. During the first half of October 2017, "more than 30 women have come forward publicly with harrowing stories of encounters with him [Weinstein]. The *New York Times* reported that Mr. Weinstein, who has denied 'any allegations of nonconsensual sex,' "[27] was under investigation by the police in New York and London.

"Well, I Guess That's One for the Memoirs"

It wasn't just Weinstein. That same month, actor Molly Ringwald wrote she had been sexually harassed in her teens. She also recounted a specific horrific episode that occurred in her twenties. "When I was asked by the director, in a somewhat rhetorical manner, to let the lead actor put a dog collar around my neck.... The actor was a friend of mine, and I looked in his eyes with panic," she wrote for *The New Yorker*. "I'd like to think that I just walked out, but, more than likely, there's an old VHS tape, disintegrating in a drawer somewhere, of me trying to remember lines with a dog collar around my neck in front of a young man I once had a crush on. I sobbed in the parking lot and, when I got home and called my agent to tell him what happened, he laughed and said, 'Well, I guess that's one for the memoirs....' I fired him and moved to Paris not long after." Her career cooled after that harrowing experience.[28]

Soon after the Weinstein accusers began going public, the stories of sexual abuse allegedly carried out by a host of other men began flooding social media. "It is estimated that across Twitter and Facebook posts, comments and reactions, #MeToo was used more than 12 million times within the first 24 hours," said David Woods-Holder, a social media analyst.[29]

The #MeToo hashtag "has appeared an average of 61,911 times per day on Twitter" from inception (October 15, 2017) through May 2018, according to the Pew Research Center.[30]

Social media also makes it easier to spread misinformation. The sad news is that we are not good at recognizing fake news on social media. A study from the University of Buffalo "examined Twitter's response to four different rumors during two disasters—the Boston Marathon Bombing and Hurricane Sandy—by examining 20,000 related tweets,"[31] according to an article written by David Wiky for the IT Technology Updates website. Fewer than 10 percent of those who responded to the false tweets expressed doubts about their accuracy.[32]

Another drawback: Social media contains no filter for importance.

Entertainment news about who is dating whom winds up in the same funnel as comments about government funding and national security issues. The only way to prioritize is to look at what gets the most likes and retweets. The challenge becomes figuring out how to separate what is important from what is not.

When you are worrying about everything, you can easily miss making progress on the problems that matter most. No one can focus on everything; we must focus on what is important. This is a big challenge when attempting to drink from the firehoses that spew information from social media platforms 24 hours per day. All too often, we are distracted by the shiny new objects that, in the long run, will not matter much—if at all.

For example, during the last week of the December 2018–January 2019 partial government shutdown, the news media focused much of its newsgathering prowess on the short video that showed the white, teenage, Catholic schoolboy who appeared to be smirking at the tribal elder who was beating a drum at the Lincoln Memorial.

We know now—with the subsequent release of the longer video—that members of the Black Hebrew Israelites appeared to be trying to instigate aggressive behavior.

That meant the original story—based on the shorter video—was not real news.

But when the longer video began to circulate, the media's focus did not move to the new party. Instead, it turned to the ways the media had covered the earlier story. It became a media event about how a story was covered. During all of this coverage, which lasted over a week on national media, attention was diverted from other major news issues.

Social media's great strength is that they provide a megaphone to everyone. That's also their weakness, since they cannot distinguish the trivial from the important. Instead, their algorithms measure interest alone. Bright, shiny, and often controversial topics (let's not forget the cat videos) are more likely to generate traffic and thereby attention. In fact, according to Pew, 77 percent of U.S. adults agree that "social media distracts people from issues that are truly important."[33]

While we may be attracted to Kim Kardashian's fashions or unsubstantiated allegations about politicians, we may also be missing the bigger and more important picture by focusing on those things to the exclusion of others, driven by our exhaustion from vast amounts of information.

So, here we are, whiling our time away on Twitter, Facebook, Instagram, and LinkedIn, liking, sharing, retweeting, and basically losing track of time (I just did it myself while writing), instead of focusing on what really matters.

News organizations know they can entice us—and earn advertising dollars—by throwing clickbait onto their sites. The result is that they may gloss over more substantive issues and fail to dig deeply into stories about issues that matter. An example of too little coverage of an important issue is the media coverage and social media focus on Trump's handling of NATO during the first years of his presidency.

As a candidate, Trump questioned the usefulness of NATO, especially since the United States is the lead funder of common expenditures and defense spending for NATO. After being elected, President Trump asked other member countries to pay their fair share. Democrats looked at this criticism of NATO as blasphemy.

After the July 2018 NATO meeting, President Trump tweeted, "What good is NATO if Germany is paying Russia billions of dollars for gas and energy? Why are there only 5 out of

29 countries that have met their commitment? The U.S. is paying for Europe's protection, then loses billions on Trade. Must pay 2% of GDP IMMEDIATELY, not by 2025."[34]

President Trump's challenge and charge elicited this response from former Sen. John Kerry, D-MA: "It was disgraceful, destructive, and flies in the face of the actual interests of the United States of America."[35] Kerry's claim was that President Trump was setting back U.S. interests.

Readers would be justified if they were confused. That's because stories about the disagreement included few of the pertinent, if mundane, facts and figures. For that, they would have had to hunt through the NATO website.

Turns out that there are two major types of expenditures that NATO tracks: common funding and defense expenditures.

"Common-funding arrangements principally include the NATO civil and military budgets, as well as the NATO Security Investment Programme (NSIP)," according to the NATO website. "These are the only funds where NATO authorities identify the requirements and set the priorities in line with overarching Alliance objectives and priorities."[36]

This is money that is contributed by the member countries and then spent by NATO. Of these funds, for the calendar years ending 2018 and 2019, the top contributor is, well, the United States, at 22.1 percent of the common funding, Germany is second at 14.8 percent, France is third at 10.5 percent.

NATO has set a goal for spending on defense of 2 percent of GDP for each of the 29 member countries. "The combined wealth of the non-US Allies, measured in GDP, exceeds that of the United States," notes the NATO website. "However, non-US Allies together spend less than half of what the United States spends on defense..." The defense spending of the United States "represents some 67 per cent of the defence spending of the Alliance."[37]

Based on NATO estimates, in 2018 the United States spent 3.50 percent of its GDP on defense, Greece 2.27 percent, Estonia 2.14 percent, the United Kingdom 2.10 percent, and Latvia 2.00 percent; the other 24 countries in NATO will spend less than the 2 percent guideline.[38]

In January 2019, NATO Secretary General Jens Stoltenberg gave Trump credit for encouraging member nations to spend more than $100 billion on defense, wrote William Cummings for *USA Today*. "NATO is united because we are able to adapt to deliver," Stoltenberg said. "North America and Europe are doing more together now than before."[39]

Billions more than previously spent in defense spending sounds like a real result, but you wouldn't know it from reading the newspapers or combing through social media sites.

Instead, the news the same week focused on speculation over when the next shutdown could occur or if it would occur, the new 2020 candidates in the Democratic primary (who are numerous), and the invitation from Senate Minority Leader Chuck Schumer, D-NY, to Stacey Abrams, who had just lost Georgia's gubernatorial race as the Democratic nominee, to deliver the rebuttal to Trump's State of the Union Address.

Does Social Media Make a Difference?

So, the news media tend to pass over real news for whatever may be the most controversial story at the time. Because all of us are attracted to what's controversial, and therefore divisive, we are more likely to retweet or share such stories. There, we have done something—or so we think. But just because we like, retweet, and share doesn't necessarily mean that we are making a difference. In fact, according to Pew Research, "71 percent of U.S. adults 'believe that social media makes people think they are making a difference when they really aren't.' "[40]

A person's race is one factor in gathering data about the importance of social media sites and their ability to connect. More than half of black social media users (54 percent), according to Pew, say social media sites are important in helping them find "others who share their views about important issues."[41]

This is almost 40 percent higher than the figure for white social media users.[42] Possibly the difference is due to white social media users having more avenues to find "others who share their views about important issues," according to Pew's report, "Social Media Conversations about Race." If so, then this would make social media more valuable and useful for black users. The same gap between black and white social media users exists for "getting involved with issues that are important to them (52 percent vs. 36 percent), or for giving them a venue to express their political opinions (53 percent vs. 32 percent)."[43]

Political party affiliations also have an impact. Some 80 percent of Democrats say social media drives sustained social change, versus 53 percent of Republicans.[44]

This difference in belief over how much social media sites make a difference in the world of politics is reflected in the use of these sites by candidates, campaigns, social movements, and everyday voters.

There are several movements whose hashtags have been used primarily on social media to raise awareness.

In July 2013, the #BlackLivesMatter hashtag sprung up after George Zimmerman was acquitted of shooting and killing Trayvon Martin, an unarmed black teen. During the five years after it surfaced, the hashtag was "used nearly 30 million times on Twitter—an average of 17,002 times per day,"[45] according to the Pew Research Center.

The hashtag representing Trump's campaign slogan, "Make America Great Again," #MAGA, rose in usage during the 2016 presidential campaign and peaked just after Election Day. "From Election Day 2016 through May 1, 2018, the #MAGA hashtag has been used an average of 205,238 times per day," according to the Pew Research Center.[46]

Those who opposed Trump grabbed the #Resist hashtag just after his election. But its usage was a fraction of that garnered by #MAGA. According to the Pew Research Center, "from inauguration day [November 8, 2016] through May 1, 2018, the #Resist hashtag [was] used an average of 59,716 times daily on Twitter."[47]

It's Personal Connections That Count

While hashtags and sharing on social media can raise awareness about a cause, it's our personal connections that resonate and create memories. Unfortunately, technology often gets in the way.

After all, smartphones are so much easier to deal with than people.

In a world where we spend more than half our waking hours watching, listening to, or interacting with technology and media, we are also experiencing less connectivity as human beings. Just think back to your last meeting or meal. Was everyone paying attention? Were some watching their phones, computers, or tablets instead? Have you had a recent experience when someone answered a phone at the table and proceeded to engage in a loud, long conversation—oblivious to the people in the room? Have you recently experienced someone interrupting a conversation to answer a text? Do you check your phone first thing in the morning, before getting out of bed, and last thing at night, before going to bed? Are you checking for emergencies (children, parents, etc.?) or are you checking social media? Have you ever simply started to check social media and gotten lost for a half hour or longer?

Many of us answer yes to many of these questions. All too often, we opt for the click or the call instead of talking to the person in front of us.

Online networks, groups, courses, and affinity groups have proliferated exponentially in the past few years. From workout groups to personal development courses to alumni associations, there are innumerable ways to connect online.

Let's take one example: the transformation of a community workout group to an online community.

In the 1990s, when I was working in the corporate world, I was also part of a running group that ran in the Virginia Highlands community on the west side of Atlanta. Anyone was welcome, and the group grew by word of mouth. We met at 7 p.m. on Wednesdays at a local bar and ran.

While we all started together, different groups ran different routes at different speeds. But all the runs ended back at the bar. From there, some would leave, but many would stay for a beer and dinner. It was a simple way to work out, exercise, catch up with friends, make new friends, and eat.

During the years I ran with the group, I met many people and made friendships that I still have today, over two decades later.

But how times have changed! Last year, our family purchased a Peloton bike with a subscription. The stationary bike tracks resistance and speed and is connected to the Internet. The subscription provides access to online, live classes as well as on-demand classes covering a wide range of interests—including cycling, strength, stretch, walking, boot camp, outdoor, yoga, and cardio.

This year, Peloton introduced a treadmill with an attached screen that is connected to the Internet so you can "run with others."[48]

Peloton has a studio for live cycling classes in New York, and when you buy a subscription, you become a member, a part of the tribe. The company tracks how many classes you have taken, rewarding you for meeting specific targets. For example, for 100 rides, they provide you with a Peloton shirt. Each time you ride or take a class, they track your progress by compiling a wealth of data, which you can pull up in your account at any time. You can follow friends' progress—or lack thereof—via usernames or Facebook. For example, I can ride at 10:13 a.m. in Atlanta with my sister in Miami. But I don't. Instead, I ride when it fits into my schedule; I rarely take the live classes, and I often choose which class to take based on the time I have available. It's incredibly flexible and convenient and I love it.

I even have my favorite bike instructor. It's great to have someone encouraging me (even if she is really encouraging others who were in her "live" class when she recorded it).

An online community that encourages you—even if it is via taped messages—is better than no community at all.

But as familiar as her face might be to me, we are not friends, nor are we likely to be friends twenty years from now. When there is a crisis in my life, I won't reach out to her. No, I'll leave that to my real friends, people with whom I have bonded in person.

However, once a personal connection has been made, it's much easier to connect meaningfully with that connection via technology. For instance, my family uses FaceTime to see each other while we talk. My daughter uses it for hours with friends while doing homework, making her bed, putting on makeup—well, just about everything. And I use it with friends and family while cooking dinner. Once a human connection has already been established, a technological connection can strengthen it.

Watch Out for "Digital Zombies"

While many of us are scrambling to cobble together online communities and connections, many others—even those who helped create the phenomenon—are doing all they can to keep their children away from devices.

Instead of pushing their children to use the growing technology, some parents and other caregivers are encouraging them to put down their smartphones and use board games or play outdoors. "From Cupertino to San Francisco, a growing consensus has emerged that screen time is bad for kids," a *New York Times* article reported in 2018. "It follows that these parents are now asking nannies to keep phones, tablets, computers and TVs off and hidden at all times. Some are even producing no-phone contracts, which guarantee zero unauthorized screen exposure, for their nannies to sign."[49]

Concern in Silicon Valley and elsewhere about screen time for children has increased over the past few years. It's created an environment where a nanny can be disciplined for using her phone while in charge of children. Remember, Silicon Valley is the home of numerous technology companies; they tend to be cutting-edge when it comes to technology. Yet some of the same people who spend their working lives creating devices, apps, and games to occupy the rest of us are working to keep their children away from those products.[50]

Possibly those of us who pore over social media for political updates and actions should take this to heart and give ourselves occasional holidays from social media, too. A bit of distance and a reframing of our minds might help us mitigate our ranting and raving.

A few years ago, some people expressed concern that a digital divide would arise in which people with more monetary resources would provide their children with greater access to technology, and that that access would give them an advantage over children from less wealthy families.

Now, many of the same people who create the technologies that foster digital interconnectedness and design the apps that occupy so many of us for so many hours per day are opting to keep their own children away from that technology so that they can focus instead on developing personal interactions. Maybe our thinking was backward.

But the people who designed these products know that keeping their children away from their products won't be easy. They know that smartphones, tablets, and computers are engrossing and an easy way to hold a child's attention. Those of us who have had or simply watched young children know that they tend to be very active and engaged with the world around them. Once they can crawl, they crawl everywhere. Once they can walk, they walk everywhere and pick up everything that they can get their hands on. Once they can talk, they ask incessant questions. They are naturally curious and want to learn. Their interaction with other people helps them create the neural connections in their brains they will need to succeed in life.

Small children can be demanding, and technology can help make them less so. Blogger Seth Godin wrote in November 2018, "If a parent uses a tablet or a smartphone as a babysitter, it's a lot easier to get a kid to sit still. As a result, parents who are busy, distracted or can't afford to spend as much 1:1 time as they'd like are unknowingly encouraging their kids to become digital zombies."[51]

Some would argue that children need less time online and more time interacting with parents, other children, and caregivers. It's the personal interactions, the dialogue, the words, the reading together that help develop their brains and socio-emotional skills. The digital divide has flipped.

The fact that tech professionals are limiting their children's technology exposure should lead us to reevaluate our own interactions with technology as well as those of our children. There is evidence to back me up.

A study at the University of Pennsylvania concluded there is a direct connection between how much time is spent connecting via social media and feelings of loneliness and depression. Maybe it's the result of comparing our own boring lives to the polished, impossibly perfect lives we see on social media; maybe it's the time spent reading the all-too-common vitriol; or maybe it's seeing others have fun while we sit alone in bed in our pajamas staring at our electronic devices.[52]

It could also be that, if we are down, we are unlikely to go out and interact with others. Whatever the reason, the connection is clear. A limit on social media leads to a better outlook on life. While the study looked at teenagers, its results might apply to others, too. Maybe we should all remind ourselves, when feeling down, to put down the smartphone, interact with humans, and spend some time with nature.

Beware of Internet Bullies

Additionally, the risk of cyberbullying is a real one, especially for children and teenagers. It can range from name calling to threats of physical violence. Bullying was common when I was a child in west Georgia, but once I left the area where the bully resided, it stopped. Home was a safe space. Now, the ubiquity of the Internet means that bullies can reach inside their target's home at any time of day or night.

According to Pew Research, "59 percent of U.S. teens have" experienced abusive behavior online. This includes name calling, being the subject of false rumors, receiving explicit images, general harassment online, or having their picture shared without their approval. The most prevalent type of online bullying is name calling, with almost half (42 percent) of American teens saying they were called a name online or via cell phone text.[53]

Household income affects the likelihood that a child will be bullied, but race and parents' levels of education do not. In households with annual incomes of less than $30,000, 24 percent of teenagers reported having received "physical threats online, compared with 12 percent [of teenagers] whose annual household income is $75,000 or more."[54]

A little over a year into her role as first lady of the United States (FLOTUS), Melania Trump rolled out her "Be Best" campaign, whose mission is "to focus on some of the major issues facing children today, with the goal of encouraging children to BE BEST in their individual paths....BE BEST will concentrate on three main pillars: well-being, social media use, and opioid abuse."[55]

FLOTUS has focused, in part, on how children should act on social media; to "choose their words wisely and speak with respect and compassion."[56]

Melania Trump's anti-bullying campaign may have been inspired by the attacks she herself has endured as first lady via social media.

On February 13, 2017, she tweeted, "Applause to all women around the world who speak up, stand up and support other

women! @emrata [twitter account of Emily Ratajkowski] Pow
erOfEveryWoman #PowerOfTheFirstLady."[57]

The first lady's tweet was in response "to model and actress
Emily Ratajkowski, an advocate for women who chose to express
their sexuality with their bodies, after she defended the first lady
amid claims she worked as an escort."[58]

No evidence has ever emerged that the first lady worked as
an escort. But she was criticized roundly in thousands of tweets
after she expressed thanks for the support she received from
Ratajkowski.

A few examples, which have been paraphrased:

> In response to @FLOTUS @Emrata:
> Hillary Clinton created the power of the First Lady. While
> she created the power—she didn't cost millions of
> taxpayers' money to stay in New York while her husband
> was working in Washington.

*   *   *

> In response to FLOTUS:
> It's not the taxpayers' problem you have marriage issues.
> Go to Washington and pay for your own security.

*   *   *

> In response to @FLOTUS:
> Ivanka is doing the job of the First Lady. How dare you
> tweet the power of the First Lady!?

As for her husband's tweets, FLOTUS has never endorsed
them. Nor do I. If the president were to ask me for my advice

(which he has not done), I would recommend that he tone down the language and the number of tweets, but then again I am not his adviser.

The president's tweets reflect his thoughts at one particular time. When criticized during the election by Sen. Rand Paul, R-KY, Trump tweeted, "Lightweight Senator @RandPaul should focus on trying to get elected in Kentucky—a great state which is embarrassed by him." He delivered that tweet on September 12, 2015.[59]

But relationships can change. On January 16, 2019, Paul showed his support for the president by tweeting, "I have never been prouder of President Donald Trump. In today's meeting, he stood up for a strong America and steadfastly opposed foreign wars. Putting America First means declaring victory in Afghanistan and Syria. President Trump is delivering on his promises."[60]

Maybe the overall lesson is that tweets are fleeting; they represent one person's thoughts at a single point in time. But relationships can evolve and thoughts can change.

Meanwhile, FLOTUS continues on her quest. In January 2019, she tweeted, "Our work in the East wing continues into 2019 with online safety, fighting opioid abuse & supporting the well-being of children everywhere! #BeBest."

Fitting Facts into the Narrative

While social media spreads information, all too often that information is shaped into a preformed narrative. In the last decade we have heard the word "narrative" over and over again as it applies to politics. "It fits the narrative." "The narrative is..." The use of the word primes us to take a given set of facts and fit them into a certain narrative rather than letting the facts fall where they may and only then deciding what they mean.

Stories (narratives) help us make sense of the world in which we live. We use them to take the data that we come across in our daily lives and fit that information into a story that makes sense to us. We do this not only for stories we believe about politics, but also for stories we tell ourselves about family, work, sports—everything and anything. It's the tool people use to make sense of what happens to them as life unfolds. When something new comes up—they automatically fit the new information into the narrative that they have already created in their heads.

Stories do not just entertain; they also educate and indoctrinate. Parents tell children stories to teach them lessons. Stories, both good and bad, are passed down from generation to generation, sometimes changing over time. Often, they are inaccurate, but nevertheless provide a window into the past. Since what we believe about the past changes how we act in the present, such stories can affect our future.

The best stories not only contain lessons, but also propel us forward to take action and make a difference.

"Stories impose meaning on the chaos," psychologist Jim Loehr wrote in *The Power of Story: Rewrite Your Destiny in Business and in Life*. Stories "organize and give context to our sensory experiences" and thereby help us understand the world around us, he said. "Facts are meaningless until you create a story around them....A story is our creation of a reality; indeed, our story matters more than what actually happened."[61]

The story you tell yourself about what happened in your life shapes your present and future actions. The same is true for stories we tell about communities, political parties, states, and nations. It's true for any group that has a cohesive identity. For nations, stories can change over time. Additionally, all nations are conglomerations of various groups (genders, ethnicities, races, countries, and origins); the more varied the groups, the harder it is for their stories to cohere into a single, national story.

According to the Merriam-Webster online dictionary, a narrative is "a: something that is narrated [a detailed account of a story], b: a way of presenting or understanding a situation or series of events that reflects and promotes a particular point of view or set of values."[62]

So, when you hear the word "narrative," remember that it's not simply a listing of facts; it's the telling of a story from a particular point of view. This is done with the goal of persuading you to embrace that particular point of view and agree with a certain conclusion. Once you espouse a point of view, then you are more likely to take new information and make it fit into the narrative you have accepted. It's human nature.

The challenge with narratives is that they create the guardrails to contain what you look for, what you see, what you pay attention to, what you consider.

Once a narrative's framework has been set, a person will find it difficult to look beyond it to accept facts or points of view that do not fit neatly into that framework.

Doing that requires the ability to step back and take a wider view—to understand that a given situation might not be as initially described. The adoption of a narrative in the political world may lead to the conclusion that there is no gray; in real life, there is a lot of gray.

Adopting a given narrative can lead to the prejudging of facts. If you believe Fact B does not fit within the constraints of Narrative A, then you might choose to dismiss or ignore Fact B.

Once a narrative is adopted, it becomes harder to recognize

and accept facts that do not fit the narrative that you have come to believe.

Mantra "Built on a Lie"

Let's take the "Hands up, don't shoot" mantra as an example.

On August 9, 2014, in Ferguson, Missouri, Police Officer Darren Wilson fatally shot Michael Brown, an unarmed, eighteen-year-old black man. Earlier that night, Brown had robbed a convenience store.

Brown's friend, Dorian Johnson, told MSNBC that he saw Wilson shoot Brown in the back. "It was then that Brown stopped, turned around with his hands up and said, 'I don't have a gun, stop shooting!' And like that, 'hands up, don't shoot' became the mantra of a movement,"[63] the *Washington Post* reported many months later. "But it was wrong, built on a lie."[64]

The media coverage and social media sharing had created a phrase that drove a movement. The hands-up action reference was supported in November 2014. At the time, according to a *Politico* story by Nick Gass, members "of the St. Louis Rams ran out on the field during pregame introductions with their hands raised above their heads." "Four members of the Congressional Black Caucus" also raised their hands on the floor of the House of Representatives on December 1, 2014.[65]

"Hands up, don't shoot. It's a rallying cry of people all across America who are fed up with police violence. In community after community after community fed up with police violence in Ferguson, in Brooklyn, in Cleveland, in Oakland, in cities and counties and rural communities all across America," Rep. Hakeem Jeffries, D-NY, said as the congressional members stood on the floor, as Lucy McCalmont wrote for *Politico*.[66]

The first march by Black Lives Matter supporters took place in Ferguson, three weeks after the Brown shooting. The Department of Justice report on the shooting, completed seven months later, showed that Johnson's account did not line up with physical evidence or other witness statements. "Brown never surrendered with his hands up, and Wilson was justified in shooting Brown,"[67] the report concluded.

However, that conclusion failed to fit the narrative of bad police attacking an unarmed black man without provocation. The incorrect story had already spread like wildfire, and remains the one many Americans believe to this day.

We have created an environment where facts are sometimes disregarded when they don't fit the narrative; opinions that reinforce the narrative are the only ones that are given credence.

The problem with relying on opinion and narrative rather than facts is that one group's opinion and narrative—created by drawing selectively from a body of facts—cannot reflect with accuracy what is going on in a nation that is geographically, ethnically, racially, and politically diverse. The narrative that is true in Wyoming will ring false in rural Alabama—even though it's true.

"What's more, people's experiences sometimes aren't wrong in the specific even if the narratives that emerge from them are wrong in the general," wrote Edward Halper, a professor of philosophy at the University of Georgia. "In a large and diverse population governed by imperfect institutions, we will *always* find victims of injustice and inequity. It is important to know how many such victims are—this can tell us if the problems are random or systemic."[68]

An additional problem, according to Halper, is that the narratives are descriptive and not proscriptive. They "neither provide nor even suggest a plan of action. Instead, they virtually insure that real problems continue to be unresolved."[69]

They give people a reason to protest—hands up, don't shoot.

And that's where we are today—mired in an interconnected, opinion-driven, narrative-oriented perspective. No wonder we don't make progress.

CHAPTER 4

Societal Changes

While technology, media, and the news have rapidly transformed, the rest of the world has not stood still. In the past half century, a number of changes in the way our society is structured have influenced the way we interact in our families, in our communities, and with our government.

"The Will of God Prevails"

As a nation, we are less religious, more urban, have fewer two-parent families, have a higher percentage of first-generation immigrants, are more racially and ethnically diverse, and have a majority of families relying on government assistance[1] to make ends meet, according to John F. Cogan, author of *The High Cost of Good Intentions: A History of U.S. Federal Entitlement Programs*. These changes have led us to a less stable, more fragile society.

Historically, we have been a religious nation. Our founding is based on our Declaration of Independence from Britain, which refers to "Laws of Nature and of Nature's God" and enumerates where our rights as humans come from.[2] This is one of the key differences between our nation and other nations. Our founding documents lay out our founders' beliefs, starting with the under-standing that there is a God, that we are made by God, and that God gives people (not kings or presidents or the pope) rights that cannot be taken away or separated from us as individuals.

"We hold these truths to be self-evident, that all men are cre-ated equal," states our Declaration of Independence, "that they are endowed by their Creator with certain unalienable Rights, that among these are Life, Liberty and the pursuit of Happiness."[3]

During the Civil War, President Abraham Lincoln often talked, wrote, and beseeched God for assistance. As president, Lincoln knew that, in the end, the outcome was up to God.

In September 1862, he wrote in a private note to himself, "The will of God prevails. In great contests each party claims to act in accordance with the will of God. Both may be, and one must be, wrong. God cannot be for and against the same thing at the same time. In the present civil war it is quite possible that God's purpose is something different from the purpose of either party—and yet the human instrumentalities, working just as they do, are of the best adaptation to effect his purpose."[4]

President Lincoln did not pass judgment on either side—but relied upon God to provide the judgment.

Peace did eventually come.

Our nation's connection to religion at a national level contin-ued during the First and the Second World Wars. During World War II, President Franklin Delano Roosevelt notified the nation of the D-Day invasion and went on national radio and asked listeners to pray with him. "Almighty God: Our sons, pride of our nation, this day have set upon a mighty endeavor, a struggle to preserve our Republic, our religion, and our civilization, and to set free a suffering humanity. . . ."[5] He asked for God's blessing and for victory, and urged the people of our nation to be con-tinually in prayer.

More recently, we have become a less religious nation, according to Gallup. In 1960, just fifteen years after Roosevelt had led our nation in prayer, when Gallup asked American adults to identify their religion, almost all [98 percent] of Americans identified with a religion of some type, with over two thirds identifying as Protestant.[6]

In 2017, according to Gallup, those identifying as Protestant had dropped to just above a third, while 20 percent identified as no religious affiliation. In 2017, 65 million Americans said they had no religious affiliation.[7]

Losing Our Shared Ability to Forgive

We are no longer a country who has a majority of the people sharing a single religion. The percentage who identify as Protestant has dropped almost in half from 1960 to 2017, while the percentage of those who do not identify with a religion has grown tenfold from 2 percent to 20 percent, according to Gallup.

This is important because a foundation in religions that are similar to one another has historically provided the majority of our country's populace with a shared understanding of morals, values, and acceptable ways of interacting with one another. The changes cited above raise the question of what happens to a common moral understanding as fewer people participate in organized religion.

As adherence to organized religion has faltered in our nation, so, too, has our shared ability to forgive, and to leave judgment and the outcome of events to God.

As the percent of Americans identifying as Protestant has declined, so, too, have congregations, both in number of attendees as well as in number of churches. Roughly 100 to 200 churches close each week in the United States, wrote Thom Rainer for

Facts and Trends, or at least 5,000 to 10,000 each year.[8] When a church closes, the people leave and the building is torn down, repurposed, or simply abandoned. The closings may leave holes in the surrounding communities from the lost activities and severed connections among the parishioners.

This loss of a centralized, physical structure has left many Americans looking for new places to congregate, new places to establish social connections. The emergence of thousands of Starbucks coffeehouses and similar places has provided physical space for people to gather. However, those spaces are not conducive to building a sense of community.

While we may have been turning our backs on organized religion, according to Gallup, we still overwhelmingly believe in God (87 percent), and a majority (55 percent) believe that "religion can answer all or most of today's problems." Still, nearly three-quarters of Americans (73 percent) say religion is becoming less influential in our country.[9]

What does this mean? It means that most Americans believe in God, but might not be religious. Perhaps it's the institution of religion that they do not find appealing. Like all institutions, it can be messy, fraught with faults, and hard to deal with. After all, it's a human institution. However, it's in the messiness in dealing with people that we can often find our connection to God.

The changes we have witnessed might also mean that Americans are ready for a religious revival. They believe in God, but possibly the current religious institutions do not make sense to them. Religious leaders might need to take a step back and see if they can find a way to serve those who believe in God—but who have not found a traditional religious home.

A community's location can affect its members' devotion, according to a March 2003 Gallup poll. Rural communities tended to self-identify as most religious, followed by suburban communities, with urban communities coming in last.[10] Why? Possibly because in rural areas there are fewer places outside of church to gather.

In comparison, urban and suburban areas often offer greater opportunities for social interaction, ways for people to connect with each other outside of church. In urban and suburban areas, commutes are often longer and the logistics of attending religious services more complicated. In smaller communities, churches often serve as the primary hub of social interaction. Many also serve as places of refuge and support, where friendly faces and a sense of belonging can always be found.

That was the case with me. I grew up in Carrollton, Georgia, a town of fewer than 30,000 residents located an hour west of Atlanta. Our family joined the First Baptist Church of Carrollton (FBC), which not only provided us with our spiritual foundation, but also served as the core of our social activities. On Sundays, after attending Sunday school and church service, we'd go home and have dinner (lunch), then return to church during the afternoon for choir and evening service.

The entire family would return for Wednesday night dinner followed by Bible study.

In addition to attending these weekly activities, my sister Kathy and I joined the youth group, which held lock-ins (the youth group would spend all night at the church), campouts, and mission trips. The church also offered Vacation Bible School and revivals. Yes, these were old-fashioned revivals held in the summer to audiences wielding paper fans to cool themselves. Both of our parents served as deacons at different times.

We had one other consistent activity in Carrollton—attendance at the local high school's Friday night football games. But it was our church activities that made up the core social structure of my formative years.

Even after Kathy and I left Carrollton for college in other cities, FBC remained the core of our mother's social life. She counted the offering, sang in the choir, and served on the finance committee. It was a two-way street. When she was ill and undergoing medical treatment in Atlanta, the pastor would drive the fifty miles that separated the two cities to visit with her. Five years after our mother died, Kathy and I still give flowers to the church to mark both her passing and her birthday.

Our country's freedom of religion is a cornerstone of our nation. In recent decades, in an attempt to uphold the freedom of religion that our Constitution establishes in its First Amendment, we have all too often strayed into freedom *from* religion.

The First Amendment states, "Congress shall make no law respecting an establishment of religion, or prohibiting the free exercise thereof."[11] This statement affirming the right to practice religion—and to not have a state-sponsored religion (as did England)—has been used increasingly to ban religion from public life.

In 1992, the U.S. Supreme Court upheld *Lee v. Weisman*, which barred "state-sponsored prayer in the public schools."[12] In the 5–4 decision, Justice Anthony M. Kennedy wrote for the majority, saying that even nonsectarian invocations violate the First Amendment.

The *New York Times*, in summarizing the ruling, quoted parts of Justice Antonin Scalia's minority view that the majority was going on a " 'psycho-journey' through the minds and emotions of adolescents who... could simply have sat through any prayer they disliked without suffering from the 'subtle coercive pressures' that Justice Kennedy had found particularly troublesome."

Scalia agreed with President Washington "that nothing, absolutely nothing, is so inclined to foster among religious believers of various faiths a toleration—no, an affection—for one another than voluntarily joining in prayer together, to the God whom they all worship and seek." It wasn't that there was a push for a state religion, but the ability to voluntarily come together in the common square and pray together. "While no one should be compelled to participate," Scalia wrote, "it is a shame to deprive our public culture of the opportunity, and indeed the encouragement, for people to do it voluntarily."[13]

No longer could a school employee lead a prayer at a school event.

Eight years later, the *Santa Fe Independent School District v. Doe* Supreme Court ruling resulted in students being unable to lead voluntary prayers at school-sponsored events.[14] It was no longer just school employees whose religious speech was curtailed, but also private citizens seeking to pray voluntarily.

While the percent of Americans who identify as being religious is waning, 1 in 5 still consider religion to be very important, according to Pew Research.[15] "Overall, 20 percent of Americans say religion is the most meaningful aspect of their lives, second only to the share who say this about family (40 percent)."[16]

The degree to which religion, faith, and spirituality give meaning to people's lives is related to their political leanings. Conservatives more often cite spirituality and faith as providing "their lives with meaning and fulfillment" (38 percent), compared to liberal Americans (8 percent). Liberal Americans more often say they find meaning in "arts or crafts (34 percent) and social and political causes (30 percent)." These figures are drastically higher for liberals than for conservatives, who cite 20 percent and 12 percent respectively for those same two categories.[17]

This disparity may help explain why liberals might be more outspoken and active than conservatives regarding social and political causes. They are substituting them for religion—it's their way to reach for higher meaning.

Driving God Out of Public Life

While they might be reaching for higher meaning for themselves, they have been spearheading an ongoing effort to drive God out of public life. In early 2019, after the Democrats took over the House of Representatives, the House Committee on Natural Resources drafted a rules package that removed "so help you God," from the "oath administered to witnesses testifying before the panel." Instead, the rules draft struck the words "so help you God" and included the words "under penalty of law." After Fox News obtained and aired the draft change in language, the final rules were submitted and accepted with the traditional "so help you God."[18]

While we have become intolerant to public displays of belief, in our quest for religious tolerance, we are subject to potential blind spots. In our quest for tolerance of religions whose adherents are a minority of our population, we ignore facts about fanatical fringe groups.

Let's take the response of the June 2016 attack inside Pulse, a nightclub in Orlando, Florida.

"I pledge allegiance to Abu Bakr al-Baghdadi of the Islamic State," the gunman, Omar Mir Seddique Mateen, said to the 911 operator he had called during the attack. His actions led to 49 people being killed and 53 wounded, Ariel Zambelich and Alyson Hurt reported for National Public Radio. "Mateen identified himself as 'an Islamic soldier,' according to the FBI, and threatened to detonate explosives, including a car bomb and a suicide vest—the kind 'used in France,' he said, referring to the terrorist attacks in Paris last November" of 2015.[19]

Afterward, President Obama noted that the attack was terrorism (a tactic—not the reason for the attack), then pivoted to his solution: gun control. "This massacre is therefore a further reminder of how easy it is for someone to get their hands on a weapon that lets them shoot people in a school, or in a house of worship, or a movie theater, or in a nightclub," President Obama said. "And we have to decide if that's the kind of country we want to be."[20]

Trump, who was the Republican nominee at the time, took a different tack. "The growing threat of terrorism inside of our borders" is the problem. He added that "many of the principles of Radical Islam are incompatible with Western values and institutions. Radical Islam is anti-woman, anti-gay, and anti-American."[21]

Obama, in response to Trump's speech, said condescendingly, "That's the key, they tell us—we can't beat ISIL unless we call them 'radical Islamists.' What exactly would using this label accomplish? What exactly would it change? Would it make ISIL less committed to trying to kill Americans? Would it bring in more allies? Is there a military strategy that is served by this? The answer is none of the above. Calling a threat by a different name does not make it go away."[22]

Being able to properly identify the fanatical group that wants to merge religion and state into one (which would be by definition against our Constitution) would not stop an attack in and of itself, but it would allow for an honest discussion of what happened.

Christian Whiton, a diplomat during the George W. Bush administration, lays out in his 2013 book, *Smart Power: Between Diplomacy and War*, that the Obama administration neither clearly identified nor articulated to the American public the definitions for two very different words: Islam and Islamism. "The former is a religion of nearly a quarter of the world's population; the latter (Islamism) is a political ideology whose central tenet is unifying government, and Islam and is advocated by a small subset of Muslims."

There is a huge difference between Islam, a religion, and Islamism, which would unify religion and government. The first is fine, the second is antithetical to our nation.

In the same speech that addressed the shooting in Orlando, Trump said that "if we want to protect the quality of life for all Americans—women and children, gay and straight, Jews and Christians and all people—then we need to tell the truth about Radical Islam."

He is right. We cannot tell the truth and have a discussion if we can't talk about the difference between Islam and Islamism.

While recently we have had to contend with enemies who live among us, how and where we live in our country has changed in the last few years.

Rural/Urban/Suburban

Over the last two decades, this nation has become less rural and more urban and suburban. Metro areas have extended their boundaries and their draw for residents. Many of those who work in metro areas are moving to areas near enough to city centers to enjoy all that they offer, but far enough away to be able to afford big houses near good schools in good communities.

The result: longer commute times and worsening suburban sprawl.

When I was growing up, Carrollton was a standalone town. People lived, worked, and worshiped there. Today, many residents of Carrollton commute an hour each way to Atlanta.

According to a Pew Research Center analysis of U.S. Census Bureau data, since 2000, the population in urban and suburban areas has continued the growth they experienced during the prior decade. "But, the total rural population has grown less than it did in the 1990s, when rising numbers fed hopes of a rural rebound. As a result, a smaller share of Americans now lives in rural counties (14% vs. 16% in 2000)." We are becoming more urban and suburban as a nation.[23]

Urban, suburban, and rural—each one a different way of life in the same nation. If you have ever spent a night on Manhattan Island, you know that the city really never sleeps.

Suburban areas tend to be different: They often include planned communities, rows of houses that look alike, cul-de-sacs, good schools, and strip malls. Often, children go to school in the suburbs while their parents work in the cities.

Both these experiences differ sharply from what happens in rural America. For instance, in Montana, it is not unusual for a person to drive for hours on a two-lane road and not see another car. Trips to grocery stores tend not to be spur-of-the-moment outings, since the local supermarket store can be an hour away. A rural person referring to a "neighbor" might be talking about someone who lives miles away.

This difference in lifestyle between rural and urban America has also been part of our political dialogue. "It's not surprising then they get bitter, they cling to guns or religion or antipathy to people who aren't like them or anti-immigrant sentiment or anti-trade sentiment as a way to explain their frustrations," then-candidate Barack Obama said in April 2008 during a fund-raising event in California. The story was broken by Mayhill Fowler, an Obama supporter who was also a stringer for the *Huffington Post*.[24]

While this comment was seized upon by then Sen. Hillary Clinton, who was Obama's opponent in the Democratic primary, it did not gain enough traction to stop Obama's eventual nomination, nor his victory in the general election.

But the rub between rural voters and the Democratic Party continued.

NPR chronicled that rub in this 2016 story. "Between 2008 and 2016, Republicans' share of the urban vote barely changed, and Democrats' share fell by four points. In the suburbs, Republicans likewise didn't change much, and Democrats lost five points. The shifts were larger in rural areas, where Republicans gained by nine points, and Democrats lost 11 points."[25]

Resentment Toward the Urban Elite

Part of the shift was due to the fact that many of those living in rural areas resented the urban elite for controlling a disproportionate share of the nation's power, money, and respect, according to Kathy Cramer, professor of political science at the University of Wisconsin–Madison, and author of *The Politics of Resentment*.[26]

Cramer talked to rural voters in Wisconsin. "They would say, 'The real kicker is that people in the city don't understand us,'" she wrote. "They don't understand what rural life is like, what's important to us and what challenges that we're facing. They think we're a bunch of redneck racists." So it was all three of these things—the power, the money, the respect. People were feeling like they're not getting their fair share of any of that.[27]

While in rural areas, Cramer noticed that many of the people who had followed in their parent(s)' footsteps in terms of profession (for instance, farmers and loggers) "were working harder than their parents, but not doing as well."[28] This reality may have led them to believe that they would be better off under a political novice, Donald Trump, rather than a known entity, Hillary Clinton.

While population growth in suburban and urban areas has exceeded growth in rural areas, that does not mean people are moving there because they want to. In fact, according to Gallup, almost twice as many people say they would like to live in rural areas (27 percent) than live there today (14 percent).[29]

Possibly it's the draw of community, safety, or less traffic, but whatever the reason, rural America remains a draw, even though not enough of a draw to attract more full-time residents.

J. D. Vance, a self-described Scots-Irish hillbilly from Kentucky, wrote *Hillbilly Elegy: A Memoir of a Family and Culture in Crisis*, about how his family's Kentucky values influenced his journey from Ohio to the Marines to Yale Law School. He provided a view into rural, working-class whites in Middle America. It's very different from the idealized version many think about.

Adverse childhood experiences "are traumatic childhood events, and their consequences reach far into adulthood," wrote Vance about his childhood, and the childhoods of many of those who grew up around him. These include "Being sworn at, insulted, or humiliated by parents, being pushed, grabbed, or having something thrown at you, feeling that your family didn't support each other, having parents who were separated or divorced, living with an alcoholic or drug user, living with someone who was depressed or attempted suicide, and watching a loved one being physically abused."[30]

He began to believe that his life had a future he could not control. He had learned helplessness.

"It's Not Your Fault You're a Loser" — The Wrong Message

For Vance, his time in the Marines changed his perspective; taught him to believe in himself and in his ability to shape his destiny. "I came a little closer to believing in myself," he wrote. "Psychologists call it 'learned helplessness' when a person believes, as I did during my youth, that the choices I made had no effect on the outcomes in my life. The Marines were teaching me learned willfulness."[31]

Vance believes that we are sending the wrong message to people. The message that is being sent to those who fail is that it's not their fault that they aren't successful, it's the fault of the government. Conservatives, who under HUD Secretary Jack Kemp, were encouraging inner city entrepreneurship, are currently too often aloof and detached.[32]

I would argue that this same message too often comes from the left, which is constantly reminding people of the various victim groups they belong to and blaming the system or those with privilege for blocking their advancement. Regardless of the intent, pessimism breeds inaction; optimism breeds action.

What did Vance see that made a difference in whether children were able to overcome the traumas they had endured? "They had a family member that they could count on. And they saw—from a family friend, and uncle, or a work mentor—what was available and what was possible.... The real problem for so many of these kids is what happens (or doesn't happen) at home," Vance noted.[33]

Part of the problem may be that the structure of families—the starting place for connections and nurturing—is rapidly changing as well, according to the U.S. Census Bureau. In 1960, 88 percent of the nation's children lived in families with two parents; by 2018, that figure had plummeted to 69 percent.[34]

In 1960, 9 percent of children lived with only their mother; and 1 percent with only their father. By 2018, the number of children who were living with mothers only had grown to 22 percent, while the number of children who were living with fathers only had grown to 4 percent.[35] This decline in two-parent households holds true for whites, blacks, and Hispanics, but there are differences.

In 1960, 91 percent of children in white families lived in two-parent households, 6 percent lived with mothers only, and 1 percent with fathers only. By 2018, the number of children living in white families with two parents had dropped to 75 percent. Two parents still overwhelmingly described white families with children.

In 1960, 67 percent of children in black families lived in two-parent households; 20 percent lived with mothers only; and 2 percent with fathers only. By 2018, the number of children living with two parents had dropped to 40 percent. More than half of all black families with children had only one parent living in the home. The percent who lived with mothers only had grown to 48 percent, while those who lived with fathers only had grown to 5 percent.[36]

In 1970, when the Census Bureau began to gather information on Hispanic children in the United States, 78 percent of them were living in two-parent families. By 2018, the percent of Hispanic children living with two parents had dropped to 67. The number who lived with mothers only had grown to 25 percent, while those who lived with fathers only had grown to 4 percent.[37]

While the percent of children living in two-parent households has drastically declined, so, too, has the percent of people who are married. From 1960 to 2017, the percent of adults who were married dropped from 69 to 53.[38]

Among whites, the percent of married adults dropped from 70 to 56 over that same time period. Figures for black adults who are married dropped from 61 percent to 38 percent. Asian adult marriage rates have remained consistent from 1990 at 2017 at 61 percent, the highest percentage for any ethnic group measured.

The percent of Hispanic adults who were married in 1990 was 57; in 2017, it was 47.[39]

"Acting Like Boys Instead of Men"

This challenge of family structure was taken up in 2008 by then-presidential candidate Obama. "But if we are honest with ourselves, we'll admit that what too many fathers also are is missing—missing from too many lives and too many homes," he said at the Apostolic Church of God in Chicago on Father's Day. "They have abandoned their responsibilities, acting like boys instead of men. And the foundations of our families are weaker because of it.[40]

"You and I know how true this is in the African-American community. We know that more than half of all black children live in single-parent households, a number that has doubled—doubled—since we were children. We know the statistics—that children who grow up without a father are five times more likely to live in poverty and commit crime; nine times more likely to drop out of schools and twenty times more likely to end up in prison. They are more likely to have behavioral problems, or run away from home, or become teenage parents themselves. And the foundations of our community are weaker because of it."[41]

Unfortunately, the left has failed to pursue Obama's call to action. Instead, they are calling for government to introduce richer social policies to alleviate the difference. But it's not just poverty that disproportionately affects single-parent households. According to Kay S. Hymowitz, a fellow at the Manhattan Institute and author of *Marriage and Caste in America: Separate and Unequal Families in a Post-Marital Age*, "Kids in single-parent homes have lower educational achievement, commit more crime, and suffer more emotional problems, even when controlling for parental income and education. Not only do young men and women from intact families (regardless of race and ethnicity) get more education and earn higher earnings than those raised with single mothers; they also do better than children who have a stepparent at home."[42]

For those who argue that if two-parent families are encouraged, then single-parent families will be marginalized—my response is that we need to broaden our minds. Think of "yes, and." To be able to understand and support one perspective (single parents) but also to do something else (encourage two-parent families). Encouraging two-parent families is not saying that single-parent families are bad—just that, statistically, the outcomes are likely to be better when both parents are involved, and that it makes sense to encourage both parents to participate in their children's lives.

Two potential caregivers, two potential breadwinners, two people to trade off childcare and household duties. Two adults to serve as role models and two parents to interact in different ways with their children. My husband and I have been married for over twenty years and we have both fully participated in raising our two children, who are now nineteen and seventeen, and it's still a lot of work and often hard.

Possibly the answer is yes, and. We should figure out how to better support single-parent households (let's say, for argument's sake, through subsidizing high-quality childcare) and also figure out how to encourage two-parent families to stay together.

Welcome to America

America is different from other countries in that it is composed mostly of settlers, immigrants, or descendants of immigrants. Native Americans and Alaskan Natives made up about 2 percent

of the U.S. population in 2018. The rest of us, or our ancestors, found our way to America from somewhere else. Some came
through South America and the Spanish explorers; some traveled over during colonial times; some were brought to America
against their will, and worked as slaves, as did their progeny.
More came over in the late 1800s and early 1900s, fleeing fam-
ine, escaping tyranny, or simply seeking to create a better life for
themselves and their children.

During the last half of the nineteenth century, we absorbed
an enormous number of immigrants as a country. Between 1840
and 1919, 32.5 million immigrants arrived on our shores. They
came primarily from European nations, fleeing wars, famines,
and religious and political persecution.[43]

In 1892, Ellis Island opened in New York Harbor as a gateway
to our country. Millions of people were processed at this location
before being allowed to enter the United States. Estimates are
that 40 percent of us in the United States today have ancestors
who came through Ellis Island.[44]

Like immigrants today, many of these arrivals were subjected
to prejudices as they entered the country. These waves of immigrants drove up the total percent of foreign-born people in our
country during that period.

In the early 1900s, when the number of foreign-born reached
15 percent of our population, Congress passed laws to restrict
the number of people who could enter the country legally; quota
systems were put in place that limited arrivals by country. These
laws favored European immigrants over people from other countries. For a time, mass immigration into America ended.

With the curtailment of immigration, the U.S. foreign-born
population fell from 20 percent in 1900 to 5 percent by 1965.
We had become less a nation of immigrants and more a nation
of native-born citizens.

This would soon change.[45]

In 1965, the United States drastically changed its system of immigration. No longer was immigration to be based on a quota system that led to most immigrants coming from Europe. The new system gave preference to applicants with skills and family already in the United States, which has led to an influx of Hispanics and Asians. It has also led to more immigrants in total, a lower median age for the United States, and a higher rate of population growth.

With the wave of new immigrants, the number of foreign-born people climbed again to 14 percent in 2015; it is predicted to reach 18 percent in 2065.[46]

According to Pew Research, from 1965 to 2015, immigration drove over half of the growth in the U.S. population. The number of immigrants in the United States more than quadrupled, from almost 10 million in 1965 to 45 million in 2015. Hispanics grew from 4 percent to 18 percent of the U.S. population between 1965 and 2015. During that same time, Asians grew from 1 percent to 6 percent of the population.

In 2015, first-generation immigrants had increased as a percent of the population to 14 percent. Second-generation immigrants were 12 percent. Combined, these two groups equaled 26 percent. In 1980, just 35 years earlier, these two groups comprised just 16 percent of the population.[47]

Immigrants are expected to continue to drive the country's population growth well into this century, at an even higher rate. Pew estimates that, by 2065, the number of immigrants will almost double and that immigration will drive "88 percent of the U.S. population increase."[48]

This current wave is composed primarily of Asians and Hispanics, with Asians taking the lead in terms of growth (35 percent) followed by Hispanics (25 percent).[49]

While the total number of immigrants has increased rapidly and demographics have changed, we are still a majority white country. But that, too, is projected to change.

Sometime between 2050 and 2055, the United States will become a majority minority country in terms of race. At that point, whites will remain the largest group but will fall below 50 percent of the population. In 1965, whites made up 84 percent of the U.S. population; by 2015, that percentage had fallen to 62.[50]

Pew estimates that, by 2065, immigrants and their children will make up more than a third of the U.S. population, double the percentage in 1965, and larger than the 26 percent in 2015. This influx of immigrants, combined with a lower birthrate among U.S. citizens, will create a demographic far different than it was in 1965. Pew estimates that, in 2065, the U.S. population will be 46 percent white, 24 percent Hispanic, 14 percent Asian, and 13 percent black.[51]

As our demographics have changed, so, too, have our laws regarding civil rights for all citizens. In 1954, the U.S. Supreme Court ruled in *Brown v. the Board of Education of Topeka* that schools could not be separate but equal. A decade later, in 1964, Congress passed the Civil Rights Act, making it illegal to discriminate based on race, color, religion, sex, or national origin.

These events, along with the historical backdrop of immigration waves that rise and fall, provide a good perspective from which to view the current debate about immigration, which has gotten out of hand. If there is no immigration reform, then the current trajectory will lead to a general population made up of a higher percent of foreign-born persons than we have had in modern history. What would this mean to our foundational and cultural framework? Would our country survive?

The issue has become politicized. Democrats have, in general, taken the "immigration is good" stand. This not only includes immigrants who came here legally, but also those who have entered our country illegally. San Francisco has begun allowing illegal immigrants to vote in local school board races if they have children under the age of nineteen.[52]

When Republicans push for security at our southern border, they are labeled racist. The discussion about how our nation can secure our borders and keep our citizens safe has devolved to name calling. We must do better.

Government Money

You know how it happens: You mean well, but the results don't turn out quite like you had hoped or anticipated. Call it the law of unintended consequences. As the Nobel Prize–winning economist Milton Friedman once said, "Government has three primary functions. It should provide for military defense of the nation. It should enforce contracts between individuals. It should protect citizens from crimes against themselves or their property. When government—in pursuit of good intentions—tries to rearrange the economy, legislate morality, or help special interests, the costs come in inefficiency, lack of motivation, and loss of freedom. Government should be a referee, not an active player."[53]

Alas, our government is a very active player in many different areas. The problem is that good intentions combined with a vast amount of money do not ensure success.

Prior to the Great Depression, which began in 1929 and continued through much of the 1930s, the federal government provided neither safety nets nor retirement benefits to the general population. That all began to change in 1933, when Franklin Delano Roosevelt won the presidency on a platform that promised swift action by the government to solve the challenges of the Great Depression. He rolled out the New Deal, a series of financial reforms and regulations, public works initiatives, and other programs.

Three decades later, President Lyndon Johnson introduced the Great Society programs. Their overall goal: to end poverty and discrimination and make our society great. Johnson said it was to provide "a safety net of assistance to the elderly, single mothers, the disabled, the unemployed, and people suffering from ill health."[54]

They were both Democratic presidents and both helped create a "complex system that now transfers hundreds of billions of dollars each month from one group of society to another, most often regardless of individual need,"[55] according to Cogan, author of *The High Cost of Good Intentions*, who is also a senior fellow at the Hoover Institution and a faculty member in Stanford University's Public Policy Program. In other words: a way to transfer wealth from one group to another.

The Great Society spawned numerous programs, each containing different requirements for eligibility and documentation. If you need assistance, you will often need assistance to get that assistance, to make sure you have properly applied to all the government programs for which you are eligible.

Roughly 180 million people in the United States receive government assistance of some sort (not including tax breaks).[56] Of these, about two-thirds receive benefits from two government programs and about half of those receive benefits from two other government programs. In total, "The $2.4 trillion the federal government currently spends on entitlements equals $7,500 for every man, woman, and child living in the United States," wrote Cogan, "an amount that is five times the money necessary to lift every poor person out of poverty."[57]

How times have changed! During Abraham Lincoln's presidency, from 1861 to 1865, the nation's sole entitlement program was for war veterans and their wives and/or children. This program would naturally run its course when the survivors died. Lincoln had fought for and won the passage of benefits for Union veterans. "During the late 1800's and early 1900's, the Republican Party used Civil War pensions as a tool to help realign the American electorate and secure unified control over Congress," Cogan wrote. This issue also led to the creation of the first national lobbying group, the Grand Army of the Republic.[58]

FDR's New Deal was paradigm-shifting. It marked the first time a government program provided benefits to citizens who had not provided a service to their country.[59] This provided a crack that has been pushed open wider and wider ever since. The challenge is there is no end to the number of people who could be determined worthy of government assistance.[60]

As the economy expanded, so did the rules and regulations covering entitlements. From 1950 until 1972, the growth was driven by political gain. The Democratic Congress used entitlements to gain votes from groups that benefited from the very entitlements delivered. According to Cogan, the crafting of such legislation was "a finely honed skill."[61] During that time, seven of the ten increases in entitlements came during election years. Not only were the benefits expanded, but so, too, was federal oversight.

Today, we have a vast network of programs that overlap and are hard to follow.

Our House in Order

For seventeen years, I have been volunteering at Our House, a homeless shelter for newborn babies and their families in Atlanta. After checking on the health of mother and baby, shelter workers seek to make sure that their clients are properly enrolled in government assistance programs.

Governments are no longer seeking to help a small number of people during times of recession. These days, they oversee an expanded web of benefits that are delivered even when the economy is roaring. And the beneficiaries now include a majority of Americans. In 2017, according to the U.S. Census Bureau, 51 percent of children under eighteen were living in households receiving government assistance. For married households, the percent receiving assistance was 41 percent; in households headed by females, 77 percent received assistance; and 41 percent of households headed by males received assistance.[62]

In providing people with cash or cash-like benefits, government programs spur the formation of interest groups that support candidates who promise to continue or to increase those payments.

As the percentage of Americans who receive support increases and the requirements to receive support loosen, the cost to our country is increasing dramatically—not only in total dollars but also as a percentage of our economy.

In 1947, entitlement spending represented less than 4 percent of the gross national product; in 2015, it was 16 percent of GNP. This means that one of every six dollars generated in our economy is going toward entitlements.

Over time, we have become a nation that has put in place a highly complex web of programs that redistribute wealth from some people to others. The Democrats who originally championed the increase in entitlements have moved past simple transfer payments and are now talking openly about moving our country in the direction of socialism.

The candidacy of Vermont Sen. Bernie Sanders as part of the 2016 Democratic primary process brought the term "socialism" into mainstream politics. Sanders, who ran as a Democrat in the 2016 presidential primary, has spent most of his time in office as an independent. He is running again in the 2020 Democratic primary.

While Sanders is the only major candidate in the Democratic primary to fully endorse the socialist label (remember he was an independent until he ran in 2016), four of the other leading Democratic candidates for 2020 have co-sponsored Sanders's "Medicare for All" bill and the "Green New Deal" resolution by Rep. Alexandria Ocasio-Cortez, D-NY, who is also a socialist.[63] These candidates, all of them senators, include Cory Booker of New Jersey, Kirsten Gillibrand of New York, Kamala Harris of California, and Elizabeth Warren of Massachusetts.

To an electorate that is used to government handouts, the move toward confiscation and mass redistribution is a seemingly small step. The Democratic Party has used this particular issue to focus their message on those with and those without—classic class warfare created to boost division and envy.

Instead of being a nation grateful to God for His blessings, and using those blessings to build upon, we are now a nation too often focused on faultfinding, leaving us divided in numerous ways: income, race, and gender, to name a few.

CHAPTER 5

Tribal Temptation

Historically, we have been a nation with multiple cultures underlying and intertwining with one another. We came from many places with different cultures and forged a single nation. The Great Seal of the United States, which is used to authenticate some federal documents, includes the Latin phrase *E pluribus unum*, which means "Out of many, one." This signifies the unity of the states under a federal government. While we came from different places and might eat different foods or dress in different ways, we have long recognized that we are, at our core, Americans.

Today, we are confronting forces that are driving us apart. Rapidly changing technology, media, and news combined with shifting societal trends have resulted in many of us yearning to belong somewhere—to be a part of something, making our environment ripe for a form of tribalization. It's identifying yourself by the group you belong to, rather than having your own personal identity.

Let's take a look at an extreme example of what belonging to a tribe can mean.

In November 2018, John Allen Chau, a twenty-six-year-old American adventure blogger and evangelical missionary, was killed by members of an isolated tribe on a remote island in the Indian Ocean.[1]

He had gone there to try to convert members of the Sentinelese tribe to Christianity.

The Sentinelese, who number fewer than 100, live under Indian jurisdiction on an island in the Andaman and Nicobar archipelago near India, Thailand, Malaysia, Sri Lanka, and Burma. The Sentinelese chased him off their island several times, the second time breaking up his canoe and forcing him to swim back to the boat of the fishermen who had transported him. The third time Chau encroached upon their island, the Sentinelese killed him. The fishermen Chau had hired to take him to the island saw the natives dragging a body on the beach and burying it. After several attempts to retrieve Chau's body, the police decided to leave him where he was buried to avoid other deaths.

An Extreme Example, but True

Tribes have been around for thousands of years. Possibly it's because we humans crave the sense of belonging and shared belief that are readily found among tribal peoples. We were hunter-gatherers before we began to settle down and raise crops about 12,000 years ago.[2] Belonging to a tribe meant safety and support. You knew who was in your tribe, who would protect you, and how your tribe operated. Lookouts would warn of strangers coming into your tribe's territory and alert your tribe of potential dangers. Some tribes would be welcoming; some, like the Sentinelese, would kill those who dared enter their territory. All tribes are different in a myriad of customs and conventions, but they all share one aspect with their members: a sense of belonging.

Being a part of a tribe provided members with physical safety as well as an understanding of how to conduct themselves both in the tribe and in relationship to people in other tribes. It provided a framework for understanding the world and a framework for living. It established customs regarding marriage, work, the raising of children, security, and worship. Some tribes were matriarchal, where the power was possessed by and passed down through women; some were patriarchal, where the power was held by and passed down by men.

Some tribes enslaved others, captured others, conquered others. Other tribes were the ones enslaved, captured, or conquered. Different tribes developed different skills; some were craftsmen, some hunters, some warriors. Tribes sometimes grew so large as to create a nation, but more often than not, numerous tribes were contained within a single nation. As it is today.

As the human population grew and tribes began to interact more closely with one another, some smaller tribes were absorbed by larger tribes; some tribes merged; some fought one another. Despite these differences, each tribe provided its members with an identity larger than that conferred by their immediate family. Some tribes required allegiance to the tribe over the family, or even the individual. "A tribe is a group of people connected to one another, connected to a leader, and connected to an idea. For millions of years, human beings have been a part of one tribe or another," wrote Seth Godin, a former dot-com business executive and American author who has written extensively about tribes and marketing. "A group needs only two things to be a tribe, a shared interest and a way to communicate."[3]

While being a part of a tribe first and foremost might have made sense when there was no other support structure, our nation was formed on a foundation of individual liberty rather than tribal liberty or identity. Our nation was founded by people who had immigrated from a variety of places or whose ancestors had done so. Individual rights come first, not the rights and values of tribes or any other type of group. This focus on the individual provides each of us with more personal freedom, but also more personal responsibility.

The Founding Fathers established this structure to ensure we would not be ruled by a king or monarchy. Prior to our declaring freedom, we were a colony of Great Britain, whose king held all of the rights and determined which of those rights he would bestow on the colonies.

This sense of tribalism and belonging can be seen today in century-long conflicts in the Middle East and in many other areas. Countries that attempt to combine tribes and sects and to govern them jointly often encounter limited success. For example, Afghanistan is so mired in tribalism and sectarianism that generations have been raised to hate and fear their tribal neighbors. The result is often open conflict with members of rival tribes.

Our country, too, has a history of tribalism, with Native Americans belonging to hundreds of tribes before their land was settled by Europeans. The tribes lived in different geographic areas, had different ways of living, and different customs. They interacted with one another in a variety of ways.

As various groups (one could call them tribes) came to North America from different parts of the world, they brought with them different customs and perspectives that also influenced our nation.

Colin Woodard, a journalist and author who has written about Native Americans, argues that we have never been a single country but rather several regions (which also edge into Canada and

Mexico). Even the name of our country, the United States, reflects the fact that it is composed not of a single unified geographic area, but a federation of states. From Woodard's perspective, there are "eleven regional nations, some of which truly do not see eye to eye with each other." They are, instead, a reflection of the people who initially lived in the various areas, the immigration that affected these areas, and the ways they changed over time.[4]

Woodard labels these eleven regions as Yankeedom, New Netherland, the Midlands, Tidewater, Greater Appalachia, The Deep South, New France, El Norte, the Left Coast, the Far West, and the First Nation. These regions extend beyond the United States into parts of Mexico and Canada. New France and First Nation are located entirely in Canada, the Midlands spans both the United States and Canada, and El Norte spans the United States and Mexico.[5]

The regions were colonized by people from different areas and—due to their religious background, economic/industrial structure, or other unique features—developed their own identities. Some regions were more likely than others to receive waves of immigrants. For instance, New Netherland—which includes New York—received millions of immigrants over the years. This has resulted in an ever-changing mix of inhabitants with different ethnicities and backgrounds, with a bias toward multiculturalism. While history does not necessarily determine the present or the future, it does provide a perspective that can help us in understanding where we came from and where we are going.

Our American experiment changed our perspective from one focused on tribal interests to one that viewed the country as a whole. While settlers from different areas and even Native Americans fought on different sides during the American Revolution, over time, we forged a more unified country.

While we might belong to different underlying groups, they, for the most part, became subordinate to our being American.

These subgroups may have been part of our identity, but they did not define our entire identity for most of us.

Without a Common Enemy, We Find It Hard to Achieve Unity

Our Civil War nearly tore our country in two. But in the end, the Union prevailed—paid for in lives, property, and treasure. World War I and World War II had a unifying effect on our country. More recently, President Ronald Reagan's leadership through the end of the Cold War against the Soviet Union provided us with a common enemy against which our nation came together. Since the end of the Cold War and the fall of the Berlin Wall in 1991, we have no clear enemy against which we can unite.

We are now a people relatively disunited.

As noted above, we have seen multiple waves of immigrants throughout our nation's history. Many arrived in our land to find themselves the objects of prejudice and discrimination, even physical attacks. According to History.com, during World War II, more than 110,000 Japanese-Americans were incarcerated in internment camps.[6]

But by the mid- to late-twentieth century, Americans believed overwhelmingly that their country was great and that our greatness could be traced to the fact that we are a nation of immigrants.

Much has changed to move us away from the tribal background of our past: Instead of riding horseback, we can travel across continents before breakfast by jumping on a plane; instead of using smoke signals, we can communicate thoughts and pictures to millions at the touch of a button on our iPhones.

Our Tribal Instincts Are Strong

Yet, as our nation's population has grown and technology has increased our ability to interconnect with one another, our tribal instincts have remained strong.

That's reflected in our growing use of the word to describe a variety of areas in our lives—from workout groups to marketing and brand management discussions and even online courses.

This constant talk about tribes could be exacerbating our problem. Yes, it's helpful to think of a community of people interested in an area as a tribe. However, when tribal members exalt loyalty to members of their own group above any other loyalty, conflict can ensue.[7] The question becomes: To what extent do we identify with tribes, and to what end?

In our country today, we divide ourselves into groups in a variety of ways—by geography, high school, college, sports teams, and political parties. By gaining membership in these loose-knit tribes, groups, or simple affiliations, we find comfort and support in belonging to a larger group, in identifying with people we admire.

We all need to belong to something. Doing so provides us with a sense of self, a foundation from which to operate, a community with which to associate. When we are isolated, we are more likely to feel lonely and more likely to become depressed. "One of the most powerful of our survival mechanisms is to be a part of a tribe, to contribute to (and take from) a group of like-minded people,"[8] Godin concluded.

Think back to the various tribes or groups you have been part of throughout your life: sports teams, social clubs, churches, volunteer groups, community organizations, and possibly a political party. Now think about those teams' rivals: Atlanta Falcons versus

Green Bay Packers, Catholic Church versus Baptist, Kiwanis versus Rotary, Coca-Cola versus Pepsi. Most of the time, your affiliations are a way to join in and cheer for your team, to be a part of something bigger. While you might believe that your team (tribe) is better than the rest, you understand that someone else might believe the opposite.

Take, for instance, football teams. In our family, there is a constant rivalry between those who root for the Atlanta Falcons and those who prefer the Green Bay Packers. My husband, son, and I are Falcons fans. My sister, her husband, my daughter, my father, and his wife are Green Bay fans. When the two teams play, each side roots for their preferred team. When that team loses, we are sad—sometimes for days. We give each other a hard time when the other team loses, but in the end we put it all in perspective and can sit together at a Green Bay–Falcons game without anyone requiring medical assistance.

But problems can occur when you join a tribe and stop thinking on your own, but instead blindly follow the tribe's belief system and understanding. This is especially dangerous when that system includes the belief that people outside your tribe are wrong or bad. We stop thinking, and we just judge those that identify with a group other than ours.

Big challenges arise when we not only prefer our group, but believe there is something inherently wrong with any other group and that the people who identify with the other group are bad just due to affiliation.

In a world of uncertainty and casual relationships, tribal membership can be so comforting that we may find ourselves tempted to support a tribal act that we don't agree with—just to avoid possible expulsion.

The current cult of tribalism is a push to the extremes, according to Godin. "All tribes are made up of partisans, and the more partisan the better. If you're a middle of the roader, you don't bother joining a tribe."[9] If we are all more partisan and are pushing for more partisans to join our side, we cannot be surprised when there are no more middle of the roaders left. If they are left, they are probably disengaged, too discouraged to join the fray.

There have been times in my life when I did not feel like I was part of any group or belonged anywhere. I felt lonely, isolated. In December 1978, a month after my father's first congressional victory, we moved to Fairfax, Virginia. My sister and I changed schools in the middle of the year, which is always challenging, so that Dad could be near Washington. I was in the seventh grade, a shy, quiet girl. I can remember that first day in my new school. I walked into the lunchroom and realized that I had no one to sit with. I looked around, alone.

Seventh Grade Angst—In the Lunchroom

Too scared to walk up to people whom I did not know, and scared of being rejected, I turned around and walked out without eating. After that, I spent most of my lunch periods reading in the school library. Reading alone was far better than risking rejection. That semester, I made it through the *Chronicles of Narnia* by C. S. Lewis and a handful of Ray Bradbury's books—at lunch.

Yes, I was shy, but that didn't fully explain my difficulty in making the transition. The new school was also a very different environment than I was used to. I had grown up in a small, rural town and attended the local public school. My new school was also a public school, but much bigger and with a more sophisticated student body. Their clothes were more expensive than mine, their language was coarser, their actions more brazen (some of my schoolmates were selling drugs on campus). I remember seeing a group of kids gathered in a hallway, exchanging pills for cash. Now, my guess is that, with money, I could have joined that group—but clearly their values were not mine and I had no interest in doing so.

At some point, I did make friends, and I am sure I sat with them at lunch—but what I most remember of that school is sitting alone in the library.

In college, many students find a sense of belonging by joining sororities or fraternities. After college, a job with a large company or membership in a business organization can fill this need, as can social clubs. Many people belong to a variety of such organizations. Most of us have no confusion about being a member of several organizations or groups. But that can change when the norms and beliefs of one group conflict with those of another.

Today, tribes are everywhere, and they form around issues of all sorts. Based on today's political standards, as propagated by the media, women, gays, and people of color should be part of the Democratic Party. Does it matter that putting entire groups (women) into one category (Democratic) is by definition prejudiced? Not if it's the current narrative.

But these narratives are being broken.

Candace Owens, the communications director of Turning Point USA, kicked off BLEXIT in 2017. According to its website, "BLEXIT is a frequency for those who have released themselves from the political orthodoxy. It is a rebellion led by Americans wishing to disrupt the simulation of fear."[10]

BLEXIT holds rallies across the country, championing blacks who have left the Democratic Party and are now Republicans.

There are others who are rejecting the notion of identifying with special-interest subgroups. For example, on February 5, 2019, Chris Barron (@ChrisRBarron) tweeted his stance, which is paraphrased:[11]

> Love our country and am gay. As for the LGBTQ group—not sure what that means. I am not a member.

Barron is a political strategist who co-founded GOProud, a political organization representing gay conservatives.

The Twitter responses he received ranged from hateful to dismissive; a few were supportive. Below are paraphrased examples:

> Who invited you anyway?

*   *   *

> The worst part of his lifestyle? Loving American—maybe that will change too.

*   *   *

> Whatever, have no idea why you tweeted this. You can't be part of a group that won't let you think on your own.

Clearly, Barron has determined that belonging to the LGBTQ group was not part of his identity, even though he is gay.

These examples are growing. The threat of adhering to subgroup identity over national identity is that, as we become more tribal and divisive, we could cause our nation to split apart. When there is no natural majority and there are no common, binding beliefs, then it is hard to have a majority rule.

In the last few decades, some people have traded their beliefs about the value of integration and assimilation for different beliefs about the value of creating and of adopting subgroup identities. Some of this has been the natural result of previously marginalized groups identifying themselves and pushing back against prejudices. But in today's society, we have moved from recognizing and confronting prejudice, which should be done, to prejudging people negatively based on the assumed privileged status someone else has assigned them based on race, sex, or any other identifier.

"A Nation of Minorities"

While integration might have been the goal for immigrants in our nation in a previous time, now we have some in our country who disdain assimilation. They have no desire to be part of a majority. They see themselves primarily as members of a minority subset or various minority subsets, with those who are not part of their subset as their oppressor.

Ethnic ideology, a set of beliefs focused on a person's ethnicity, which occasionally became more important than other identifying attributes, became the vogue decades ago. The result, according to Arthur M. Schlesinger, Jr., a Democratic organizer, historian, and writer who died in 2007, was the cult of ethnicity. It produced "a nation of minorities—or at least minority spokesmen—less interested in joining with the majority in common endeavor than in declaring their alienation from an oppressive, white, patriarchal, racist, sexist, classist society."[12]

The challenge is that, by simply labeling a group's members based on their attributes, "victims" of the opposite group (now termed privileged) can lead those labeled as victims to have lower expectations for themselves, and for others to lower their expectations of those who are in the supposed "victim" group. Additionally, those who are labeled privileged can end up having their accomplishments dismissed. Of course they should have done well—they are privileged! If they are successful, it is not due to their own effort, and if they are not successful, then they are stupendous failures since they are "privileged."

During the process, this identification based on physical attributes has created a hierarchy of victimhood and oppressors. In today's structure the top of the privileged pyramid would be white males. In order for them to be accepted by those who view themselves as victims, they would need to acknowledge their "privilege."

Jonathan Haidt, a social psychologist at New York University, talked about intersectionality operating in academia under the guise of identity politics on the *Charlie Rose Show* on PBS in March 2017. His take: "What's happening now in a few departments is they are being taught one perspective to look at everything. 'Let's divide everybody up by their race and gender and other categories. We'll assign them moral merit based on their level of privilege, being bad, and victimhood, being good. Now let's look at everything through this lens.' So it's this one totalizing perspective, all social problems get reduced to this simple framework."[13]

The problem with this simplistic structure is that it labels one group bad (the so-called oppressor) and the other good. This is done over and over again to get ranking of merit based on victimhood. While this might have come about as a way to discuss and overcome discrimination, it has instead created ways to categorize people based on their particular race, sex, ethnicity, etc. According to Haidt, "Once victimhood becomes the new lens, victimhood trumps anything else. It becomes a struggle about power—not justice. For example, regarding Israel, the Palestinians are the victims. So, therefore, they are the good and the Jews or the Israelis are the bad."[14]

This, too, is a social exclusionary tactic. For those who believe in this social construct, if you don't agree (that you have white privilege and acknowledge it), then you are ****. Fill in the blank with whatever derogatory term you would like. No matter the unique characteristics of the individual in question. So what if the white male is from a broken home in West Virginia, was raised in poverty, and is addicted to meth? Those convinced of the truth of intersectionality will cry white male privilege, or possibly toxic masculinity.

Another example—a black woman born into a millionaire household, who goes to an Ivy League college and works on Wall Street, would still be a victim of toxic white masculinity.

Something just doesn't make sense. Yes, our country has discriminated in the past based on race, and discrimination should not be allowed. But to create and use another way of sorting people into groups based on race and sex, and then judging individuals based on a group's attributes—well, it's prejudiced.

But wait, someone will argue, we are also the nation that enslaved blacks and killed the indigenous people. Yes, that's true, but we had a Civil War and the Union won. We've passed the Civil Rights Act. Are we a perfect country? No. But if we work together for the benefit of all Americans, we can get better. However, if we decide that progress is possible only by tearing down those who were born male and white, then we will rip our country to pieces.

The real challenge to us is whether we both appreciate the good parts of our history and acknowledge the bad without enduring the ongoing self-flagellation that is all too often the approach of those on the left. While one side of our country beating up on the other side might provide temporary relief—and a temporary outlet for our national self-loathing—it would do nothing to help us reach our goals of creating a better country for all.

What should we do? Reject prejudice of any type, and be grateful that we live in a country that is based on individual rights, while putting those rights into action.

CHAPTER 6

Party versus Party

O ur society is undergoing rapid changes in media and technology. Add humans' propensity for tribalism, and the result is polarization of our political parties. There are fewer voices in the middle, and the voices of extremists on both sides are amplified, so much so that they drown out nearly all else. The center is largely silent, disengaged, or possibly afraid to voice their opinions, and we are pulling apart—toward the extremes. At the same time, each party blames the other for the polarization.

Several forces are fueling the polarization and resulting rage between Democrats and Republicans. They include the sorting of both parties by ideology, the widening of gaps between the parties on many of the major issues, the effect of people using political ideology as a substitute for their personal identity, the fact that the news media rewards extremist voices by focusing their coverage on them, and the coverage of politics as though it were a sport.

Should we care about the two parties becoming more polarized? Yes, and here's why: In order to solve problems, legislators must pass legislation and the president must sign the legislation into law. Then, the administrators who implement the law have to do so in a way that follows its spirit and intent. In the best of times, with good intentions, this is not easy. It wasn't intended to be. If the process were, then one person or a single political faction could more easily wrest control of the government. In fact, our Founding Fathers designed our government to be inefficient and hard to maneuver to ensure that legislation contained a balance of various points of view, perspectives, and interests.

Our government has two legislative bodies, one that is slower-moving and gives equal representation to each state (the Senate) and one in which each state's number of representatives is based on its population (the House of Representatives). This structure (a bicameral legislature) ensures that there is a balance between the interests of large and small states.

This, combined with the two other branches of government (executive and judicial) makes our government inherently inefficient in the short term. But in the long term, this structure is effective in reflecting the will of the people, and in preventing any one person or group from gaining control. While government might be inefficient, the people of our nation still want it to make progress, even if the progress is slow.

And slow it is. In an increasingly polarized, and greatly divided country, it is hard to make any progress at all. The more ideologically split the two sides, the less room for compromise. Any representative who dares compromise by ceding an inch to the other side risks attracting the kind of backlash from his or her own party base, who could oust them from power in the next primary election.

That's not just a theoretical musing. From 1994 to 2012, several incumbents on both sides lost in their respective primaries, rejected by their own parties for not being sufficiently pure ideologically. In 1994, David Levy, R-NY, lost by 54 votes to Dan Frisa,[1] who went on to win the general election. Frisa had lost to

Levy in 1990, but Levy's success was short-lived. The Republican Revolution in 1994 helped fuel Frisa's win.

In 2000, Matthew Martinez, D-CA, lost to Hilda Solis, who then won the general election. Martinez had supported a "gun-control measure backed by the National Rifle Association. and his efforts to help ban late-term abortions had made him vulnerable to a challenge," according to his obituary in the *Los Angeles Times*.[2]

In 2002, Thomas Sawyer, D-OH, lost to Tim Ryan, who also won the general election. Sawyer had voted with Republicans on free-trade measures and paid the price in the primary.[3]

In 2006, Joe Schwarz, R-MI, who supported abortion rights, lost in the primary to the more conservative Tim Walberg, who argued that Schwarz did not represent his constituents.[4] They must have agreed. Walberg also won the general election.

In 2008, three incumbents, Al Wynn, D-MD; Wayne Gilchrest, R-MD; and Chris Cannon, R-UT, lost in the primaries to more extreme opponents. Their opponents were Donna Edwards, Andrew Harris, and Jason Chaffetz, respectively. Edwards attacked Wynn "for his initial support of the [Iraq] war, even though he has since called for withdrawal of troops,"[5] reported CBS News.

Edwards "also criticized his vote for a 2005 bankruptcy-reform bill that [she] said exacerbated problems for homeowners facing foreclosure."[6] Edwards went on to win the general election, too.

Harris attacked Gilchrest for voting with Democrats on a timeline for withdrawing troops from Iraq.[7] Harris lost in the general election. Chaffetz beat Cannon by focusing on Cannon's more liberal stance on immigration. Chaffetz also won the general election.

Two years later, in 2010, Bob Inglis, R-SC, lost to Trey Gowdy, who also won the general election. Inglis, who stated he believed in climate change, had come out in favor of a carbon tax to reduce emissions.[8] In 2012, Tim Holden, D-PA, and Jean Schmidt, R-OH, lost to Matt Cartwright and Brad Wenstrup, respectively, both of whom won the general election.[9] Wenstrup had called out Schmidt's votes in favor of raising the debt ceiling.[10]

Yet some coalitions are attempting to reach across the aisle. In the Democratic House, the Blue Dog Coalition is composed of "pragmatic Democrats, appealing to the mainstream values of the American public." Their focus is on "fiscally-responsible policies, [and] ensuring a strong national defense."[11] With 27 members in 2019, the coalition represents 11 percent of the 235 Democratic House members.

On the other side, the Republican Main Street Partnership has "a commitment to conservative, pragmatic government as well as compassion in our communities and character in our national leaders." Its "members are solutions-oriented fiscal realists and defenders of national security, advancing positive policies that can command bipartisan support."[12] Its 2 Senate and 68 House members represent 4 percent of the GOP senators and 29 percent of its representatives.

There is a huge disparity between the number of moderate voters and the number of moderate elected officials. Over a third of our electorate claim the moderate label, according to Gallup.[13] But only 11 percent of nationally elected Democrats and 29 percent of nationally elected Republicans align with moderate coalitions.

When compromises do occur and legislation is passed, it's rarely reported or talked about. That may be because there is no controversy, and controversy sells in the news. Combine this with the overall mainstream media bias against Republicans and you'll find scant coverage of bipartisan success under the Trump administration.

Instead of celebrating bipartisan successes, we tend to focus on the issues that drive us apart. It's these issues that drive viewers to the cable news programs and readers to newspaper websites. After all, these are the items that people will rant and rave about.

There has been a recent shift in party composition and ideological makeup. Party identification (Republican and Democrat) is not the same as ideological identification (liberal, moderate, or conservative). When I was growing up in the 1970s, it was common to have some conservative Democrats and some liberal Republicans. The result was that both parties had more ideological diversity than they do today. This meant that, even though two people might belong to different parties, they often held similar views on specific issues. Take Senator Sam Nunn from Georgia, who served from 1973 until 1997. While a Democrat, he was a moderate, voting with Republicans for school prayer and in favor of a constitutional amendment to balance the budget.

When there were people in opposite parties with similar ideological views on issues, they could work on those particular issues together, and come up with bipartisan solutions, even though they might have disagreed on other issues. There was always some issue that someone in the other party could work with you on solving.

This ability to work on problems together allowed politicians from both parties to get to know their counterparts in the opposite party in a nonadversarial way. They talked to them, spent time with them, occasionally worked together with them, and successfully solved problems with them. The end result—a connection made with another person and a problem solved. This experience of working together and solving a problem would help the two officials build a foundation of trust and mutual respect that could prove crucial later on. When the next problem popped up, there would be someone on the opposite side of the issue with whom you had worked successfully before. Someone to whom you could reach across the aisle and work with again. It was possible to build bridges between parties.

Bipartisan Legislation? Yes, It Exists

Recent examples of bipartisan legislation include the historic Veterans Administration reform, legislation that addressed the opioid crisis, the Farm Bill, and Criminal Justice reform. None of these received much media coverage.

The VA Mission Act of 2018, signed by Trump June 6, 2018, was approved by 92 percent of Republicans and 94 percent of Democrats in the Senate. In the House, it was approved by 99 percent of Republicans and 60 percent of Democrats.[14] When I looked up "VA Mission Act" on the *New York Times* website for the week of the signing, I found no mention of this historic legislation. It was covered by CBS News, which reported that the bill provided "military veterans' access to private-sector health care, should they choose to seek medical care outside of that provided by the Department of Veteran Affairs."[15]

The Patients and Communities Act, which addressed the opioid crisis, passed in the Senate with 98 percent of Republicans and 100 percent of Democrats voting for the bill. The support in the House of Representatives was almost as high, with 91 percent of Republicans and 94 percent of Democrats voting yes. President Trump signed the bill on October 24, 2018. There was no mention of this legislation in the *New York Times* during the time of the signing and little coverage in other mainstream news.

The Agriculture Improvement Act of 2018, signed on December 20, 2018, was approved in the Senate by 75 percent of Republicans and 100 percent of Democrats. In the House, it was approved by 77 percent of Republicans, and 95 percent of Democrats. The *Washington Post* reported that President Trump signed "the $867 billion farm bill that provides billions in aid to U.S. farmers while rejecting deep cuts to the federal food stamp programs sought by some House Republicans."[16]

" 'We have to take care of our farmers and ranchers, and we will take care of them,' Trump said at the signing ceremony, going on to praise Democrats in Congress for their work on the bill."[17]

The *New York Times* had its own take on the bill's passage: "a sweeping, $867 billion farm bill—a result of rare bipartisan compromise that critics say [President Trump's] administration is already seeking to undermine by using regulatory power to restrict access to food stamps." I guess no good bipartisan deed goes without some criticism. Instead of praising the bipartisanship and passage of the important bill, the *Times* noted "the fact that it managed to slip through a hyperpartisan Congress currently battling over whether or not to shut the federal government down was hailed as a positive, if slightly dissonant, development."[18]

Criminal justice reform, or the First Step Act, was approved by 75 percent of Republicans and 100 percent of Democrats in the Senate. In the House, 77 percent of Republicans and 89 percent of Democrats approved. Trump signed the bill December 21, 2018.

The coverage in the *New York Times*, based on a search for the bill's name during that time period, came up with two opinion articles. One was titled, "Donald Trump Is Doing Something... Good?"[19] Which makes it seem as though the *Times* was trying to make something good seem like something bad.

While the bills mentioned above might have been passed on

a bipartisan basis—they were not provided much media coverage, and if bipartisanship was mentioned at all, it was often with skeptical coverage.

So, while there is some, limited bipartisanship, the media's focus is on what tears us apart. Searching for viewers and readers, maybe?

With both parties increasingly becoming more ideologically pure, members of each side are finding fewer potential allies across the aisle, because the ideological overlap has decreased. Additionally, with less ideological diversity within each party, there is less exposure, and therefore less understanding of different ideologies.

Take a Democrat to Lunch

It's hard to understand another side's perspective if you have never even met with someone from the other side, much less sat down to dinner with them. This is why, in international affairs, it's so important to go and meet other countries' leaders. These meetings often include not only time for discussion of the issues, but also time to share a meal.

Pew Research tracks ideology in relationship to ten political values, to test the overlap between the two parties and views on specific issues. In 1994, when the parties were more ideologically diverse, there was considerable overlap on the issues. Based on the answers for the ten areas, almost a quarter "of Republicans were more liberal than the median Democrat." There was also overlap on the Democratic side, with 17 percent of Democrats "more conservative than the median Republican."[20]

This meant, in 1994, that people from two different parties might nevertheless be relatively close from an ideological perspective. For instance, many Southern Democrats in the 1990s were fiscally conservative and identified as conservative Democrats. Today, members of the Blue Dog Coalition in the House of Representatives are more fiscally conservative than the rest of the party, but their numbers are small, holding just 27 (11 percent) of the 235 Democratic seats. Nathan Deal, who was a founding member, switched to the Republican Party in 1995 and went on to serve as governor of Georgia from 2011 to 2019.[21] He is applauded by members of both parties for his work on criminal justice reform and early education while he served as Georgia's governor.

Democratic President Bill Clinton was able to work with my father, Speaker of the House Newt Gingrich, R-GA, during 1995 and 1996 to pass legislation that led to welfare reform, the largest capital gains tax cut in history, and four consecutive balanced budgets. This was the last time that our country balanced the budget, and the only time in my lifetime. The negotiations resulted in the government shutting down a few times as part of the process, but in the end both sides came to an agreement and moved forward. While plenty of pundits have blamed my dad for creating this polarized environment (which he is not responsible for), he is rarely given credit for balancing the budget with Clinton.

As the number of lawmakers in the center has shrunk, the number of lawmakers on the extremes has grown—from majority to super majority. In 1994, 64 percent of Republicans were to the right of the median Democrat, and 70 percent of Democrats were to the left of the median Republican.[22] By 2017, 97 percent of Republicans were to the right of the median Democrat, and 95 percent of Democrats were to the left of the median Republican.[23]

These days, the overlap of ideologies on issues is tiny. Only 1 percent of Republicans are more liberal than the median Democrat, and only 3 percent of Democrats are more conservative than the median Republican. This means there are almost no issues where the two parties' beliefs overlap, making it harder to find common ground, work together, and create solutions that most of the country will agree with. This widening gap in ideology has led to fewer opportunities to work across the aisle. As a result, each side is spending less time with people who have different political beliefs. This widening gap in ideology and the reduction of time together have led each side to view the other side's members as different, or even bad.

Some specific issues have driven this divide wider over the past few years. For example, the number of Democrats and Democratic-leaning independents who say government should help the needy has risen sharply—from 54 percent in 2011 to 71 percent in 2018; while Republicans and Republican-leaning independents barely moved on the topic—from 25 percent to 24 percent. The gap between the two parties in their belief on this topic has moved from 29 percent to 47 percent—almost entirely due to shifts in the Democratic Party.[24]

This gap can be seen in the approach the country has taken to help those in need. Some Democrats on the left are arguing for a universal basic income, regardless of whether a person works. Some Republicans are arguing for shortening the amount of time a person can receive welfare benefits and adding work/education/training requirements. Democrats seek to fix problems with more government intervention, Republicans by encouraging individual responsibility and less government intervention. Both see a problem—but differ on the solution.

Partisan Differences over Racial Discrimination

The partisan difference in views about racial discrimination against blacks has almost quadrupled, increasing from a 13-point gap in 1994 to a 50-point gap in 2019. The percent of Democratic and Democratic-leaning independents who say "racial discrimination is the main reason many blacks cannot get ahead" has risen from 39 percent to 64 percent, while the percent of Republicans and Republican-leaning independents who say the same thing has declined from 26 to 14 percent.[25]

This large gap is driven largely by Democrats embracing the concept of blacks being victims and the belief that it is not a lack of individual effort but an oppressive system that is to blame when there is a lack of progress. Many Democrats believe that systems have to be changed for individuals to make progress. This view is opposite to that held by Republicans, who believe that individual effort is what makes the difference, even though the system might not be perfect.

In 1994, Democrats and Republicans held near-identical views regarding the belief that "immigrants strengthen the country because of their hard work and talents," with 30 percent of Republicans and 32 percent of Democrats agreeing with that statement. Since then, more people in both parties have come to agree with this view, but the gap between the two parties has grown dramatically. Today, 84 percent of Democrats and 42 percent of Republicans say immigrants strengthen our country—a 42-point gap.[26]

Today, many Democrats have embraced not just legal immigration, but illegal immigration, creating sanctuary cities (and potentially states) and reacting with the reflexive "racist" accusation whenever someone suggests stopping illegal immigration. This is a ridiculous stance and has resulted in some odd optics. For his 2019 State of the Union Address, President Trump invited Debra Bissell, whose parents were shot and killed by an illegal immigrant. Rep. Bonnie Watson Coleman, D-NJ, invited an illegal immigrant to be her guest.[27]

During the same speech, Trump laid out his agenda for immigration reform. "Now is the time for Congress to show the world that America is committed to ending illegal immigration and putting the ruthless coyotes, cartels, drug dealers, and human traffickers out of business,"[28] he said.

He then said why border security was needed.

"As we speak, large, organized caravans are on the march to the United States. We have just heard that Mexican cities, in order to remove the illegal immigrants from their communities, are getting trucks and buses to bring them up to our country in areas where there is little border protection."[29]

Trump spoke of our country's "moral duty to create an immigration system that protects the lives and jobs of our citizens." He added, "I want people to come into our country, but they have to come in legally."[30]

Everyone Pays a Price for Illegal Immigration

It's not only citizens and legal immigrants who pay the price of illegal immigration, according to Trump, but also those who are coming illegally. They pay the price by becoming victims of sexual assault. "Human traffickers and sex traffickers take advantage of the wide-open areas between our ports of entry to smuggle thousands of young girls and women into the United States and to sell them into prostitution and modern-day slavery."[31]

An unsecure border results each year in needless deaths. "Tens of thousands of innocent Americans are killed by lethal drugs that cross our border and flood into our cities, including meth, heroin, cocaine, and fentanyl,"[32] he said.

"The savage gang, MS-13, now operates in at least 20 different American states, and they almost all come through our southern border. Just yesterday, an MS-13 gang member was taken into custody for a fatal shooting on a subway platform in New York City. We are removing these gang members by the thousands. But until we secure our border, they're going to keep streaming right back in."[33]

His goal: "My administration has sent to Congress a common-sense proposal to end the crisis on the southern border. It includes humanitarian assistance, more law enforcement, drug detection at our ports, closing loopholes that enable child smuggling, and plans for a new physical barrier, or wall, to secure the vast areas between our ports of entry."[34]

The Democratic stance is that there is no need for a wall, that we should look at women and children at the border from a humanitarian perspective and that any attempt to stop migrants from coming to our nation is racist. I am sure that there are both Democrats and Republicans who could work together to solve the problem. Unfortunately, they are not the ones getting media coverage.

What's also not getting much national media coverage are comments like this one, from Mark Morgan, a former Border Patrol chief in the Obama administration, who said this about President Trump: "The president is right. The wall works."[35]

In addition to the gap in issues and beliefs between the parties, there is also a difference in the demographic makeup between the parties. While both parties have become more diverse in the past four decades as our country has become more diverse, the Democratic Party has changed more rapidly.

Those who identify as Democrats or Democratic-leaning independents tend to be higher-educated, younger, more racially diverse, and include a higher percentage of women than those who identify as Republicans or Republican-leaning independents.[36] More than half (56 percent) "of women identify as Democrats or lean Democratic, while 37 percent affiliate with or lean toward the GOP."[37] Certainly part of this discrepancy can be traced to the ongoing media bashing of women who are not Democrats.

African-American voters identify with the "Democratic Party or lean Democratic by an overwhelming margin (84 percent Democrat to 8 percent Republican), according to a 2018 Pew Research report. Hispanic voters align with Democrats by greater than two-to-one (63 percent to 28 percent), while Asian-American voters also largely identify as Democrats or lean Democratic (65 percent Democrat, 27 percent Republican)."[38]

The size and strength of each party's dislike for the other intensified from 1994 until 2017. In 1994, two thirds (68 percent) of Republicans (and leaners), and more than half (57 percent) of Democrats (and leaners) held a negative view of the opposite party. The percent who responded very unfavorably were close, with 17 percent for Republicans and 16 percent for Democrats.[39]

By 2017, 81 percent in both parties held an unfavorable opinion of the opposite party. Those who hold a very unfavorable view increased over 2.5 times with almost half in each party saying they held a very unfavorable view (44 percent of Democrats and 45 percent of Republicans) of the other party.

Picking Friends by Their Party Affiliation

Unfortunately, this animosity is directed not only against the opposite party, but against the people who make up the opposite party. This has led to a majority in both parties determining their friendships based on party affiliation. Both Republicans (57 percent) and Democrats (67 percent) have a lot of close friends in the same party. But 64 percent of Democrats and 55 percent of Republicans say they have few or no friends in the opposite party.[40]

When people talk about political ideology, it's normally about whether someone identifies as a liberal, a moderate, or a conservative. Recently, as the parties have become more ideologically pure, the labels have become less about issues (issue ideology). People have begun to identify with the political party itself; think of this as identity-ideology.[41]

The catch with identity-ideology is that it is not about values, issues, or policy; it's about belonging, being a part of something bigger than yourself. With belonging, there is an automatic determination that you are part of a group (included) as opposed to being outside of a group (excluded). This view of who is in and who is out creates an us-versus-them mentality. In its most simplistic form—my group good, your group bad. It is this identity-ideology that "drives liberal-versus-conservative rancor,"[42] according to Dr. Lilliana Mason, assistant professor of government at the University of Maryland, and author of *Uncivil Agreement: How Politics Became Our Identity* (University of Chicago Press, 2018).

Yes, each group dislikes the other just because they are the other group. It sounds like we are reverting back to middle school; it often feels that way.

This shift from an issues-based identity to a social one has far-ranging consequences. When you join a social group, you may take on the group's identity as your own. For example, when someone joins a fraternity or sorority, it's not unusual for that person to adopt the attributes of the group as a whole. For example, if your son goes to college and joins a fraternity where the men wear khaki pants and golf shirts, don't be surprised to see him wear khaki shirts and golf shirts more often. This is why parents often warn their children, especially those of an impressionable age, to watch the company that they keep.

The next step is to prefer people who are part of your group over people who are not part of your group. This is due, in part, to simple familiarity (you know them) and to fear (you know your group will accept you, but you are not sure if those who are not in your group will accept you). Now that you identify with, resemble, and prefer being around members of your group—the next step is that you decide that those who are "in" your group are better than those who are "out" of your group.

Welcome to the all-too-human curse of feelings of moral superiority. We love to feel like we are better than others—perhaps morally superior to an entire group. This is not due to facts but to the connection between the status of the group you belong to and your concept of your identity. You decide that your group is better, because you think it is.[43]

Let's take a few recent examples.

In October 2018, much of the nation watched as Christine Blasey Ford testified in front of the Senate Judiciary Committee stating that she had been assaulted sexually by Brett Kavanaugh in 1982, when she was fifteen and the Supreme Court nominee was seventeen.[44]

It was important that the allegations were heard and taken seriously. It was equally important that the accused had the opportunity to respond. Due process and the presumption of innocence make up the foundation of our country's legal system.

Ford's testimony was raw, emotional, and compelling.

She said she had gone to a party in a house where there was drinking. She said she was pushed from behind into a bedroom, and that Kavanaugh and another boy, named Mark Judge, entered the bedroom and locked the door. She said Kavanaugh then groped her, tried to remove her clothes, and put his hand over her mouth. Eventually, she freed herself and left the room and the house.[45]

To me, Ford was credible; I believe she was molested at the party.

However, investigators uncovered no corroborating evidence that Kavanaugh was the attacker, or that he was even present at the event she described.

According to Ford, one of her best friends was with her at the party. This friend, Leland Ingham Keyser, said in a statement that she did not know Kavanaugh and did not believe she ever saw him at a party. One of the other males Ford remembered being at the gathering—whom she absolved of wrongdoing— said in a statement that he did not remember any such event.

Ford could not identify a fourth male she remembered being there.[46]

These statements were given to the Senate Judiciary Committee. It's a felony to lie to the committee.

I believe Ford's testimony; I believe this is her memory.

I also believe Kavanaugh.

As he said, "Allegations of sexual assault must be taken seriously. Those who make allegations deserve to be heard." He made clear that he believed Ford had been assaulted "by some person in some place at some time"—but not by him.[47]

Kavanaugh's initial statement was emotional, defiant, and raw. He talked about the toll this public airing of accusations by Senate Democrats and the media had had on his family—and how he wanted to testify and clear his name as soon as possible. His voice cracked. He was moved to tears, but he would not quit. In his words, he "would not be intimidated into withdrawing from this process.... You may defeat me in the final vote, but you'll never get me to quit. Never."[48]

Kavanaugh "categorically and unequivocally" denied that he had ever sexually assaulted Ford—or any woman. He said clearly that he believed she experienced the trauma she described, but in no uncertain terms, he added, "I am innocent of this charge."[49]

Kavanaugh acknowledged having participated in normal high school antics, saying he was "not perfect in those days," and that he "did things in high school that make me cringe now."[50]

Yet, during the course of the hearing, senators added into the record letters signed by hundreds of women who knew Kavanaugh throughout his high school, college, and professional careers, and who described him as a man of impeccable character.

Senator Dianne Feinstein, D-CA, did not notify the Senate Judiciary Committee on July 30, 2018, when she received the letter from Ford that made the allegation and requested a confidential investigation into the matter. If Feinstein had been concerned about the victim and wanted to provide privacy to the victim, rather than play politics, she would have notified the committee so they could have investigated the allegation privately. Instead, it turned into a media circus.

Flatulence References in the "World's Greatest Deliberative Body"

It is depressing that Ford and Kavanaugh and their friends and families had to endure Feinstein's orchestrated media circus due to her putting politics first.

And it is sad that we had to watch Democratic members of the Senate, which is sometimes referred to as the "world's greatest deliberative body," ask a U.S. Supreme Court nominee about references to flatulence and inside jokes that were written in a high school yearbook.

I am sorry for what Ford had to endure—both in 1982 in high school and in 2018 in the Senate.

The hearing itself was an example of the most partisan of partisan politics. Sen. Cory Booker, D-NJ, condemned Kavanaugh during the nomination process, claiming that anyone who did "not oppose his confirmation is 'complicit in evil.'"[51]

At this writing, Booker is seeking the Democratic nomination for president. With him was Senator Elizabeth Warren, D-MA, who is also seeking her party's presidential nomination. With Warren at his side, "Booker described the Kavanaugh confirmation battle as a 'moral moment' that demands that all who oppose evil also oppose the constitutional originalists' confirmation,"[52] wrote Jack Crowe, a news writer at the *National Review*. Performing for a primary audience maybe?

After Ford testified, a number of women rushed to state that they "believed in her," ignoring the fact that believing in something is not the same as following due process and looking for evidence. Senator Kamala Harris, D-CA, yet another candidate for the Democratic presidential nomination, used the confirmation hearing as a testing ground. "By deliberately insinuating that Kavanaugh was somehow connected to the Trump administration's efforts to defend itself against the Russia-collusion probe led by Robert Mueller, Harris not only gained the kind of publicity that is fundraising gold for a potential candidate, she also made it clear that she would stop at nothing in her efforts to smear opponents,"[53] reported Jonathan Tobin, a contributing writer for the *National Review*.

The Senate confirmed Kavanaugh. As it should have.

Muted Reaction to Virginia Political Scandals Involving Democrats

A few months later, when a series of scandals broke in rapid succession in Virginia implicating Democratic politicians, the party's reaction was more muted.

It began with Virginia House of Delegates hearings on legislation proposed by Democratic Delegate Kathy Tran. During a hearing in late January 2019, Republican House Majority Leader Todd Gilbert asked her if the legislation that she had introduced that "would loosen restrictions on third-trimester abortions would allow a pregnancy to be terminated while the mother is in labor." Tran responded, "My bill would allow that, yes."[54]

The legislation was tabled.[55]

Two days later, during a televised interview, Virginia Governor Ralph Northam (Democrat) was asked what would happen under the legislation to a fetus that was not viable or had severe deformities.

"The infant would be delivered; the infant would be kept comfortable; the infant would be resuscitated if that's what the mother and the family desire, and then a discussion would ensue between the physicians and the mother,"[56] Northam said.

The resulting furor from the Republicans and right-to-life groups was immediate and national in scope.

Two days later, a picture appeared on the Twitter feed of Big League Politics, a media website founded by former Breitbart News employees, that showed Northam's yearbook page from 1984, when he was in medical school. One of the pictures was of two men, one in blackface and one dressed as a Ku Klux Klan member in a white robe and pointed hat.

The photo was given to Big League Politics by someone who was mad about the abortion comments, according to Patrick Howley, its editor-in-chief.[57]

Northam initially apologized for having been in the picture, but later recanted, saying he did not think he was either of the men depicted.

The interesting thing to me is that the furor over the man in

blackface was greater than the furor over the man in the KKK outfit. While blackface is degrading to and demeaning of black people, the KKK outfit represented a group that killed black people.

The Virginia saga continued.

On February 3, 2019, Big League Politics published an allegation of sexual assault by Virginia Lt. Governor Justin Fairfax
(Democrat). The next day, Fairfax—who was next in line had
Northam resigned—denied the allegation. The accusation came
from Vanessa C. Tyson, an associate professor of politics and an
expert in black history at Scripps College in California.

The location of the alleged sexual assault was the 2004 Democratic Convention in Boston.[58]

Fairfax's second accuser spoke out on February 8, accusing
Fairfax of a "premeditated and aggressive" sexual attack when
they were undergraduates at Duke University in 2000.[59]

While Democratic leaders and activists eventually called for
Fairfax to resign, their numbers and strength were sparse and
weak compared with those who were vocal during the Kavanaugh hearing.

While the rapid response to the KKK/blackface photo on
Northam's yearbook page included condemnations and calls
for his resignation, the response to the allegations against Fairfax was slower. This could be a 2020 presidential race preview
of "a potential collision of two powerful forces in Democratic
politics—the battle to combat racism and the movement to stop
sexual harassment," wrote Jenna Portnoy, Gregory S. Schneider,
Neena Satija, and Laura Vozella of the *Washington Post*.[60] The
point: When you are constantly trying to appeal to victimization
(racial or gender-related in this case), it becomes hard to determine who has been victimized the worst when events conflict
with one another.

After the second accuser came out against Fairfax, calls for

With both parties becoming more ideologically pure, the expanding gap regarding issues, the increase in identity ideology, and identification of party by color, political coverage often appears similar to coverage of, well, a horse race.

Election night coverage provides viewers with breathless, wall-to-wall updates on who is winning where, and which party is ahead or behind at any given moment.

The news coverage during election season is more likely to be about the latest poll among likely voters rather than about coverage of the issues themselves, even though the polls themselves are often inaccurate. That's likely because the reporters themselves pay so much attention to the day-to-day, superficial stuff that they themselves often appear to have a poor grasp of the issues.

When they do focus on issues, they often do little more than review how a given candidate may have changed his or her opinions about a given issue over time rather than delving into thoughtful coverage about the issue itself. Since people increasingly identify with ideology and party based on social identification rather than issues, this non-issue-based coverage amplifies the view shared by many that politics is a team competition.

The Sportification of Politics

Think of it as the sportification of politics. Winning at all costs, focusing on outcome rather than process, and vilifying the other at any opportunity. It's an "us good, you bad" mentality. What we have learned is that, due to this focus on winning and social identity, "levels of partisan bias, activism and anger have increased,"[71] according to Mason.

As social-based identity overwhelms the importance of issue-

his resignation increased. Over a month later, both Fairfax and Northam were still in their seats.

These examples of different takes on alleged sexual assaults (Kavanaugh and Fairfax) illustrate how perceptions change based on whether the person being accused is in or out of the group with which people identify.

Take, for instance, Trump's State of the Union Address in 2019. "And exactly one century after Congress passed the Constitutional amendment giving women the right to vote," Trump said, "we also have more women serving in Congress than at any time before."[61] A true factual statement. But NPR's fact check noted that "There are more women in Congress than ever before, but that is almost entirely because of Democrats, not Trump's party."[62] Trump never mentioned what party the women belonged to, so his statement was correct!

Now that politics has become a social identity, people respond to it socially. Just knowing that someone is a member of the other party can lead to anger or dislike. Stacey Abrams, the Democrat whose bid to be governor of Georgia proved unsuccessful, used Democratic identity to generate enthusiasm and action among her supporters. People wanted to vote for her because she was a minority woman candidate—her gender and color created enthusiasm among Democratic voters.

People often disagree with and dislike each other based on where they stand on specific issues—but it's less than half the size of the hatred and dislike people have for one another due to their belonging to the other party.[63]

Know Which Team You Belong To

The overlap of issue-based ideology and identity-based ideology has led people to distance themselves (within friend groups, social groups, and neighborhoods) from those in the other groups and move toward those in the same group. In our greatly divided nation today, it's not important that you and your team hold the same views on all the issues; it's just important that you know which team you belong to and therefore which team to hate.[64]

This does not require that people disagree on the issues. In fact, they might not even be aware of the issues. "The passion and prejudice with which we approach politics is driven not only by what we think, but also powerfully by who we think we are,"[65] concluded Dr. Lilliana Mason.

In their book *Mistakes Were Made (But Not by Me)*, Carol Tavris and Elliot Aronson wrote about blind spots in party issues and support. They included research by Geoffrey Cohen that revealed that Democrats supported a traditionally conservative, restrictive welfare policy proposal when they believed it was promoted by their party and that Republicans would support a more liberal or expansive welfare program when they believed it was promoted by their party. "Conservatives and liberals alike will bend over backward to reduce dissonance in a way that is favorable to them and their team," wrote Tavris and Aronson. "Our efforts at self-justification are all designed to serve our need to feel good about what we have done, what we believe, and who we are."[66]

Part of the increase in ideology-based perspective has been fueled by the identification of a single color for each party, a further indicator of who is on and off our political team. Election night television coverage first featured a map of the United States with states identified by color of the winning party on November 3, 1976. At 3:30 a.m., NBC Anchor John Chancellor called Mississippi, which locked the win for Jimmy Carter. The state turned red (yes, red in those days), and Carter won. This

was the first year that results were displayed on a map a the newscast.[67]

The map was fourteen feet tall, made of plastic, with bulbs behind the states. During practice prior to election some of the map melted from the heat—a cooling system to be installed to prevent a meltdown. The colors reflected political leanings of the British Parliament—whose Labour P identified with red and Tories with Blue.

"If you studied the ratings that night you will see the audien share for NBC grew as the night went on," said Bill Wheatley, former NBC News executive. After ratings increased for NBC two other networks added maps to their election coverage during the next election cycle. CBS used the same colors as NBC, but ABC flipped the colors—red for Republicans and blue for Democrats.[68] During the next few election cycles, the colors for the parties would flip back and forth. There was no consistency between election years.

The digital touch screen (magic wall) was debuted by John King on CNN in 2000. After that year's contentious election between Senator Al Gore, D-TN, and Governor George W. Bush, R-TX, the election hung in the balance for over a month. In order to track the results, the *New York Times* and *USA Today* printed color-coded maps. Republicans were red and Democrats were blue.[69]

Throughout the days and weeks following the election, there was nonstop coverage, with the colored maps giving viewers a quick way to grasp what team, party, and candidate was in the lead. Since then, the colors have stuck.[70]

The color party connection is so great that I know of a Republican candidate who was told not to wear blue—the over-the-top advice was ignored.

based identity within the political arena, winning becomes about more than issues—it's a reflection of who you are as a person and if your team—the group you identify with—is winning. If you lose, it's personal. The loss is not about a specific candidate, but is about you. You lost. If your candidate or party wins, it's also personal, a sign that you are better than those on the losing team. "The ultimate consequences of this psychology of competition are an uncivil attitude about elections and increased mobilization," according to Patrick Miller and Pamela Johnston Conover, political scientists who have written about partisan hostility and voting.[72]

Because the identification is social and personal, those who closely identify with a party may judge members of the other party to be "rivals who are fundamentally immoral and cannot be trusted; likewise, they are enraged at each other for 'destroying American democracy.'"[73] It's never our fault, it's someone else's, and that someone else belongs in the other party.

As partisanship and social identity increase, the anger at the "other" party, which is destroying America, can be used as leverage to mobilize voters to campaign and to get out the vote. If this mobilization were more issues-based, it might prove helpful toward creating solutions. But since it's driven more by social identity and being considered part of the "in" group that is working against the "out" group, the political polarization continues.[74]

When elections are not decisive, but close, the competition between the two parties only increases. Just think of your favorite sports team—when it competes annually with a close rival, the stakes are high. Imagine if there were no other rivals to play, but you played only the one opposing team over and over again, with the outcome hanging on a small percent of the total vote. The competitive focus would become more important than the game itself.

These close elections drive up the competition, with the result that the "strongest partisans express the greatest rivalry and anger, predisposing them to take uncivil actions," according to Miller and Conover.[75] The overall result is that political behavior of the masses reflects these uncivil actions.

So here we are, driven by labels and colors and ideology with many people unaware of the actual issues underlying either party or ideology structure. But that does not matter. What matters is that they know what color represents their party, and what subgroup with which they identify is part of which larger political party. The motivation and mobilization of the bases on both sides of the political spectrum is now based more on who people think they are than in what they actually believe.

This was clearly on display during the 2019 State of the Union Address. When President Trump talked about securing borders, record low unemployment, rapid economic growth, U.S. Immigration and Customs Enforcement success, and the rights of babies to live, the majority of the Democrats remained seated. When Trump mentioned how many women had been elected, they stood.

Rep. Liz Cheney, R-WY, tweeted early the next morning, "Things my Democrat women colleagues wouldn't clap for at #StateOfTheUnion2019 tonight: America, freedom, free enterprise, law enforcement heroes, record low unemployment for women & minorities, the right of babies to live. Things they did clap for: themselves."

Because people currently use political party identification as a way of identifying where they fit in society, most people believe the party they belong to reflects who they are as people. Even more important, they believe that the party another person belongs to reflects that other person's social values. This belief affects not only what we do in the political arena, but what we do in all areas of our lives. Politics is the new way to interact socially. Think of it as my party good, your party bad—for both sides. This conflating of party with social acceptance and value is making politics more divisive and uncivil, not better.

CHAPTER 7

Outrageous Outrage

Political outrage is everywhere. Whom are we to believe? What are we to believe? Whom can we blame?

Let's back up to election night of 2016. I was in New York at the Trump victory party. When the night began, I thought a Trump victory was possible, but not probable. As the night wore on, I knew that he would win the election. How could I tell? By watching the mainstream media's coverage of the election. The expressions on the anchors' faces were sour and sad. Even though the TVs were on mute, I could tell the anchors were not happy.

It was as if they were hoping—believing—that if they just delayed their reporting, that the Democratic Party's candidate, former Secretary of State Hillary Clinton, would win.

When the networks began delaying calling the states for one party or the other, combined with the anchors' sad looks and their broken demeanor, I knew that Trump would emerge triumphant.

While the anchors and media pundits appeared stunned by the concept of Candidate Donald Trump becoming President Donald Trump, I was not. The Democratic nomination process had been ridiculous and, quite frankly, should have elicited outrage from those on the left, but it didn't.

Based on a WikiLeaks report, it is my opinion that the Democratic National Committee (DNC) had effectively rigged the nomination process in favor of Hillary Clinton. As a result, DNC Chair Debbie Wasserman Schultz, a congresswoman from Florida, resigned her DNC post. Donna Brazile, who was then working as a contributor to CNN, resigned after they found out she had leaked debate questions to the Clinton campaign before a CNN town hall debate.[1] (In March 2019, Brazile became a contributor to Fox News. Odd that they hired her, knowing that she leaked the CNN questions.)

So, what happened? Trump won the election; Democrats were beside themselves; many of them still can't understand how Trump could have won. They searched for reasons outside themselves and found one. Ah must be collusion.

The investigation started with information about George Papadopoulos, a campaign adviser, and was fueled by a fake dossier. This dossier was funded by Team Clinton and the DNC (Sen. John McCain, R-AZ, leaked it to the press). This investigation started before the 2016 election and continued until March 2019. For over two years the U.S. Justice Department investigated potential Russian collusion.

During this time, media outlets were constantly covering the so-called collusion and obstruction investigation, alleging Trump's involvement.

The investigation was massive, with more than 2,800 subpoenas issued, almost 500 search warrants executed, and about 500 witnesses interviewed. According to Attorney General William Barr, this was led by a team of 19 lawyers who were supported by "400 FBI agents, intelligence analysts, forensic accountants, and other professional staff." Cost? Over $24 million.[2]

The result of the investigation? No proof of collusion.

Based on the findings of the investigation, no one from the Trump campaign organization had been shown to have conspired or coordinated with the Russians—despite the Russians' best efforts. With no collusion, the obstruction inquiry also fell flat.

Throughout the ordeal, President Trump expressed his outrage over the coverage. With the report of no collusion—his outrage makes total sense.

This real-life example provides us with two examples of political outrage.

The first—the outrage displayed by Democrats when what they expected did not happen (Clinton lost, Trump won).

Second, the outrage expressed by President Trump over the media's focus on the investigation into his campaign for potential collusion, where there was no collusion. Charlie Kirk, founder and president of Turning Point USA, kept a running tally of the nonstop coverage. His tweet from this spring is paraphrased:

> More than 2,300 stories from the Washington Post and New York Times. More than 6,000 stories run by MSNBC and CNN. So many thousands of stories about the Mueller investigation, with a lot of speculation and no grounding in reality.

It seems that, during the coverage of the Department of Justice investigation into Russiagate, the media was jumping at any movement, shadow, or sound and reporting on it unendingly. I call this a Bunny Bark.

It's what our six-year-old, twenty-pound rescue dog, Bunny, does when she takes after a squirrel, bird, walker, or shadow, which she does with equal amounts of enthusiasm. She goes flat out, full speed ahead, with no concern about whether the shadow she is chasing is real.

She just barks, and barks, and barks.

When we jump and bark—all too often we are not sure what we are barking at, we are just certain that barking is our job. In our case, we express ourselves not by barking, but through our human expressions of outrage. Some of them are justified, some might be useful, but most accomplish nothing more than make the world a more outrageous place.

I blame our outrageous outrage on all of us. We are all Bunny Barking.

The Merriam-Webster online dictionary offers three definitions of the noun "outrage." One, "an act of violence or brutality"; two, "an injury, insult; an act that violates accepted standards of behavior or taste"; and three, "the anger and resentment aroused by injury or insult."[3] Most often in our political arena today, we use the word for its second or third definition. But in today's world, acts of political outrage often end up so extreme—so over the top—that they are unbelievable. The outrage is expressed through acts, or words, that are way outside the bounds of acceptable behavior, and the outrage is a result of the anger and resentment due to a real or perceived injury. We are almost constantly outraged about politics.

When the outrage gets out of hand, which it can easily do, violence can ensue.

We have all been outraged at some point in our lives. When you were young, your parents may have enraged you; your siblings, too. Add to the list friends, co-workers, neighbors, relatives—you name them—they have probably led you at some point to become outraged. It's part of the human condition; the very act of being in community with others means that you interact with them. If you interact with them, then you are bound to experience points of abrasion, contention, and misunderstanding. The question becomes: How do you handle this conflict? Is your default reaction one of outrage? If so, it becomes very hard to remain in community, in harmonious relationship with others. Who wants to be in a relationship where the other party is always outraged?

Sometimes we become outraged due to a perceived injustice, either to ourselves or to someone else. This is understandable, and sometimes warranted. Sometimes an expression of outrage is helpful. It can start movements, attract attention, fuel action. As an example, Rosa Parks's decision in 1955 to refuse to surrender her seat to a white passenger on a city bus in Montgomery, Alabama, proved to be a productive way for her to express her outrage at segregation.

The Rev. Dr. Martin Luther King, Jr., channeled his outrage at segregation to fuel the passion with which he gave his "I Have a Dream" speech at the Lincoln Memorial in 1963, a speech that proved so powerful that it helped bring about the passage of the Civil Rights Act of 1964.

But allowing oneself to be outraged all the time and about everything is unlikely to result in such successes. More likely, it will simply result in exhaustion. People tend to ignore the outrageous outrage, and it's not helpful at all.

That's all too often where we are today in our political arena. Beset by ongoing outrage, which is itself outrageous and exhausting.

Learning to Control Our Outrage Begins as a Toddler

The hard part is determining when outrage is helpful and when it is not helpful. Most of us learn this over time. Children have no filter, no way to stop simply reacting to how they feel. Babies scream when they want something. Over time, they learn when this screaming works and when it does not, and adjust their behavior accordingly. Toddlers throw fits. There are various ways that parents can handle these fits when they occur in public: Pick up the child and take him away or placate the child so she will be quiet. The first teaches the child that their fits will not result in their getting what they want; the second tells her that fits will result in placating actions from her parents. If parents take the second route, their children will learn to throw better fits to get even more of what they want.

If you reward bad behavior—you will get even more of it.

As people mature, they usually learn to control their emotions, not to deny them, but to channel them productively. Some people throw fits as adults, and in some circumstances, those fits are looked on as part of the job—Nick Saban, the head football coach of Alabama, threw his headset to the ground during the Alabama-Oklahoma game at the 2018 Orange Bowl—while his team was ahead 28–10. The reason for his lost temper? The Alabama team had "committed three pre-snap penalties with the ball down at the Oklahoma 15-yard line late in the first half of the Orange Bowl,"[4] according to *USA Today*. This is part of how Saban coaches. Alabama won 45–34 and thereby earned another trip to the national championship.

Political outrage was visible in March 2019 when the Cook County State's Attorney's Office announced it had dropped charges against actor Jussie Smollett for sixteen counts of allegedly lying to police about an alleged hate crime he had reported. Prosecutors concluded that Smollett's account was not true, and a grand jury had already indicted the actor when the prosecutor's office dropped the charges. Chicago Mayor Rahm Emanuel expressed his outrage at a news conference after the news broke.[5]

"This is without a doubt a whitewash of justice and sends a clear message that if you're in a position of influence and power, you'll get treated one way," Emanuel told reporters. "There is no accountability, then, in the system. It is wrong, full stop."[6]

The prosecutor's office announced that the charges were dropped and that Smollett had forfeited his $10,000 bail and had voluntarily completed sixteen hours of community service.

Emanuel was outraged that hours of taxpayer-funded police work had been for naught and that the reputation of the City of Chicago had been stained. As he spoke, Chicago Police Superintendent Eddie Johnson and other officers stood next to him.

"We'll have conversations after this," Johnson said. He was direct regarding his belief about the identity of the true culprit: "At the end of the day it was Smollett who committed this hoax," he said.[7]

Both of these events, Saban and Emanuel, are examples of acceptable outrage, in my opinion.

But the definition of acceptable behavior can vary, depending on the context in which it occurs. For example, some football fans may consider throwing a headset to the ground in disgust to have been acceptable behavior. But if the CEO of a Fortune 100 company were to do the same thing, he or she might wind up getting fired.

As I've gotten older, I have noticed that, even when I feel outraged or upset, I am more able to separate my feelings from my behavior. I might feel outraged, but do I act that way? If I am rested, present, and in the moment, then I am typically more able to let the wave of emotion associated with feelings of outrage rush through me without reacting. Once the wave has receded, I can then choose how to react.

But still, too often, I react too rapidly—becoming outraged at something someone else did or said. I have often told my children that they may not be able to control what happens to them, but they can always choose how they react; that a reaction based on emotion allows the other person to control you; that a sign of maturity is to take a breath and choose how to act on your own. When I do forget to follow my own advice, my children are glad to remind me to do so.

How is your own outrage triggered? And in cases where it is triggered, are you able to control your outrage to use it productively? Think about how you react when you hear a negative comment from a person regarding a group you identify with. Does it outrage you? How closely you identify with the group that is the target of the comment can make a difference. Was it a personally directed insult, an insult directed at your family, or an insult directed at a group to which you belong?

If a disparaging comment is directed at a group, whether you take the insult personally will be determined, in part, by the number of groups you belong to. When you are a member of multiple groups that don't wholly overlap, you're not defined by any single group. If one group you belong to is the target of the offensive comment, then you might shift your perspective to that held by members of another group.

Establish a Broad Range of Friendships

But those individuals who have only one set of friends and no other groups with which to identify, may find their personal identity tightly woven into the single group's identity. This may make those individuals "less psychologically equipped to cope with threat and [they] may feel [a] higher level of negative emotions when confronted by threat"[8] against a group, according to Lilliana Mason, an assistant professor of government and politics at the University of Maryland and author of " 'I Disrespectfully

Agree': The Differential Effects of Partisan Sorting on Social and Issue Polarization."[9]

This is why parents often encourage their children to join groups that have sprung up around different areas of their lives, so that when a problem or confrontation arises in one group, they can fall back on other groups for support.

For example, if a middle schooler has friends in school, ballet, and choir, and the groups are made up of different people, the student can socialize with several different groups. If there is a fracturing of camaraderie among members of one group, the other two will likely still operate as normal. There will be no blowback from the other two groups. This provides the child with a buffer to ease the impact of conflict within one group. If all three groups have the same people as members, then a conflict in one group will carry over into the other two as well.

Now, let's apply these schoolyard lessons to our political systems. In recent years, as political parties have become less ideologically diverse, many of us have chosen to associate primarily with people who think politically like we do. This means that, for most people, their friends are part of their political party identity. These factors have led people in both political parties to think of members of their own party (or group) as good and those in the opposite party (or group) as bad.

Research on political parties has found that, instead of judging people who are members of political parties as individuals, we tend to judge them based on the way we feel about their party. For example, we tend to judge people in opposing parties as bad, even though we may not know them as individuals. And the converse is also true: We tend to like those who are in our own party, even if we don't know them as individuals.

According to research conducted by Professors Shanto Iyengar of Stanford University and Sean J. Westwood, who was then at Princeton, this bias toward our party and against the other party "has increased substantially over the past four decades."[10] This correlates with a decline in the diversity of party ideology and a decline in the number of people who have friends with different political beliefs.

This is not bias that we are even aware of, but it is so automatic and without thought that "hostile feelings for the opposing party are ingrained and automatic in voters' minds," wrote Iyengar and Westwood. It's feelings without thought. According to their research, the bias against people who are in the opposite party "may be more sizable than race—but hard to tell if as frequent."[11]

If reading about this research produces a feeling of outrage in you…let that feeling just sit for a while. Should you become outraged when your potential biases are questioned? If you do, what does that mean?

People Feel Free to Discriminate Against People in Opposing Parties

In recent years, political polarization and subsequent rage against the other party have become normalized and are now viewed as acceptable within our society. It's not okay to discriminate based on any other criteria, but according to Iyengar and Westwood, people "feel free to express animus and engage in discriminatory behavior toward [people in] opposing parties."[12] They argue that there is social pressure not to discriminate based on race, sex, ethnicity, or a host of other attributes, but that there is no social pressure to "temper disapproval of political opponents."

The result: You can't hate me because of my race or gender, but it's fine to hate me because of the political party I support.

For example, President Donald Trump is known for his outrageous tweets and speeches against his detractors. For example:

> @realDonaldTrump Mar 28
> "The Fake News Media is going Crazy! They are suffering a major "breakdown," have ZERO credibility or respect, & must be thinking about going legit. I have learned to live with Fake News, which has never been more corrupt than it is right now. Someday, I will tell you the secret!"

Democrats also use Twitter to spread outrage. Here's an example from Rep. Maxine Waters, D-CA:

> Maxine Waters @RepMaxineWaters
> "Kellyanne Conway, the "alternative fact" is your husband George is absolutely correct. Who do you support, your loving husband or this unhinged president?"
> 11:04 AM - 21 Mar 2019

Celebrities express their outrage as well:

> The last two years, Donald Trump has made our nation sad, sick, perplexed, and dead. We are a nation at war. We are debilitated, unable to function, and furious that he will not be punished.

So, based on those few entries, hatred can be okay, as long as it is directed toward the other party. This is the real danger of political polarization. It not only allows for hate, but promotes hate as a way to galvanize people who are in your group against those who are not in your group. It relies on pushing down the people in the opposing group to improve one's own group.

This is contrary to what courses in business leadership teach us. What we should be doing is developing others and improving the world for all of us—not just a portion of us. But this requires us to be balanced and secure in ourselves. It requires that we shrug off personal attacks by others, meet them where they are, and help them end up in a better place. This is my working definition of grace.

High on Self-Righteousness

But still we often push down someone else to make ourselves feel better. Maybe we respond so often with self-righteous indignation because it makes us feel good. This theory was written about in 2012 in a *Wired* piece titled "Why David Brin Hates Yoda, Loves Radical Transparency."

Brin's argument? "There's substantial evidence that self-righteous indignation is one of these drug highs," that we are self-righteous toward others because it makes us momentarily feel good about ourselves, "and any honest person knows this."[13]

The last time you acted in a self-righteous manner, did you feel superior to, even better than, the other person? Have you ever spiraled out of self-righteous control, convinced yourself that you are better in each and every way? Possibly, if we were aware that our displays of self-righteousness are motivated more by a desire for pleasure than by anything else, then we might stop being so self-righteous.

But why do overt displays of outrage appear to be becoming more frequent and more dramatic—let's call them outrageous outrage. Here's why: connectivity, social media, amplification, corporatization, and tribe building all play a role, and they are all increasing. There is the increase in connectivity due to technology; anyone can share their outrage at any time with anyone else.

Social media provides a variety of platforms on which to share outrage and to jump on the outrage bandwagon. How better to prove you are a member of your group, or tribe, than by adding your voice of outrage to theirs?

Amplification comes not only from social media, but also from traditional media. In their continual ratings chases, mainstream media outlets prize controversy, even if that means they have to manufacture it. Corporations have also become part of the outrage machine, both in support of and in protest against those who amplify outrage. Corporations pick and choose which groups and/or individuals to support. The tribalization of group identification amplifies the outrage.

Our current lack of real community building fuels overt expressions of outrage in two ways. First, being part of the outrage machine gives us a way to fit into a group we select for ourselves. Second, a lack of real communities means that there are fewer places where adherence to societal norms can prevent outrage from erupting into full view in the first place.

Let's explore the first: Let's say someone decides to identify with a group online. Then the group we identify with dislikes something. We then determine that we, too, dislike that same something. If the group can't claim us, at least we can claim them, by adhering to their values and reinforcing their beliefs, words, and actions. So they tweet, we tweet. They attack someone, we jump on board.

Second, with fewer real communities, when we act or react outrageously, there is no pushback, since those who see our expressions of outrageous outrage tend to be strangers or people whom we seldom see. There is little chance that we will see them again and that they will remember our outburst of outrageous outrage. Additionally, once we become outraged, those who are near us and watch our eruption with no social pushback are more inclined to express their outrageous outrage as well.

Children stop throwing tantrums, at least in part, because their parents tell them the behavior is unacceptable. Then, if a child does throw a fit, the parents take the child out of the situation where the fit is being thrown. If there is no one in the groups with which you socialize to provide you with behavior guidelines, to reinforce the message that expressing outrage is not acceptable, you might be led to believe that expressing your outrage does work.

If many of us identify tightly with one political party or the other, what do we do when we are confronted with opinions or beliefs that are opposed to what we or our party believes?

Cognitive Dissonance

Such a situation results in cognitive dissonance, "a state of tension that occurs whenever a person holds two cognitions (ideas, attitudes, beliefs, opinions) that are psychologically inconsistent," according to Carol Tavris and Elliot Aronson, social scientists and authors of *Mistakes Were Made (But Not by Me): Why We Justify Foolish Beliefs, Bad Decisions, and Hurtful Acts.*[14]

This means that, if your personal identity is tied to a group you not only belong to, but identify with personally, you will view insults to that group as insults to you personally.

Once you get mad, you are likely to try to justify your anger. After all, if you believe that only bad people get angry for no reason, and you believe you are not a bad person, you must find a reason for your anger. This can also lead to self-justification for any of your other thoughts, deeds, or acts, especially in today's world where we all too often view mistakes as signs of failure, rather than as precursors to learning.

The problem with self-justification, according to Tavris and Aronson, is that it "is more powerful and more dangerous than the explicit lie. It allows people to convince themselves that what they did was the best thing they could have done. In fact, come to think of it, it was the right thing."[15] It also gives us a pass for our bad behavior because, of course, we had no choice. It allows us to overlook our mistakes because they, of course, are not our fault. Cognitive dissonance drives people to confirm their beliefs, even when confronted with evidence that their beliefs are not correct. We select facts that confirm our beliefs. This is confirmation bias.

The result, forming an opinion—any opinion—means that we are less likely to accept new information that supports a view contrary to the one that we hold. Once we decide which side is right or wrong, the potential for us to understand or empathize with the other side is diminished.[16]

Once we have formed an opinion, we prejudge all subsequent information we receive, without even being aware of the filter, to see if it fits our opinion. The result? We continue to believe whatever it was that we believed before we got this new information, and we see everything in that light, feeling better about ourselves along the way.

When we are challenged, we can both feel and vent our outrage, even if we do so in an outrageous way, as there are no societal norms preventing us from doing so. In theory, we once again seek to justify our actions by telling ourselves that not only are we entitled to express rage, but that doing so makes us feel better. Of course, that is just not true. Expressing outrage only increases outrage.

In our own lives, when we behave poorly, we experience dissonance. But to feel good, we need to feel innocent and virtuous.

To resolve our dissonance, we become outraged at the faults of those we have harmed and thereby make ourselves feel better.

Rage Feeds upon Itself, Resulting in More Rage

While expressing rage or outrage might cause us to feel good, doing so does not mitigate our rage. Research by Tavris and Aronson found that expressing rage, participating in outrage (letting your rage show), serves only to increase the rage, the anger.[17]

Self-justification applies not only to individuals and groups, but to nations. Tavris and Aronson wrote about the Iranian Hostage Crisis of 1979–1980, when 52 Americans were held hostage in Tehran for 444 days.[18] What the authors found is that most Iranians chose answers that justified their anger at the United States, and most Americans chose answers that justified their anger at Iran.[19] The result: Each side chose facts that supported the anger that they felt toward the other.

Our attempt to align how we view ourselves and how we think and act leads those who perpetrate acts of outrage to "reduce their moral culpability." On the opposite side, it also leads victims to maximize their "moral blamelessness."[20] This leads to simplistic thinking. If I do something bad, it has to be someone else's fault; if something bad happens to me, I am blameless. They are bad. In either case, the result is that they are bad, I am good.

While the attempt to reduce cognitive dissonance is human nature, it's also the result of simplistic thinking. In a series of articles titled "The Crack-up" and published by *Esquire* in 1936, F. Scott Fitzgerald wrote that "the test of a first-rate intelligence is the ability to hold two opposed ideas in mind at the same time and still retain the ability to function."[21]

Unfortunately, few people today take the time to exercise and share their first-rate intelligence. We are all too often intellectually lazy.

Now, before you become outraged at this discussion of outrage, you should note that there is sometimes a benefit to be derived from harnessing and using those passions, the emotions that arise when something outrageous happens. Sometimes, but not all the time. Passion is energy—and the world needs more energy, but energy for good. Energy that builds and creates rather than destroys.

Think about the last time you felt outraged. What caused you to feel this outrage?

Outrage often begins with a sense of certainty. Certainty that you are absolutely, undeniably right in whatever you believe or do, and that the other person or group is absolutely, without question, wrong. If these two facts are true, then there are two possible responses: outrage or openness.

Outrage is the easy response. It is outrageous that someone dares to question your rightness, or dares even to ask you a question. That feeling of outrage can lead you to push back against others without looking within yourself. Outrage is a reflexive response—something that you can claim has been caused by another—another person or group. It allows you to become the victim and accuse the other of being the aggressor.

Slow Down, Let the Other Person Speak

Openness is hard. It requires work, it requires time. Openness allows for the free exchange of ideas, which requires that, even if you are absolutely certain you are correct, you slow down and allow the other person to speak while you listen. You don't simply wait for that person to finish speaking, but you truly listen to their perspective and allow for the possibility that you might be wrong, even if, in the end, you conclude that you are indeed correct. Openness also provides the space needed for the other person to take a step back, take a breath, and possibly begin to understand your point of view, to see your perspective.

It's this ability to listen to others, to allow them to speak, even when you are sure the other side is wrong—especially when the other side is wrong—that is at the core of who we are as a nation. A century ago, Justice Oliver Wendell Holmes's dissenting opinion in *Abrams v. United State* "gave birth to modern First Amendment jurisprudence, with its veneration for the marketplace of ideas," wrote Richard Dooling in a *Wall Street Journal* opinion piece in 2017. "The problem, Holmes realized, is that we are almost always absolutely certain of our premises, but sometimes we are wrong," wrote Dooling.[22]

It's this possibility—the possibility that we are wrong—that led Holmes to push back against those who would censor a person's opinion even when that opinion seemed to be absolutely, definitely wrong at a particular point in time. Holmes understood that information, knowledge, and understanding change over time, and to censor speech is to remove the possibility of learning and growth.

If you have to quash dissent, especially of ideas or ideals, to ensure that your idea gains acceptance, then it's not really acceptance—it's force. This would also mean that there would be no end to the censoring of speech. Once you begin to regulate speech, the next step would be to regulate thought, and the only way a government can control thought is to control people.

This shift to people/mind control would require that we flip our Constitution on its head and put the state on top, instead of the individual. In order to control speech, and eventually thought, the state would have to define what was right and what was wrong. Eventually, it would need to reach into the population to identify and suppress anyone who spoke differently or thought differently. Does this sound familiar? You cannot control speech or thought without controlling people, and to control people, you need an authoritarian government.

The idea of defending the right to free speech was so integral to the foundation of our country that Holmes said we should defend that freedom, even for speech we hate. "The best test of truth is the power of the thought to get itself accepted in the competition of the market, and that truth is the only ground upon which their wishes safely can be carried out," he wrote. "That at any rate is the theory of our Constitution. It is an experiment, as all life is an experiment....I think that we should be eternally vigilant against attempts to check the expression of opinions that we loathe."

Think of it this way: I can hate what you say, but I will also fight for your right to say it, out loud and in public.

Throughout our country's history, people have needed to speak up to move our country toward a more perfect union. President Abraham Lincoln did this when he led the Union through the Civil War and freed the slaves. The Rev. Dr. Martin Luther King, Jr., did this when speaking out about the evils of segregation and prejudice. But speaking out does not mean that the espoused position should be accepted without discussion, argument, and controversy.

How to Protect the Minority

And if the idea of protecting those in the minority from exposure to hate-filled and hurtful speech is your goal, it is a goal you might want to rethink. "The Bill of Rights doesn't offer freedom from speech," wrote Arthur M. Schlesinger, Jr., whose book *The Age of Jackson* won a Pulitzer Prize for history. "To silence an idea because it might offend a minority doesn't protect that minority. It deprives it of the tool it needs most—the right to talk back."[23]

It was by exercising this right to speak up, to talk about uncomfortable topics, that Dr. King was able to change the trajectory of the nation. Had he not been able to respond to criticism from those who opposed him, he would not have been able to press onward and our nation would not have taken the steps it has taken to address the evils of segregation and prejudice.

The recent focus of many college campuses to limit speech to that which reflects the views of the left is un-American and unhealthy. This process, claiming to protect students, moves to equate words with weapons, such that the words themselves can make someone feel assaulted or brutalized. This improper equation leads to suppression of speech that those in power don't agree with. This results in students needing safe spaces so they won't feel threatened, and trigger warning labels before hard-to-deal-with topics, just in case they might be offended.

Nadine Strossen, a past president of the American Civil Liberties Union and a constitutional law professor at New York Law School, argues that college campuses must include minorities who have historically been discriminated against, but they must also welcome ideas that are "unpopular." She believes that the exposure to and debate regarding "'unwelcome' ideas, including those that are hateful and discriminatory, is essential for honing our abilities to analyze, criticize, and refute them."[24]

"The Antithesis of Comfort"

In an article for the Daily Beast, Strossen includes the words from the first address given by Ruth Simmons, who served as president of Brown University from 2001 to 2012—the school's first female president and the first black president of an Ivy League school. Simmons talked about speech that does not make students feel good about themselves. "I say, 'That's not what you're here for'...I believe that learning at its best is the antithesis of comfort. [I]f you come to this [campus] for comfort, I would urge you to walk [through] yon iron gate.... But if you seek betterment for yourself, for your community and posterity, stay and fight."

While it might seem helpful to censor hate speech, Strossen argues that censoring hate speech has not worked historically. "That is why so many hatemongers—from the Nazis in Germany to the neo-Nazis in Charlottesville, provoke and welcome efforts to silence them, in order to increase the attention and support they receive,"[25] Strossen wrote.

As the call for censorship increases, so, too, does the outrage felt by those who feel put upon by speech they do not like. The thought process goes something like this: If I believe the speech I don't like should be censored, then my outrage makes sense. Instead of increasing their ability to defend themselves and their ideas through a free exchange of ideas, and thereby becoming more powerful by winning the argument, they become more outraged by having to think and argue. The more speech is censored, the less able people are to think robustly about their ideas and to defend them.

This is exactly opposite to the theory of resilience. Resilience occurs only when you confront issues and make your way through them successfully—something that is not possible if you are constantly being shielded and told that you need to be protected from troublesome words; that you are unable to defend your thoughts; that you are unable to take a stand for yourself. Instead of becoming more resilient, we are becoming intellectually soft—unable to defend our own thoughts without resorting to screaming.

A few examples:

New York City Police Department Commissioner Raymond Kelly went to Brown University on October 29, 2014, at the school's invitation, to give a presentation and talk with students. After protesters interrupted his talk with boos and prevented him from resuming, the speech was canceled.[26]

In response, the school's president, Christina Paxson, condemned the actions of the crowd. "The conduct of disruptive members of the audience is indefensible and an affront both to civil democratic society and to the university's core values of dialogue and the free exchange of views,"[27] she said in a statement.

In May 2014, Condoleezza Rice (secretary of state under President George W. Bush from 2005 to 2009) pulled out of a speaking engagement that was to have taken place during Commencement at Rutgers University. According to a *New York Times* article titled "Rice Backs Out of Rutgers Speech after Student Protests," by Emma Fitzsimmons, the faculty was against her speaking. "In late February, the faculty council for the university's New Brunswick campus approved a resolution asking officials to rescind the invitation because Rice, the council charged, had played a prominent role in misleading the public about the reasons for the war in Iraq."[28]

While the university administration stood behind their invitation, Rice decided to cancel her appearance and issued a statement. "Commencement should be a time of joyous celebration for the graduates and their families. Rutgers' invitation to me to speak has become a distraction for the university community at this very special time."[29]

In March 2017, author Charles Murray was shouted down as he was attempting to address students at Middlebury College in Vermont, according to an article written by Katharine Seelye of the *New York Times*. The protesters included hundreds of students and ended with an "encounter that turned violent and left a faculty member injured." Murray had co-written *The Bell Curve: Intelligence and Class Structure in American Life* in 1994 and had written *Coming Apart: The State of White America, 1960–2010* in 2012. He had been invited to speak by the American Enterprise Institute Club, a student-run organization.

After being shouted at for twenty minutes, Murray moved to another room, where he was interviewed by Allison Stanger, a Middlebury professor. The interview was livestreamed.[30]

"From my perspective as a professor of political science, if we can't have someone like Charles Murray on campus, who's an influential voice in the Republican Party, well we can't be a department of political science, we become a department of indoctrination if we can only allow Democrats to speak on campus," Stanger told the *Middlebury Campus*, which is the school newspaper. "So for me on principle it's extremely important that he be allowed to speak and I be allowed to engage him, along with my students."[31]

On March 27, 2019, Erik Prince, founder of the security company Blackwater, arrived at Beloit College in Wisconsin to speak to the Young Americans for Freedom Club. This is a student-run club that had followed school procedures for inviting a guest speaker. Due to security concerns, members of the Beloit Police Department were on hand at the campus venue, which was open to the public.

But some students showed up carrying drums and cymbals; they pushed their way into the venue, where they refused to be quiet, while others stacked chairs on the stage in protest. The event was canceled.[32]

In February 2019, Hayden Williams, a field recruiter for the Leadership Institute, a conservative, grassroots training organization, was punched in the face as he sought to recruit members on the campus of the University of California–Berkeley.

"The message that provoked my attacker was our sign that read 'Hate Crime Hoaxes Hurt Real Victims,' a reference to the recent case of Jussie Smollett, who was charged by Chicago police with filing a false police report about an apparently fictitious attack," Williams wrote in an op-ed published by *USA Today*. "My attacker said we were promoting violence, which, in his view, gives him permission to use any means necessary to shut us down."[33]

It makes no sense to hurt someone physically because he was offended by words.

"Make It De Facto Impossible to Be Conservative in Public"

Williams recounted how he and others had been treated, and what he had seen and heard on campuses nationwide. "Conservative students across the country have suffered verbal and physical assault, social ostracism and even academic persecution for voicing their opinions on political topics," he wrote. "This is because young liberals believe that they are on the morally righteous side in a culture war and, in order to win, they must silence any form of dissent." Their goal—"make it de facto impossible to be conservative in public."

Years ago, I was with my dad when he made a speech at Harvard College. During our visit, I met a politically conservative student at the school. I asked him why he had decided to go to Harvard, which has a reputation for being a relatively liberal school. His response: "I knew that if I could argue and win at Harvard, I could win the argument anywhere." He understood that only free speech and debate allow for free exchange of ideas, which is the foundation of a free country. Speech can be controlled only by controlling people—and only a totalitarian regime can attempt to do so.

Yet, to maintain our democratic republic, we need public debate to determine the best ideas to put into practice. It's this very skill, the ability to think and debate ideas, especially those you may think are wrong, that is integral to our country's very survival as a working, representative democracy.

CHAPTER 8

Civil War—What Could Happen

No one on any point along the political spectrum will deny the increasing partisanship and divisiveness in our country; it is a fact. We are a country in crisis. It's almost impossible to have a civil discussion about politics without emotions overflowing and people erupting into tears or anger or both. I'm not talking just about politicians having a tough time getting along with each other. I'm talking about your circle of friends, your family, too.

The changes in technology have increased our ability to connect with everyone everywhere, and social media has accelerated the rapid spread of information and allowed for the rapid and widespread dissemination of stories, real and fake.

Networks and newspapers are labeled "liberal media" or "right-wing thinking," and often carry more opinion than facts and figures. Their quest often appears to be to find facts that fit narratives, rather than to report the facts as they are. Our political parties have become less ideologically diverse, leading to more polarization, resulting in each of the major parties disparaging the other. Compromise has become a bad word and both sides penalize those in their parties who attempt to reach across the aisle.

Where will this partisanship lead us? If we want to avoid another civil war, we would do well to learn a little about them.

Civil wars have been around for all of human history, but the term "civil war" did not appear until the Romans. They described it as a war against the citizens of the state "within Rome itself." Rome was used to fighting "just" or proper wars against external enemies—to fight a war against its own citizens was almost unthinkable. "Even Julius Caesar, Rome's most famous civil warrior, doesn't use the term 'civil war' in the context of his own history, an indication of his reluctance to deploy this deeply unsettling description of contention among the Romans who themselves invented it," wrote Thomas Ricks in his *Foreign Policy* article titled "What a New U.S. Civil War Might Look Like."[1]

The phrase "civil war" joined two words together in a way that did not, and still does not, make sense to many. "Civil" meant relating to ordinary citizens, and "war" typically referred to an armed conflict against a "just" enemy. To make war against your own citizens was to fight yourself. If you are fighting yourself, then which side is the just side? Is there a just side? And what could be the justification for a civil war?[2]

An Internal Battle for Control

This internal fighting can end in two ways: with the two opposing factions forming two separate nations (the American Revolutionary War of 1775–1783 was termed the American Civil War at the time it occurred), or with one side winning and reabsorbing the other (as occurred after the American Civil War of 1861–1865).

The aftermath of a civil war where one side wins and reabsorbs the other is typically long, hard, and fraught with issues that other wars do not have. Once the war is over, the divisions may be closed over, but tend to be slow to heal. Even today, more than 150 years after our own Civil War, unhealed wounds and divisions remain. In civil wars, the enemies are not unfamiliar, far away, or unseen. The enemies are those with whom you have worked, played, and fallen in love. For both the victor and the defeated, there is no returning to life as it had been before the civil war. It rips a country in two, creating an unmendable break with the past.[3]

Once a nation engages in a first civil war, it's more likely to engage in another, according to David Armitage, author of *Civil Wars: A History in Ideas.* "The rawness of history and memory within communities and families means that it's always easy to touch off high passions about old conflicts," he wrote.[4]

Most Conflicts Today Are Civil Wars

While hundreds of conflicts around the world have become wars within the last seventy years, the vast majority of those have been civil wars, with "barely 5 percent of the world's wars hav[ing] taken place between states."[5] Civil wars not only pit one part of the population of a nation against another, but also drive people from their nation in their efforts to find a place of peace to live. Since 2012, almost five million Syrians have left their home country in search of peace and opportunity.[6]

While historians can recite facts and figures about any number of events in the past, wars and civil disturbances have proven particularly difficult for them to agree on. That's no surprise, given that there are layers upon layers of interactions, histories, differences, and perspectives about the impact and legacy of such conflicts.[7] We have often heard that history is written by the victors, but the reality is that the defeated often hold grudges and use informal social networks to spread those grudges to the next generation and beyond. Both sides tell their sometimes conflicting versions of the conflict.

Rome Was Founded on Conflict

Rome was founded on conflict, and familial conflict was referenced in the founding story about Romulus and Remus, the twin sons of Aries, the god of war. The twins were raised by a wolf. Romulus killed Remus after Remus stepped over a line Romulus had drawn. Rome created a civil society structure, with rules and procedures to make life work, to smooth over the rough edges and the passions of human nature. The process of civil war, where citizen fought citizen, brought all the savagery and viciousness of human nature to the forefront.[8]

Initially, the threats of violence in Rome were personal and specific: swords drawn by one person against another. These could be dismissed as arguments between men, civil disturbances. Eventually, they grew into conflict between groups of people and could no longer be dismissed as personal conflict— but conflict between citizens, and therefore civil war.

Edward Gibbon, the eighteenth-century English historian, said Rome's decline should have been foretold "from civil wars, that ensued after the fall of Nero or even from the tyranny which succeeded the reign of Augustus," according to Armitage.[9] An empire that is unable to keep peace within itself is an empire that will inevitably collapse. Rome did not die at the hand of another empire; it died through internal strife and conflict.

Sound familiar?

While one incident of internal conflict might not signal disaster, it would not bode well if the civil unrest were to recur again and again, as was the case in Rome, according to Armitage. "Explanations turned into justifications. And events settled into a narrative stretching deep into Rome's past—to its very beginnings—projecting a shadow onto its future, to rise up again at moments of political strain." Leading ultimately to its demise.[10]

We should study our own history if we hope to avoid a similar fate.

Our country was created when our forefathers declared their independence from Great Britain. It was not a hasty decision, but one that was reached after decades of subjugation to King George's overreaching rule, taxation without representation. We simply had had enough.

After the Seven Years' War of 1756–1763, Great Britain was heavily in debt. British Prime Minister George Grenville reduced the tax on sugar and molasses imports in 1763, but began to require—for the first time—that it be paid. The net effect was a tax increase on the colonists. Unsurprisingly, this did not make the colonists happy.[11]

"British Parliament passed the 1764 Currency Act which forbade the colonies from issuing paper currency [they were required to use British Sterling]. This made it even more difficult for colonists to pay their debts and taxes."[12] Soon after, the Stamp Act was passed, which required "colonists to purchase a government-issued stamp for legal documents and other paper goods."[13] These laws were passed an ocean away, in Great Britain, but enforced in the colonies, adding additional pressure to the daily lives of the colonists and leading many of them to resent being governed by those who lived overseas.

The colonists pushed back, with the Virginia House of Burgesses pushing back on the authority of Britain to tax the colony by passing resolutions. The thirteen colonies came together to protest a common enemy—the British Parliament and its taxation of the colonies, who had no representation. The Stamp Act was repealed a year later to appease the colonists.

But the British Parliament was not to be deterred from raising money from its subjects, so more taxes were added just a few years later with the Townshend Act in 1767. The Boston Tea Party—a protest over the East India Company's favorable tax treatment, included in the Tea Act—was held on December 16, 1773. Britain responded by imposing additional controls and taxes on the colonies. It was a struggle between those who wanted to control the economy of the colonists and the colonists themselves.

Patrick Henry's call to action on March 20, 1775, at the Second Virginia Convention, was the first strong public statement that acknowledged that our freedom would come only if we fought and won against Britain. The choice he articulated, "Give me liberty or give me death,"[14] made it clear that accommodating Britain was not going to work. His was the first open statement that we would prefer to fight than to remain under British control.

"In July 1775, the same month that Bernard Romans' 'Map of the Seat of the Civil War in America' appeared, the Continental Congress issued its first declaration, almost exactly a year before the much more famous Declaration of Independence," according to Armitage.

"Also drafted by Thomas Jefferson, the 'Declaration...Setting Forth the Causes and Necessity of Their Taking Up Arms' justified the move to armed resistance against British forces. The members of Congress tried to reassure 'the minds of our friends and fellow subjects in any part of the empire...that we mean not to dissolve that Union which has so long and so happily subsisted between us, and which we sincerely wish to see restored.' Their stated aim was 'reconciliation on reasonable terms...thereby to relieve the empire from the calamities of civil war.'"[15]

"Reconciliation on reasonable terms" did not work. We declared our independence through the signing of a document on July 4, 1776. Our Declaration of Independence included three distinct areas. First, it declared our freedom and our understanding of the natural order of authority and power. Second, it listed our grievances, explaining to the world and reinforcing to ourselves that we had no choice but to declare our independence as a free country. Third, it committed those who signed it to defend each other with their lives, their fortunes, and their honor. Our founders understood that if they signed the declaration, they could be killed.

The first section is often quoted, and you may know it by heart: "We hold these truths to be self-evident, that all men are created equal, that they are endowed by their Creator with certain unalienable Rights, that among these are Life, Liberty and the pursuit of Happiness.—That to secure these rights, Governments are instituted among Men, deriving their just powers from the consent of the governed,—That whenever any Form of Government becomes destructive of these ends, it is the Right of the People to alter or to abolish it, and to institute new Government, laying its foundation on such principles and organizing its powers in such form, as to them shall seem most likely to effect their Safety and Happiness."

The Core of American Exceptionalism

We are exceptional as a nation not because our citizens are better than other countries' citizens (people are the same everywhere), but because our government is built on a different foundation. Our founders created a foundation that started with their belief in a creator (God). People are given rights by God. They then loan their God-given rights to the government. These are loaned in order for the government to secure individual rights (life, liberty, pursuit of happiness).

We have managed to work through our differences with relative civility, with the exception of the mid-1800s, when our country was torn in two by a vast and all-encompassing civil war. As we look into our future, it is up to us to decide if we will be able to continue to work together through the political process, or if we might—just might—end up in another civil war.

Our civil war was—and still is—the deadliest war our country has endured. With North fighting South, casualties on both sides were Americans. During the war, we lost more than 600,000 American military members. The American Battlefield Trust estimates that "Approximately one in four soldiers that went to war never returned home."[16] Take a moment and imagine that. Of all the men who marched off to war, a quarter of them never returned, a truly staggering statistic.

While the Civil War was won by the Union, and the states were reunited, there remain today reflections of division and divisiveness in our nation. The lesson is clear: We need to do everything possible to resolve our differences without resorting to another civil war.

The reasons are vast and varied for our current state of political polarization, according to David Blankenhorn, founder and president of the nonpartisan Institute for American Values. In "The Top 14 Causes of Political Polarization,"[17] published in May 2018 in *The American Interest*, he notes the lack of a common enemy after the end of the Cold War, a shift from values to identities in both political parties, a change in the country's religious makeup, growing racial and ethnic diversity, self-sorting by geography and political alliance, weakening of regular rules of procedure in Congress, the emergence of megadonors focusing on issues and ideas, the creation of more politically homogeneous districts, a reduction in journalistic standards, and a general propensity of many of us to think the worst of each other, along with his term of "media ghettos" (outlets where polarized narratives are reinforced without challenge).

"Mixed Company Moderates"

"Mixed company moderates," wrote Bill Bishop and Robert Cushing in *The Big Sort: Why the Clustering of Like-Minded America Is Tearing Us Apart* (Houghton Mifflin Harcourt, 2008). "Like-minded company polarizes. Heterogeneous communities restrain group excesses; homogeneous communities march toward the extremes." Their point: If we interact only with people who believe as we do, we never have the chance to learn and grow. Whom do you spend time with?

What a Civil War Could Look Like Today and What It Could Mean for Our Country

According to a poll by Rasmussen, almost a third (31 percent) of likely U.S. voters "say it's likely that the United States will experience a second civil war sometime in the next five years, with 11% who say it's Very Likely."[18]

It's becoming increasingly clear that incidents of the kinds of violence that could lead to a second civil war are a strong possibility. In fact, a majority of "voters [59 percent] are concerned that those opposed to President Trump's policies will resort to violence." This is an increase of 6 percentage points from the 53 percent recorded at the same point under President Obama's administration. "Women and those under 40 are more worried about a possible civil war than men and older voters are," reported Rasmussen. "Forty-four percent (44 percent) of blacks think a second civil war is likely in the next five years, a view shared by 28 percent of whites and 36 percent of other minority voters."[19]

Some political commentators believe that we are already in the beginning stages of a civil war. Conservative radio talk show host Dennis Prager believes that our historical foundation is crumbling. Prager argues that, without a common belief system, "there will be unity only when the left vanquishes the right or the right vanquishes the left." Prager then argues that, since the current left "holds Western civilization and America's core values in contempt," there is no possibility for common ground. In his mind, the civil war has already begun.[20]

During the first Civil War, states took sides and generals led their troops into battle along a variety of physical fronts. A second civil war would be much different and would be fought by networked, interconnected small players, according to Thomas Ricks, who wrote "What a New U.S. Civil War Might Look Like," for *Foreign Policy Magazine*.[21]

Instead of two distinct sides with relatively clear lines, it would be more ideologically and financially based with the spark being set by "marginalized communities whose suffering and fear is wielded by cunning global actors," Ricks wrote. There would no longer be two clear sides, but factions would spring up "that push violence to become a necessary solution."[22]

A new American Civil War would not be a full-scale, two-sided war, as occurred with the last conflict, but would instead be made up of relatively small conflicts from a variety of groups and factions with their own specific demands. It would be ideologically based, not territorially based.[23]

With the proliferation of technology, mobile communications, and the ability to network, interconnect, and hide one's own identity, the war would be based not on territorial control but on ideology. Instead of attacking and taking over geographically, the focus would more likely be on destabilizing information, commerce, and communications nationally. Uncertainty and instability would reign. There would be no geographical, clear-cut front; instead, the enemy could be anywhere, including living next door.[24]

With small sects opposing one another, "the outcome (and probable goal) would likely be a fragmentation of the republic into smaller, more manageable alliances, though it may just as easily harden an increasingly authoritarian federal government," according to Ricks.[25]

A Recipe for Civil War

What holds us together now is the belief that we have a better economy when we work together, and the threat of arrest, and possible incarceration, if we rebel. If the economy takes a dive, especially a deep one, and if we no longer reject violence and the risk of arrest and/or incarceration diminishes, then the unrest could more likely lead to civil war. The left's class warfare and attacks on capitalism are leading many of us to doubt that we are better off economically when we work together. If an economic collapse were to occur, resulting in the spread of violence, authorities could clamp down on civil liberties in an attempt to suppress protesters.

Keith Mines, a former Special Forces officer turned diplomat, noted that several attributes support Ricks's position: "entrenched national polarization, with no obvious meeting place for resolution; increasingly divisive press coverage and information flows; weakened institutions, notably Congress and the judiciary; a sell-out or abandonment of responsibility by political leadership; and the legitimization of violence as the 'in' way to either conduct discourse or solve disputes."[26]

With part of the Democratic Party rejecting Trump's election as illegitimate, since he did not win a majority of the popular vote, we face the possibility of a large internal split. The left is pushing for voting rights for illegal immigrants, lowering the voting age to sixteen, and eliminating the Electoral College. All of these moves would shore up their base, which is immigrant, young, and urban.

With the recent rise in support for socialism, the potential for civil conflict over economic systems has increased. In the fall of 2018, a Gallup Poll found that, "For the first time in Gallup's measurement over the past decade, Democrats have a more positive image of socialism than they do of capitalism."[27]

What drove this was the Democrats' having "a less upbeat attitude toward capitalism, dropping to 47 percent positive… lower than in any of the three previous measures." Young adults are driving this change. "Americans aged 18 to 29 are as positive about socialism (51 percent) as they are about capitalism (45 percent)," according to Gallup. "This represents a 12-point decline in young adults' positive views of capitalism in just the past two years and a marked shift since 2010, when 68 percent viewed it positively."[28] Clearly, capitalism's allure has decreased in the eyes of young adults and that of socialism has increased, supporting the downward swing in support for capitalism across all fronts.

Centralization Is Not the Answer

But we learned long ago that government control of the economy is not the answer. In his October 1964 speech, Ronald Reagan laid out what was at risk: "You can't control the economy without controlling the people," Reagan said. "We either take responsibility for our own destiny or we abandon the American revolution and confess that an intellectual belief in a far-distant capital can plan our lives for us better than we can plan them ourselves."[29]

Reagan did not believe that government could solve problems through centralization. "This was the very thing the Founding Fathers sought to minimize," he said. "They knew that governments don't control things…And they knew when a government set out to do that, it must use force and coercion to achieve its purpose."[30]

Theoretically, government or central control might sound good, but it doesn't work. The only way to control the economy centrally is to take control away from people and give it to the government. Unfortunately, there are many who look toward a theoretical utopia and ignore the ugly realities faced in the Soviet Union, North Korea, Cuba, and Venezuela.

Reagan knew that good intentions can lead to bad consequences. "Regardless of their sincerity, of their humanitarian motives, those who would trade our freedom for security have embarked on this downward course,"[31] he said.

"The Venezuelan case is a textbook example of the evolution of socialism," wrote Kevin Williamson in "Venezuela's Future— And Ours," published June 24, 2018, in the *National Review*.[32] "Venezuela had essentially one big plan: Use the profits from state-run oil companies to fund a massive welfare state, and use the leverage thus gained to fortify support for [former Venezuelan President] Hugo Chávez and his political party until they achieved power sufficient to move Venezuela's assets and its people around like pawns on a chessboard. The problem is that people are not chessmen. Chávez et al. turned out to be pretty poor chess players, but even if they had been grandmasters, it would not have been enough. Economies cannot in fact be controlled and managed in the way that socialists imagine."

Unfortunately, as a result, the citizens of Venezuela are flee-ing, children are starving—the country is in a state of collapse.

So what is the difference between capitalism and socialism? Capitalism is about individual freedom and incentives to build and create. Socialism focuses on central control and divvying the results among people according to a central plan. To be success-ful for the long term, a country must build. If it changes focus from creating to dividing up the results, overall growth will fall dramatically while people fight one another for the remaining pieces.

"When central planning fails—and it always fails—the result is almost never the relaxation of political regimentation," wrote Williamson, "but the redoubling of efforts to impose the plan by increasingly brutal application of force."[33] It becomes not a system of production, but an application of power.

The problem is that once you begin to divide people into different groups and communities within a nation, and then pit them one against the other, the outcomes that they focus on are no longer about moving the country ahead together, but about how one group can take from the other.

In an article published in November 2018 for Stratfor, histo-rian Ian Morris concluded that, despite this period's volatility, a new American Civil War was unlikely due to the strength of our military and its allegiance to political control.

But the cycle of "polarization/regionalism/financial crisis/ political violence" has occurred many times before; sometimes ending in civil war, according to Morris.[34]

But there have been numerous instances dating back to ancient times where the same "polarization/regionalism/financial crisis/ political violence package" did not lead to civil war.[35]

In Rome in the 130s BC, "Tiberius Gracchus . . . tried to can-cel the debts of poor farmers and redistribute elite properties to them. A constitutional crisis ensued, splitting the ruling class. To conservatives, Gracchus seemed to be rallying the impoverished peasants of Etruria [a region of central Italy] against Roman urban interests to make himself king,"[36] wrote Morris.

"A meeting of the Roman Senate in 133 BC ended with conservatives breaking up the wooden benches on which they sat and using the pieces to beat Gracchus and 300 of his followers to death. Twelve years later, his brother Gaius also died in political violence over much the same issues. Yet civil war did not erupt in either case." However, the Rome Empire did indeed fall.

Look also at Henry VIII's break with the Roman Catholic Church and the United States in the 1960s. In none of these three cases did civil war break out.[37]

Rome was tied up in civil wars in AD 69, "The Year of the Four Emperors," driven not by polarization but by ambitions of rulers and potential rulers. England's period termed "The Anarchy" was driven by "a royal succession crisis and fragile state institutions."[38]

So what about us? What will happen in the United States? With a strong military and a strong economy—the probability of another civil war occurring in the near future is low. But as trust declines, polarization and incivility increase, and we increasingly pit ourselves against each other—in our own nation—that probability increases.

CHAPTER 9

What We Can Do

Citizenship is what makes a republic—monarchies can get along without it.

—Mark Twain

Ours is an incredibly diverse nation—economically, geographically, racially, ethnically, and ideologically—we face a variety of options regarding who we, as a nation, can become. We are in the midst of re-sorting our political parties and our identity. Think of this phase as our country's challenging adolescence—that awkward time between childhood and adulthood, a time to try on different outward appearances and roles as we figure out who we are and who we want to become. This time period may prove to be tumultuous, but worthwhile in the end, if we work together to find our way through to a better future.

This transitional period will doubtless be challenging and fraught with turmoil, difficult decisions, and real consequences. But it has to happen. As citizens of a democratic republic, we have a great responsibility. If we don't use this responsibility wisely, then we can lose our republic.

If we do choose wisely, we can remain the safest, freest, and most prosperous nation on earth. If we, as citizens, fail to make smart decisions and instead simply meander along, our nation will face the real possibility of entering a period of slow, steady decline. If we make the wrong choices, then we may accelerate our nation's demise and potentially split our country into new nation states.

While the last option may not sound likely, it is possible. The first option is also possible, but not probable—unless we really make an effort. It's very possible that we will meander about, not reaching our potential as a country, but getting by.

The current environment of ranting and raving and the resulting political polarization is dangerous and has led us to be a greatly divided nation. Our nation is in crisis. But our nation is also exceptional and therefore worth saving. Yes, there are deep divisions in our country. All too often, we identify more with these respective subgroups than we do with Americans in general. As citizens, we hold the power to effect positive change, but currently many of us are failing to use that power. By not voting, by blindly agreeing with one party or another, by hoping that the government, instead of we the people, will solve our problems. We must do better, and we can.

Let's just assume for a minute that we want to make our country better, to do what we must to remain the safest, freest, most prosperous nation on the earth. What could each of us do to ensure such a future?

We can choose gratitude over grievance, create a positive national narrative, and work together to solve real problems.

Choose Gratitude over Grievance

We all have problems in our lives and we all get to choose how we think of them. All too often, we choose to complain, to blame someone else, and to air our grievances. We might think this makes us feel better, but scientific studies have shown that expressing gratitude is a better way to approach life. Gratitude leads to more happiness and deeper connections with other people. When you are grateful, you are aware of the positive impacts that other people have on your life. You appreciate the connections you have with others, and therefore search to establish more connections. When you dwell on resentment or ingratitude, the opposite occurs, you begin to look to see how someone else might have gotten ahead, which can lead to feelings of anger toward others, irritability, and isolation.

Gratitude "changes the molecular structure of the brain, keeps the gray matter functioning, and makes us healthier and happier," according to UCLA's Mindful Awareness Research Center. "When you feel happiness, the central nervous system is affected. You are more peaceful, less reactive, and less resistant."[1] Gratitude lowers our anxiety, allows us to think in a much broader fashion, to think about positive solutions—solutions that include others, not only ourselves or the groups with which we identify.

Why shouldn't we focus on grievance? After all, there is plenty of room for improvement. Our country is riven by wealth disparities, prejudice, and unfair court decisions. But according to Dr. Dennis Kimbro, author of *The Wealth Choice: Success Secrets of Black Millionaires*, our country is also full of opportunity—it just has to be seized. "Eighty percent of all [black] millionaires can be classified as first generation," Kimbro wrote. "In other words, these wealth creators built their fortune with little to no capital, savings, or inheritance." In 1965, there were five black millionaires in the United States, according to Kimbro; in 2013, there were 35,000 black millionaires.[2]

Filter Out the Ranting and Raving

Today's political culture is all about grievance. If you listen to politicians talk, you'll see that they tend to pit one group against another. This will not, cannot, lead to long-term success. Instead, it leads to internal strife, more ranting and raving. Taken to the extreme, it might just lead to another civil war. Only by working together, thinking through and implementing more expansive solutions, can we be successful.

How do we change our focus? We can begin by filtering out ranting, raving, and other generally unhelpful noise. Understand where your news comes from and what biases are built into the information you consume. In 2014, a Pew Research report laid out the "Ideological Placement of Each Source's Audience."[3] On the left were *The New Yorker, Slate, The Daily Show,* the *Guardian, Al Jazeera America* (which closed in 2016), NPR, CBS's *The Late Show with Stephen Colbert,* the *New York Times,* BuzzFeed, PBS, BBC, *HuffPost,* the *Washington Post, The Economist,* and *Politico.* On the right were Breitbart, *The Rush Limbaugh Show, The Blaze, The Sean Hannity Show, The Glenn Beck Program,* and *The Drudge Report.*

Most of the major news outlets lean liberal. The outlets closest to the center are the *Wall Street Journal* and *Yahoo! News.* Understanding the ideological bent of the outlet allows for proper filtering of information received from them. As a resource, Allsides .com is a news aggregator that lays out political news issues and categorizes news stories as being from the right, center, or left. It allows readers to see the same story reported from different perspectives.

Take a Walk

Cable shows on both sides of the political spectrum focus on conflict and personality. The same is true regarding social media. If you do watch cable or participate in social media, don't do so to confirm your own thought patterns. We know that simply reinforcing our beliefs means we are not open to new thoughts; that we are addicted to reinforcing our feelings of intellectual superiority, making ourselves feel better by making ourselves feel smart.

If you do watch the cable shows with their ranting and raving, then watch with a critical eye to see if there is anything new to learn, any new insight to be gained. If not, maybe your time would be better spent reading, volunteering in the community, breaking bread with neighbors, or taking a walk outside.

Asking positive questions of each other reorients group members to build trust in each other and confidence that a solution might be possible. According to David L. Cooperrider, a professor of social entrepreneurship at Case Western Reserve University, negative issues and facts will inevitably arise as part of the process, but positive ones might be overlooked if not focused on.[4]

The same holds true for nations.

All too frequently, we focus on the grievances one group has against another in our nation. Instead of focusing on the booming economy and brainstorming about how to continue to improve opportunity for all, we complain about how the economy is divvied up. Instead of being amazed by the innovation in health care, and the improvements in medicine, we focus on cost. Instead of being grateful that our nation is so wonderful that people want to migrate here both legally and illegally, we argue that we're not good enough and we don't do enough for those who choose to break the law to enter our country.

It's not that there is no longer prejudice, there is—it is not acceptable and it needs to be solved.

We should not become complacent and we must address our problems (more on that later); it's just that, if we always focus on the negative, we tend to develop a negative outlook on life in general. This is the foundation of the Positive Psychology Movement's approach. Recently, the World Congress on Positive Psychology highlighted various research projects conducted in different countries with different populations to determine whether positive psychology works.

Successes include "exploring ways to improve the resilience for girls from low-resource settings in India," according to an article written for *Psychology Today* by Michelle McQuaid, a positive psychology coach. Members of the organization also worked "to boost wellbeing with both teenagers and retirees in China and to try and halt child-bride abductions in Ethiopia."[5]

What this approach promotes is greater focus on the positive actions than the negative actions. This is reminiscent of the saying "You catch more bees with honey than vinegar." When looking at group performances, those who focus on negative (one strength for four deficits) tend to be the lowest performers, while those who focus on strengths (four strengths for one deficit) tend to be the highest performers. It doesn't work to ignore problems nor is it helpful to focus on one grievance for every strength. But the four-to-one ratio appears to lead to the best outcome.[6]

No Wonder We Can't Move Forward

Based on the overwhelming negativity of media coverage and political attacks, it's no wonder we cannot move forward—we're too busy tearing our country down. Our ratio must be somewhere in the thousand-negatives-to-one-positive category.

According to research by Cooperrider and Frank J. Barrett published in the *Journal of Applied Behavioral Science*, focusing on problems can magnify them. When managers were asked "why they see one another as troublesome or problematic… the belief is actually strengthened. Therefore, if one were to say one sees a co-worker as crabby and unapproachable because the co-worker is selfish, moody, and insecure the chances would be greater that, merely because one formed and articulated this causal explanation, one's belief about the co-worker would be stronger. One becomes even more convinced that the co-worker is selfish, moody, and insecure."[7]

The simple articulation of a belief strengthened the belief that it was true. Just imagine what we are doing as a nation in our constant airing of grievances about one group or another. Our constant complaints that Democrats or Republicans are bad in one way or another simply strengthen our beliefs that that is true. The lesson is that, if we continue to articulate negative beliefs about one another, we will cement those beliefs.

"The Power of Appreciation"

Instead of going negative, we should go positive.

In "The Power of Appreciation," posted on the Chartered Financial Analyst (CFA) Institute website, CFA Jim Ware writes, "Appreciation is a powerful cultural tool for positive change." Ware argues that a focus on appreciation leads to the creation of organizations that work better than those that focus on fixing the negative. "The big differentiator is the focus of attention. Traditional problem solving homes in on the defects, on what's wrong. Appreciative inquiry focuses on the successes, on what's right." Ware continues, "The research is clear: What you focus on grows. So, if you focus on problems, they get bigger!"[8]

We are prone to search for the negative, and it's a lot easier than searching out and magnifying the positive. For a few days, try it yourself; notice the focus of the media you ingest. Then notice your thoughts—are you focusing on grievances or gratitude? What is the result of your focus? Are you a better person? Is your organization or country better off? As citizens, we have to be able both to work to fix our country's problems and to act as constant promoters and cheerleaders.

The hard part is to turn around our traditional grievances. For example, if you are a black American and have been told— and believed—all your life that Republicans are racist, and then you meet a Republican whose actions do not support your belief, then either you believed something that was never true or what you are experiencing is not real. When this type of cognitive dissonance happens, it's easier psychologically for a person to confirm his or her original belief, even when there is evidence to the contrary—this is confirmation bias.

Dissonance also arises when we behave poorly against others. We need to feel innocent and virtuous. To resolve our dissonance, we become outraged at the faults of those we have harmed. For example, if we believe we are in the right and another group is in the wrong, then even if presented with facts that prove we are wrong, we will ignore those facts and continue to believe that we are right, while blaming those in the other group.

Just look back to the examples regarding the press coverage over Russiagate. Mainstream media fit any information into their collusion, obstruction narrative.

While this can create a cycle of incorrect beliefs and thoughts, dissonance can also create a cycle of virtue. "When people do a good deed, particularly when they do it on a whim or by chance, they will come to see the beneficiary of their generosity in a warmer light," wrote Tavris and Aronson. Why? Because if they did a favor for someone, then their thought process is that that person must have deserved the favor; he or she must be good. They think, "He is a pretty decent guy who deserves a break."[9]

Because of the current focus on ranting, raving, and grievance, we have to champion free speech to change our perspective from one of grievance to one of gratitude.

Free speech is the bedrock of our country. If we don't engage in active and open dialogue, then we are subject to censorship and chilling of speech. This is achieved by controlling people's thoughts and you can't control thoughts without controlling the people themselves.

The movement to create safe spaces and halt hate speech on campuses may be well-meaning, but it is ineffective and can be used to censor all types of speech not countenanced by whoever happens to be in charge. Instead of trying to safeguard someone's feelings by censoring the words to which he or she is exposed, we should be arming our students and our children with the ability to think, discuss, and disagree while maintaining their sense of self.

While some argue that those who belong to groups that have been historically privileged should be stripped of the ability to talk to allow for those who are in some way disadvantaged to talk, "silencing the privileged doesn't help the disadvantaged. It deprives them of chisels. It strips away their access to antifragility," wrote Tricia Beck-Peter for the Foundation for Economic Education. "It reduces them to perpetual victimhood, stripped of the autonomy to confront true oppression....Silencing the privileged doesn't empower the disadvantaged; it perpetuates the notion that the disadvantaged can't compete in an equal contest."[10]

One way to support free speech is to encourage institutions of learning to adopt the Chicago Statement regarding free speech.[11]

The University of Chicago is leading the way in reaffirming the need for free and open debate on campus. In January 2015, a committee formed by the president of the university, Robert J. Zimmer, and Provost Eric D. Isaacs released this statement:

> The University is committed to free and open inquiry in all matters, it guarantees all members of the University community the broadest possible latitude to speak, write, listen, challenge, and learn . . . the ideas of different members of the University community will often and quite naturally conflict. But it is not the proper role of the University to attempt to shield individuals from ideas and opinions they find unwelcome, disagreeable, or even deeply offensive. Although the University greatly values civility, and although all members of the University community share in the responsibility for maintaining a climate of mutual respect, concerns about civility and mutual respect can never be used as a justification for closing off discussion of ideas, however offensive or disagreeable those ideas may be to some members of our community.

Since then, the Foundation for Individual Rights in Education (FIRE) has championed free speech, encouraging other educational institutions to endorse the Chicago Statement. By 2017, according to FIRE, the statement had received support from "over fifty-five institutions including Princeton University, Purdue University, American University, Columbia University, Georgetown University, and the University of North Carolina at Chapel Hill, among others."[12]

In an effort to support free speech, President Trump signed an executive order on March 21, 2019, requiring that "institutions that receive Federal research or education grants promote free inquiry, including through compliance with all applicable Federal laws, regulations, and policies."[13] The test will be if any lawsuits result from educational institutes allegedly limiting free speech.

According to a *Washington Times* article by S. A. Miller, "Nearly three in four voters—73 percent—favor[ed] Mr. Trump's order . . . that required U.S. colleges to protect free speech or risk losing federal research dollars."[14] Most Americans understand that the right to speak freely, even if you are wrong, is the cornerstone of our strength as a nation.

If we were to equip people with the ability to think for themselves, to develop a sense of self, to disagree respectfully with others, and still know exactly who they are, we would have served them so much better than if we had cleansed their environment of anything that might make them sad, mad, or frightened. We cannot remove all potential points of conflict—we must instead arm our young people with the tools they will need to defend themselves intellectually.

Without the ability to talk freely and openly, to debate how our country should solve problems, we will be limited in the progress we can make, and where we will end up. "First, you win the argument," said Margaret Thatcher, the former prime minister of Great Britain, "then you win the vote." Making and winning the argument is the way for a free society to move forward. Once the argument is won—then the vote is yours. Without making the argument, you can't win over the other side.

Instead of seeking to forge a future together, we often find ourselves looking backward. We focus on our past errors and the resulting terrors. As we continue to look backward, we forget to reach out today and create bridges between ourselves. These bridges must be formed if we are to have any hope of creating a better future together.

We can be grateful that we live in a country where we elect our leaders, have the rights to free speech, to own property, to travel freely, to make our own associations, to create our own futures, and to argue over how to create and implement policy that provides opportunity and encouragement for our citizens.

As we discuss our differences and argue about our futures, we should also be grateful for those who offer opposing perspectives. It is their efforts that push us to hone our messages and communicate them more effectively. The better the competition, the better the outcome.

Just imagine the possible outcomes if we could be more grateful and focus less on grievances.

Change Our National Narrative

As humans, we love stories; they teach us about life and help us make sense out of what we are experiencing. Stories help us to understand the world around us.

Throughout our history, what held us together was not that we were people who shared a common background, because we have never been a common people. Instead, it was our shared belief in the ideals of our nation. The story of why our nation is great. It's not that the story was 100 percent true, but that it inspired us to purpose-filled action—made us want to strive forward.

The ideals of our country, based on research by the Associated Press–NORC Center for Public Affairs, include "the country's fair judicial system and rule of law, individual freedoms and liberties as defined by the Constitution, and the ability of people to get good jobs and achieve the American dream." Additionally, many "consider the shared use of English as important."[15]

We are an exceptional country not because of our differences, our diversity of backgrounds, but because of our similarities of belief.

For more than two centuries, these shared, core beliefs have held us together. Additionally, our history of assimilating new arrivals to America has helped us create and maintain a common culture and identity. According to the same AP–NORC research, most Americans believe that "the United States should be a country with an essential American culture and values that immigrants take on when they arrive [60 percent], compared to just 40 percent who say the country should be made up of many cultures and values that change when new people arrive."[16]

People who say that Americans should change to reflect the values of immigrants are speaking for a minority of Americans. The reality is that if we change ourselves for migrants, then we lose our identity, and that identity explains, at least in part, why people have sought to come to this country in the first place.

We are the United States because, so far, we have always found a way to unite ourselves through a chosen identity, by focusing on agreed-upon ideals rather than the identity we were given at birth. It's the decision to adhere to the underlying beliefs of our foundational structure, and exercise our rights and responsibilities as citizens that makes our country different from others. If our nation splits into factions that no longer share a common identity, then the chances rise that our country will become Balkanized or face an existential threat due to a constitutional crisis.

Self-identification and the shouldering of responsibility are important to the core identity of American citizens. But this does not preclude identifying with other groups—religious, ethnic, racial, or other. Part of what makes our country strong is the fact that it is home to people from multiple underlying and interlocking cultures: people whose family traditions have passed from generation to generation, people who celebrate various holidays, people who march in all kinds of parades (what would New Orleans be without Mardi Gras?), and people who eat all kinds of food from different countries. "It is these strands of particularity that lend richness and texture to our society,"[17] wrote Arthur M. Schlesinger, Jr., author of *The Disuniting of America: Reflections on a Multicultural Society.*

It is this multidimensional overlay that makes our nation more interesting and more resilient than other countries, but this happens only if we use our differences to weave ourselves into a cohesive union rather than sort ourselves into separate groups that harbor grievances against one another.

America is more than a nation; it's an ideal founded on the belief that its citizens determine who governs them; its system of justice is equal; and opportunity is abundant. This ideal cannot be achieved if we are constantly attempting to make everyone equal by pulling some people down while attempting to push others up. Instead, we become great as a nation when we raise the bar for all—reach down and pull people up, encouraging and helping them to live their lives to the fullest. This hard, person-to-person work cannot be done at the national or even the state level; it must be done at the individual and community level.

As citizens, we need to ask ourselves several questions about the narratives we tell ourselves, according to Edward Halper, professor of philosophy at the University of Georgia. "Ask whether or not they actually achieve their goals on their own terms,"[18] he wrote in the *Weekly Standard*. Does the story lead to action and results that are anticipated?

Stories with Purpose

Halper then breaks down the complexity of each narrative between the political parties. For example, the Democrats may believe that the policing tactics used in black communities are "unfair because they are indiscriminate," while Republicans may believe that it is unfair to "the people who live in these communities to be subject to high crime."[19] The Democrats ignore the breakdown of the family; Republicans often ignore that racism does still exist.

"Yes, racism is real, but the most insidious sort of racism is an attitude," Halper wrote. "It's hard to address, and its victims are not necessarily benefited by dwelling on it." His point is that, if we continually tell a group of people that they cannot achieve success due to some barrier, some will simply give up without trying. "By pointing to crime rates, the counter-narrative [often mentioned by Republicans] reinforces the racial stereotypes that too many African-Americans have, tragically, internalized."

The end result is that "both narratives discourage African-Americans from developing their considerable talents."[20] If our goal is to make sure every citizen in our country reaches their full potential, then both sides have fallen short.

The stories we tell should have purpose, be true, and lead to hope-filled action. Some will argue that stories do not resonate with them because the people in the stories do not look like them. My response is simple: Look deeper. We are all the same in God's eye, and yes, you can understand and grab hold of the ideal—no matter your sex, ethnicity, or skin color. I believe it's yours—you simply have to claim it as your own.

So What Are Our Nation's Stories?

We believe in freedom of religion—our forefathers fled religious persecution, and came to a new world. We have a tradition of belief in God. The Pilgrims held the first Thanksgiving and gave thanks to their Creator. This belief is also reflected in our founding documents. We value hard work. There was no other way to survive in the new world. Without hard work, the Pilgrims would have perished.

Revolutionary War leader Patrick Henry understood and articulated the inevitability of our revolt against the British, even while others were hoping for resolving our differences peacefully. Addressing the Virginia Convention in March 1775, Henry made it clear that his individual rights were not negotiable. Confronting those who were hesitant to go to war against the king to preserve such rights, Henry famously bellowed: "Is life so dear, or peace so sweet, as to be purchased at the price of chains and slavery? Forbid it, Almighty God! I know not what course others may take; but as for me, give me liberty or give me death!" His passion swayed a wavering legislature to adopt a resolution for preparation of militia.

President Lincoln, who campaigned against the expansion of slavery, decided to engage in civil war rather than let the Union dissolve. He also ended slavery—the question that had led to the war. We value unity and equality. In November 1863, one of the darkest periods of the Civil War, Lincoln approached the dais of the Gettysburg National Cemetery at its dedication and spoke about our country's resolve and the debt owed to those who died for our freedom.

"It is rather for us to be here dedicated to the great task remaining before us," Lincoln said in conclusion, "that from these honored dead we take increased devotion to that cause for which they gave the last full measure of devotion—that we here highly resolve that these dead shall not have died in vain—that this nation, under God, shall have a new birth of freedom—and that government of the people, by the people, for the people, shall not perish from the earth."

After a childhood marked by sickness and asthma, Theodore Roosevelt was determined to become physically fit. He served as a Rough Rider, loved the outdoors, established the national park service, and championed what he termed "the strenuous life." In his famed "Strenuous Life" address in 1899, he challenged his audience to strive not only for themselves, but for their nation:

"Above all, let us shrink from no strife, moral or physical, within or without the nation, provided we are certain that the strife is justified," he said. "For it is only through strife, through hard and dangerous endeavor, that we shall ultimately win the goal of true national greatness."[21]

In August 1963, the Rev. Dr. Martin Luther King, Jr., delivered his "I Have a Dream" speech as he stood on the steps of the Lincoln Memorial in Washington. The speech was the close of a day-long Jobs and Freedom March. The crowd was made up of 200,000 Americans—blacks and whites, Northerners and Southerners, children and adults. King used imagery, scripture, and history to connect with his audience, just as Lincoln had in his lifetime. King delivered an optimistic view of the future of our country. He called for us to work together toward a higher purpose. The vision he shared called on us, and still calls on us, to be more and to do more.

In a 1987 speech in Berlin, President Ronald Reagan challenged Mikhail Gorbachev, the general secretary of the Communist Party of the Soviet Union, to "tear down this wall!" Reagan, who believed freedom, free speech, free elections, and free markets would win over the totalitarian regime—was passionate about which side would win. He was right.

In perhaps the darkest moment in American history since the Japanese attacked Pearl Harbor in 1941, President George W.

Bush talked about what he had seen in the ten days following the September 11 attacks on New York, Washington, and Pennsylvania—tough, unwavering Americans who had graciously risen to support one another and were eagerly prepared to defend their security.

"In the normal course of events, presidents come to this chamber to report on the state of the union," Bush said. "Tonight, no such report is needed; it has already been delivered by the American people.... My fellow citizens, for the last nine days, the entire world has seen for itself the state of union, and it is strong."

For a brief moment, we were unified as a country, and it appeared that Americans were willing to put aside their political differences. But soon, it was back to partisan politics.

Today, we face many challenges as a nation, and the best way to meet those challenges is to believe that they can be met—and solved; to remind ourselves that we are able to overcome obstacles when we work together; and to tell ourselves over and over again that we can once again rise to the challenges ahead.

Make Your Enemy Your Partner

Do you think what we are doing in politics is working? What I see is incivility, partisanship, and pre-judgment. We are a nation greatly divided. The way to make progress is to put aside preconceived notions about people in the other party and work together on fixing the issues that our country faces.[22]

How do we improve our country? Not through increasing government control in an attempt to secure power, responsibility, and work, but through building our families and our communities. It requires hands-on, real work, connection, and cooperation. Currently, we move rapidly, sometimes erratically, as a nation, and spend an enormous amount of money but make little progress. It is as if we are flailing in panic. We are frantic, afraid, too scared to slow down, to be methodical, which we must do to make sure that real progress is made.

What we have to realize is that, as humans, we often seek to justify our behavior, both bad and good. The only way to make real progress is for both sides to drop such self-justification and work together to solve problems. "If you want to make peace with your enemy, you have to work with your enemy," said Nelson Mandela, the South African anti-apartheid leader who was imprisoned for twenty-seven years and then was elected president of his country. "Then he becomes your partner."[23]

One possible approach is to use Appreciative Inquiry to address challenges in communities. The process focuses on building connections and capitalizing on "shared strengths by discovering the best of their pasts, dreaming of what might be possible, designing pathways forward and deploying actions that create sustainable changes,"[24] according to McQuaid. While the steps might appear incremental, small changes can, over time, exert long-lasting influence.

First, we have to get out of the ideological bubbles that envelop many of us. Reach out to those who are different from you, politically, racially, ethnically, ideologically, and otherwise. It's impossible to learn if everyone you associate with shares the same opinions. Get involved in conversations with friends and family about politics—even if it's hard. Focus on listening and learning. Change your goal from telling someone how wrong they are to learning about their perspective and why they believe what they do. The goal is not to give in to their point of view but to understand why they believe what they do. Even if you do not change your mind, you will probably learn a lot along the way.

Speak up, even when you know that you will be the lone voice on an issue. What's most important is that we hear and truly listen to a multitude of voices—not that we agree with all or even any of them. This requires that we speak up when our perspective differs from those of the people around us. If those who disagree with us are silent, then we cannot begin to understand their perspectives; if we are silent, they cannot begin to understand ours.

There are ways to have differing opinions yet to retain respect for one another. This ability to agree to disagree, to work together civilly, will help us move forward as a country and make changes that benefit our entire nation. It also helps to remember that each of us is human, and therefore fallible. Take a breath and look for the spark of the divine, the spark of God, that resides in even our enemies.

Part of working together requires that we leave judgment to God and focus on what we can do, whom we can help, rather than seeking to apportion blame. Many times, the rush to judgment is a rush to make ourselves feel correct, better, superior. Remember, when throwing a stone, even a verbal one, what Jesus said in John 8:7: "Let any one of you who is without sin be the first to throw a stone at her."[25]

A week before the 2018 midterm elections, Pete Davidson, a comedian on *Saturday Night Live*, made a passing reference to Dan Crenshaw, a former Navy SEAL and then-Republican candidate for the Second Texas Congressional District. As the show broadcast a picture of Crenshaw wearing an eye patch, Davidson said he looked like a "hitman in a porno movie." The backlash was fast and intense and led Davidson to appear on the program the following week and apologize. Crenshaw later penned an opinion piece in the *Washington Post*. It read, in part:

How, then, do we live together in this world of differing ideas? For starters, let's agree that the ideas are fair game. If you think my idea is awful, you should say as much. But there is a difference between attacking an idea and attacking the person behind that idea. Labeling someone as an "-ist" who believes in an "-ism" because of the person's policy preference is just a shortcut to playground-style name-calling, cloaked in political terminology. It's also generally a good indication that the attacker doesn't have a solid argument and needs a way to end debate before it has even begun.[26]

It's a good reminder (an example) that personal attacks are not helpful responses to personal attacks. Instead, ignore the attacks and return the focus of discussion to the issues at hand. Crenshaw and Davidson ended up appearing on *Saturday Night Live* together, with Davidson apologizing and Crenshaw not only accepting his apology, but teasing him as well. A perfect example of how to make up and move on.

Let's challenge ourselves to reach out, not over Twitter or Facebook, but in our communities, to one another, not to point fingers and blame, but to join hands and help. If you're active in communities that exist on social media, that's okay, too. My point is we also need to carry on those relationships off the screen—in our streets, churches, and homes. Social media can be a great way to connect, but it is essential to remember that those connections must extend beyond the screen to foster true understanding.

Be open to being wrong; when talking with others, start with the statement "I could be wrong, but…" This simple statement, often used by Benjamin Franklin, tends to put the other person at ease, makes the discussion more about issues than about personalities, and opens you to learning something new and potentially even altering your opinion.[27]

Instead of being stubborn and never changing your opinion, or flip-flopping every time you get a new piece of information, consider this: Between these two options lies "intellectual humility," which balances "the willingness to change, plus the wisdom to know when you shouldn't." Pepperdine University researchers came up with four building blocks for creating this intellectual honesty: "Having respect for someone else's point of view, not being intellectually overconfident, separating one's ego from one's intellect, and a willingness to revise one's own viewpoints."[28]

Throughout our nation's history, when most needed, inspirational leaders have emerged. They would articulate their belief that our foundation as a country is different, that our future is bright. Their optimism was based on their belief that the American people would rise to the challenge. I believe this is still true today.

Here's how you can take steps to make sure that happens: Go out into your neighborhood, find a problem to solve with someone else, and then share the solution with others. What we do know is that we can't simply sit back and scream until something gets done. We have to get up and take action to achieve solutions ourselves. Together, we can stop ranting and raving, and bridge the great division within our country.

ACKNOWLEDGMENTS

Writing a book is a process that includes a lot of people at different points along the way.

To my husband, Jimmy, and our children, Maggie and Robert: Thank you for your support, encouragement, and patience. My sister Kathy and her husband, Paul, deserve extra credit. Kathy served as not only my agent, but also my coach, confidante, and sister. This book would not have happened without her support. Huge thanks to my dad and his wife, Callista, for their assistance and support. His foreword and her photo make this book a family project. My mother-in-law, Elkin Alston, sister-in-law, Elkin Taylor, and her husband, Roger, have been incredibly supportive and are deeply connected in the Atlanta community, providing great examples of civic engagement.

I have no doubt that my mother, Jackie Gingrich, and my father-in-law, Jim Cushman, are in heaven smiling down at my attempt to inspire others to engage civically as they both did during their lives.

I am so grateful Carly Evans from 2 Market Media contacted me. Steve Carlis had the initial idea for this book. Many thanks to the 2 Market Media team, including Hank Norman, Devin Bramhall, Clare Edgerton, Danielle Kessler, Graziana Mirabile, Jani Moon, Lauren Pringle, Anna Roberts, Arestia Rosenberg, and Jessica Tanir.

Gingrich Productions 360 provided valuable advice and guidance. Special thanks to Audrey Bird, Louie Brogdon, Joe DeSantis, Woody Hales, Christina Maruna, and Debbie Myers.

Huge thanks to Kate Hartson, who believed in this project, acquired it for Center Street, and shepherded it through completion. Special thanks to Rolf Zettersten, publisher; Patsy Jones, VP of marketing and her team; and Bob Castillo, managing editor for the project.

Aidan Gannon, Patrick Lanier, and Dr. Amy Steigerwalt provided valuable research assistance. Trisha Downs, Christina Maruna, and Maxwell Billieon reviewed the manuscript and provided excellent advice. Michael Morris, Michael Jacobs, Rodney Cook, Jr., and Bea Perez provided advice, encouragement, support, and assistance. Thank you to Kim Mallen and Jeno Luckett for keeping me organized and on track—you make my life so much better!

Leadership Atlanta and the class of 2018 (the Best Damn Class Ever) gave me an opportunity to meet and work with people all across our city, greatly enriching my life. Special thanks to Victoria Seals and Tracey Lloyd, who literally lifted me over their heads on our retreat; and to David Brand, who will answer any question I ask.

This book would not have been finished, nor would it be nearly as good, without the long hours, hard work, and thoughtful editing by Tom Watkins. A friend for decades, he is incredibly talented and patient, and I am grateful for his friendship and help.

Special thanks to my girls' groups that have provided support, encouragement, and a friendly ear when needed. Thanks to the flying pigs tennis team, Mimosa Garden Club, the best book club ever, and of course to my fairy godmother, Rayna Casey.

A few years ago I began appearing as a guest on *Political Rewind* with Bill Nigut on Georgia Pubic Radio. Bill's thoughtful approach to political discussion paved the way for this project. Job Creators Network, led by Alfredo Ortiz and Elaine Parker, has sharpened my thinking and led me to work on better communicating the importance of economic freedom and activity.

Finally, to all of my children's friends who have spent time or will spend time at Cushmania (our family's home). I wrote this book so that we can disagree without being disagreeable. I love you all so much, and I want you all to feel free to disagree—which I know you will!

NOTES

Introduction: Who Am I, Why I Care—Why You Should, Too

1. Associated Press–NORC Center for Public Affairs, "The American Identity: Points of Pride, Conflicting Views, and a Distinct Culture," March 2017, p. 5. http://apnorc.org/PDFs/American%20Identity/APNORC_American _Identity_2017.pdf. Accessed December 10, 2018.
2. Associated Press–NORC Center for Public Affairs, "The American Identity: Points of Pride, Conflicting Views, and a Distinct Culture," March 2017, p. 5. http://apnorc.org/PDFs/American%20Identity/APNORC_American _Identity_2017.pdf. Accessed December 10, 2018.
3. The Atlantic, "The Man Who Broke Politics," by McKay Coppins, November 2018. https://www.theatlantic.com/magazine/archive/2018/11 /newt-gingrich-says-youre-welcome/570832/. Accessed April 8, 2019.
4. Ibid.
5. PBS, "1978 Speech by Newt Gingrich," by Newt Gingrich, June 24, 1978. https://www.pbs.org/wgbh/pages/frontline/newt/newt78speech.html. Accessed April 8, 2019.

1: The Proposition

1. American Thinker, "Covington Teens Put In…," by Catharine Evans, January 25, 2019. https://www.americanthinker.com/blog/2019/01/covington _teens_put_in_psychological_woodchipper_while_media_and_holly wood_hacks_coddle_the_haters.html. Accessed May 12, 2019.
2. Townhall, "So Called Adults Apoplectically…," by Timothy Meads, January 20, 2019. https://townhall.com/tipsheet/timothymeads/2019/01/20 /so-called-adults-apoplectically-over-react-to-the-covington-high-school -kids-n2539329. Accessed May 21, 2019.

3. Cincinnati Enquirer, "Report: The Black Hebrew Israelites...," by Mark Curnutte, January 21, 2019. https://www.cincinnati.com/story/news/2019 /01/21/black-hebrew-israelites-believe-african-americans-gods-chosen -people/2636154002. Accessed January 24, 2019.

4. Southern Poverty Law Center, "Intelligence Report," August, 29, 2008. https://www.splcenter.org/fighting-hate/intelligence-report/2008/racist -black-hebrew-israelites-becoming-more-militant. Accessed June 25, 2019.

5. Washington Post, "It Was Getting Ugly...," by Cleve Wootson, Jr., Antonio Olivio, and Joe Helm, January 20, 2019. https://www.washingtonpost .com/nation/2019/01/20/it-was-getting-ugly-native-american-drummer -speaks-maga-hat-wearing-teens-who-surrounded-him/?utm_term =.ed5b4698469a. Accessed March 11, 2019.

6. Today, "Nick Sandmann on Encounter...," by Eun Kyunk Kim, January 23, 2019. https://www.today.com/news/nick-sandmann-interview-today-show -s-savannah-guthrie-encounter-native-t147242. Accessed March 3, 2019.

7. CNN, "Nick Sandmann Files Lawsuit," by An Phung, February 20, 2019. https://www.cnn.com/2019/02/19/media/nick-sandmann-washington -post-lawsuit/index.html. Accessed March 3, 2019.

8. Media Research Center News Busters, "Martina Compared to Nazi...," by Jay Maxson, March 4, 2019. https://www.newsbusters.org/blogs/culture /jay-maxson/2019/03/04/martina-compared-nazi-goebbels-after-clarifying -position. Accessed June 25, 2019.

9. CBS News, "Attorney General Pam Biondi Responds...," June 25, 2018. https://www.cbsnews.com/news/florida-attorney-general-pam-bondi -confronted-mr-rogers-movie/. Accessed January 23, 2019.

10. Ibid.

11. U.S. News and World Report, "Nebraska GOP Office Windows...," by Grant Schulte, July 3, 2018. https://www.usnews.com/news/best-states /nebraska/articles/2018-07-03/vandals-throw-bricks-through-nebraska -gop-office-windows. Accessed March 23, 2019.

12. The Daily Caller, "Eight Violent Attacks on Republicans Just This Year," by Peter Hasson, October 17, 2018. https://dailycaller.com/2018/10/17/ republicans-attacked-2018-list/. Accessed November 3. 2018.

13. The Daily Caller, "Ted Cruz Chased Out...," by Amber Athey, September 24, 2018. https://dailycaller.com/2018/09/24/ted-cruz-protested-dc-restaurant/. Accessed March 12, 2019.

14. Laramie Boomerang, "Man to get 3...," Boomerang Staff, January 4, 2019. https://www.laramieboomerang.com/news/local_news/man-to-get-years-in

-prison-for-gop-fire/article_2d58080f-183b-5025-93f8-f670264a08fc.html. Accessed June 25, 2019.

15. The Daily Caller, "Eight Violent Attacks on Republicans."

16. Associated Press News, "Protesters Target Home of..." by Ashraf Kalil, November 8, 2019. https://apnews.com/5aa41068747f4e41b39947f761462f96?utm_source= Twitter&utm_campaign=SocialFlow&utm_medium=AP. Accessed June 25, 2019.

17. Washington Post, "They Were Threatening Me...," by Allyson Chiu, November 8, 2018. https://www.washingtonpost.com/nation/2018/11/08 /they-were-threatening-me-my-family-tucker-carlsons-home-targeted-by -protesters/?utm_term=.05394814c499. Accessed May 7, 2019.

18. Ibid.

19. Washington Post, "The Latest Sign of Political Divide: Shaming and Shunning Public Officials," by Mary Jordan, June 24, 2018. https://www.washing tonpost.com/politics/the-latest-sign-of-political-divide-shaming-and -shunning-public-officials/2018/06/24/9a29f00a-77bc-11e8-aeee-4d0 4c8ac6158_story.html. Accessed November 3, 2018.

20. Newsweek, "Maxine Waters, 'No Peace, No Sleep ,'" by Benjamin Fearnow, June 24, 2018. https://www.newsweek.com/maxine-waters-trump-harass -kirstjen-nielsen-stephen-miller-sarah-huckabee-993173. Accessed May 7, 2019.

21. The Daily Caller, "Eight Violent Attacks on Republicans."

22. Huffington Post, "Maxine Waters Cancels Event...," by Mary Papenfuss, June 29, 2018. https://www.huffingtonpost.com/entry/maxine-waters-cancels -events-death-threat_us_5b357256e4b08c3a8f68e124. Accessed March 12, 2019.

23. New York Times, "Black Female Lawmaker in Vermont Resigns after Racial Harassment...," by Liam Stack, September 26, 2018. https://www.nytimes .com/2018/09/26/us/politics/kiah-morris-vermont.html. Accessed November 25, 2018.

24. Newsweek, "Mail Bomb Suspect Cesar...," by Reuters, October 27, 2018. https://www.newsweek.com/mail-bomb-suspect-cesar-sayoc-charged-over -sending-pipe-bombs-donald-trump-1190341. Accessed May 7, 2019.

25. AM New York, "Bombs Sent to Democrats, Trump Critics: What to Know," by Nicole Brown, October 29, 2018. https://www.amny.com/news/bombs -sent-to-democrats-1.22434938. Accessed January 23, 2019.

26. CNN, "Mail Bomb Suspect Cesar...," by Erica Orden and Nicole Chavez, March 24, 2019. https://edition.cnn.com/2019/03/21/us/cesar-sayoc-guilty -plea/index.html. Accessed, June 25, 2019.

27. Washington Times "Eric Holder: 'When They Go Low, We Kick Them,'" https://www.washingtontimes.com/news/2018/oct/10/eric-holder-when -they-go-low-we-kick-them/. Accessed November 3, 2018.

28. Pew Research Center, "The Partisan Divide on Political Values...," October 5, 2017. http://www.people-press.org/2017/10/05/the-partisan-divide -on-political-values-grows-even-wider/. Accessed November 23, 2018.

29. Stacey Abrams website, "Immigrant Justice." https://staceyabrams.com /immigrantjustice/ Accessed May 7, 2019.

30. "Religion." https://news.gallup.com/poll/1690/religion.aspx. Accessed December 8, 2018.

31. Congressional Budget Office, "The Distribution of Household Income, March 19, 2018. https://www.cbo.gov/publication/53597. Accessed March 19, 2019.

32. *The High Cost of Good Intentions: A History of U.S. Federal Entitlement Programs*, by John F. Cogan, Stanford University Press, Stanford, California, 2017.

33. Ibid.

34. National Archives, "Declaration of Independence: A Transcription." https:// www.archives.gov/founding-docs/declaration-transcript. Accessed November 23, 2018.

35. National Archives: "The Constitution of the United States: A Transcription." September 24, 2018. https://www.archives.gov/founding-docs/constitution -transcript. Accessed November 23, 2018.

36. "Guide to the Constitution—The Heritage Foundation." https://www.heritage.org/constitution/. Accessed November 23, 2018.

37. National Archives, "The Constitution of the United States: A Transcription."

38. The Conversation, "Which Countries Have the Most...," by Gilles Pison, March 10, 2019. http://theconversation.com/which-countries-have-the-most -immigrants-113074. Accessed May 6, 2019.

2: The Death of News

1. PBS, Public Broadcasting Service. www.pbs.org/opb/historydetectives/feature/radio-in-the-1930s/. Accessed March 19, 2019.

2. "The Fireside Chats: Roosevelt's Radio Talks—White House Historical..." https://www.whitehousehistory.org/the-fireside-chats-roosevelts-radio -talks. Accessed November 3, 2018.

3. PBS, Public Broadcasting Service.

4. Ibid.

5. Ibid.

6. "The Fireside Chats: Roosevelt's Radio Talks—White House Historical..."

7. Ibid.

8. Ibid.

9. Ibid.

10. Gallup, "Presidential Debates Rarely Game…," by Lydia Saad, September 25, 2008. https://news.gallup.com/poll/110674/presidential-debates-rarely -gamechangers.aspx. Accessed March 3, 2019.

11. History.com, "The Kennedy-Nixon Debates." https://www.history.com /topics/us-presidents/kennedy-nixon-debates. Accessed March 12, 2019.

12. Ibid.

13. Ibid.

14. Washington Post, "Republican Presidential Debate…," November 10, 2011. https://www.washingtonpost.com/politics/republican-debate-transcript /2011/10/11/gIQATu8vdL_story.html?utm_term=.119974be740f. Accessed June 25, 2019.

15. *Bias: A CBS Insider Exposes How the Media Distort the News*, by Bernard Goldberg, Regnery, Washington, DC, 2002, p. 93.

16. CCTA, "History of Cable." https://www.calcable.org/learn/history-of-cable/. Accessed March 19, 2019.

17. Verizon, https://www.verizon.com/about/our-company/wireless-network. Accessed March 4, 2019.

18. Pew Research Center, "Mobile Fact Sheet," February 5, 2018. http://www .pewinternet.org/fact-sheet/mobile/. Accessed March 4, 2019.

19. Nielsen, "Mobile Kids: The Parent…," February 28, 2017. https://www .nielsen.com/us/en/insights/news/2017/mobile-kids--the-parent-the-child -and-the-smartphone.html. Accessed March 4, 2019.

20. Knight Foundation, "Americans' Views of Misinformation in the News and How to Counteract…," June 20, 2018. https://knightfoundation .org/reports/americans-views-of-misinformation-in-the-news-and-how -to-counteract-it. Accessed November 3, 2018.

21. Time, "The Story Behind Time's…," June 21, 2018. http://time.com/5317522 /donald-trump-border-cover/. Accessed March 14, 2019.

22. Daily Kos, "New York Daily News Depicts…," by Leslie Salzillo, June 16, 2018. https://www.dailykos.com/stories/2018/6/16/1772405/-This-NY-Daily -News-cover-that-demonizes-Trump-should-be-the-model-for-every -newsgroup-in-the-nation. Accessed March 14, 2019.

23. Daily Mail, "Honduran Father Reveals Daughter Was Never Separated from Her Mother," by Daniel Bates and Karen Ruiz, June 21, 2018. https:// www.dailymail.co.uk/news/article-5869829/Father-two-year-old-face -child-separation-crisis-speaks-out.html. Accessed November 8, 2018.

24. Ibid.

25. Daily Kos, "New York Daily News Depicts…"

26. "The Truth Behind This Photo of an 'Immigrant Child' Crying Inside a Cage…," June 18, 2018. https://www.cnn.com/2018/06/18/us/photo-migrant-child-cage-trnd/index.html. Accessed November 25, 2018.

27. Twitter, Jose Vargas, posted June 28, 2018. https://twitter.com/joseiswriting/status/1006397160622055429?lang=en. Accessed May 7 2019.

28. Geo Group, "GEO World," Second Quarter 2016. https://www.geogroup.com/userfiles/1de79aa6-2ff2-4615-a997-7869142237bd.pdf. Accessed March 4, 2019.

29. Gallup, "Media Use and Evaluation: Gallup Historical Trends—Gallup News." https://news.gallup.com/poll/1663/media-use-evaluation.aspx. Accessed November 3, 2018.

30. Ibid.

31. Ibid.

32. Ibid.

33. Ibid.

34. Ibid.

35. "Americans Struggle to Navigate the Modern Media…—Gallup News." https://news.gallup.com/poll/226157/americans-struggle-navigate-modern-media-landscape.aspx. Accessed November 3, 2018.

36. Ibid.

37. Ibid.

38. Pew Research Center, "Political Polarization and Media Habits," by Amy Mitchell, Katerina Eva Matsa, Jeffrey Gottfried, and Jocelyn Kiley, October 21, 2014. http://www.journalism.org/2014/10/21/political-polarization-media-habits/. Accessed March 4, 2019.

39. Ibid.

40. Washington Post, "Is Glenn Beck's Network…," by Avi Selk, June 28, 2018. https://www.washingtonpost.com/news/arts-and-entertainment/wp/2018/06/24/is-glenn-becks-network-collapsing-he-walked-out-of-a-cnn-interview-when-asked/?utm_term=.adc8f8d855b2. Accessed March 14, 2019.

41. Ibid.

42. Ibid.

43. MRC News Busters, "TV News Buries Trump's Defeat…," by Bill D'Agostino, October 23, 2018. https://www.newsbusters.org/blogs/nb/bill-dagostino/2018/10/23/tv-news-buries-trumps-defeat-isis-iraq-and-syria. Accessed January 23 2019.

44. Ibid.
45. "Anti-Trump and Anti-GOP: How TV News Is Spinning the Midterms," October 30, 2018. https://www.newsbusters.org/blogs/nb/rich-noyes/2018 /10/30/anti-trump-and-anti-gop-how-tv-news-spinning-midterms. Accessed November 25, 2018.

3: Media/Technology and Interconnectedness
1. Nielsen, "Time Flies: U.S. Adults Now Spend Nearly Half a Day Interacting with Media." https://www.nielsen.com/us/en/insights/news/2018 /time-flies-us-adults-now-spend-nearly-half-a-day-interacting-with-media .html. Accessed December 23, 2018.
2. Ibid.
3. Ibid.
4. New York Times, "Alexa and Siri Can Hear This Hidden Command...," by Craig Smith, May 10, 2018. https://www.nytimes.com/2018/05/10 /technology/alexa-siri-hidden-command-audio-attacks.html?module =inline. Accessed March 19, 2019.
5. Ibid.
6. Washington Post, "Chinese Hack of Federal Personnel Files...," by Ellen Nakashima, June 12, 2015. https://www.washingtonpost.com/world/national -security/chinese-hack-of-government-network-compromises-security -clearance-files/2015/06/12/9f91f146-1135-11e5-9726-49d6fa26a8c6_story .html?utm_term=.1dc772cf3534. Accessed March 14, 2019.
7. Wall Street Journal, "Chinese Hackers Target Universities...," by Dustin Volz, March 5, 2019. https://www.wsj.com/articles/chinese-hackers-target -universities-in-pursuit-of-maritime-military-secrets-11551781800. Accessed March 14, 2019.
8. Pew Research Center, "Social Media Fact Sheet," February 5, 2018. http:// www.pewinternet.org/fact-sheet/social-media/. Accessed March 14, 2019.
9. Ibid.
10. Ibid.
11. New York Times, "Facebook Was Hacked: Here Are 3 Things...," by Brian X. Chen, September 28, 2018. https://www.nytimes.com/2018/09/28 /business/facebook-was-hacked-here-are-3-things-you-should-do.html. Accessed March 14, 2019.
12. Pew Research Center, "Social Media Use in 2018," by Aaron Smith and Monica Anderson, March 1, 2018. http://www.pewinternet.org/2018/03 /01/social-media-use-in-2018/. Accessed March 5, 2019.

13. Washington Post, "Here's How the First…," by Juliet Eilperin, May 18, 2015. https://www.washingtonpost.com/news/politics/wp/2015/05/26/heres -how-the-first-president-of-the-social-media-age-has-chosen-to-connect -with-americans/?utm_term=.0c0069d177dd. Accessed March 5, 2019.

14. Ibid.

15. Ibid.

16. Investor's Business Daily, "Social Media: Is Trump…," September 21, 2018. https://www.investors.com/politics/editorials/social-media-trump-con servative-bias/. Accessed March 5, 2019.

17. National Review, "Viewpoint Discrimination Against Algorithms," by Ben Shapiro, March 7, 2018. https://www.nationalreview.com/2018/03/social -media-companies-discriminate-against-conservatives/. Accessed March 5, 2019. See also PJmedia, "96 Percent of My…," by Paula Bolyard, August 25, 2018, https://pjmedia.com/trending/google-search-results-show-pervasive -anti-trump-anti-conservative-bias/. Accessed July 3, 2019.

18. Gizmodo, "Here's the Full…," by Kate Conger, August 5, 2017. https:// gizmodo.com/exclusive-heres-the-full-10-page-anti-diversity-screed -1797564320. Accessed March 5, 2019.

19. Ibid.

20. Ibid.

21. CNBC, "Fired Google Engineer James…," by John Shinal, August 14, 2017.https://www.cnbc.com/2017/08/14/fired-google-engineer-james -damore-says-this-.html. Accessed, June 26, 2019.

22. Twitter, Real Donald Trump, January 24, 2019. https://twitter.com /realDonaldTrump/status/1088430717611245571. Accessed May 12, 2019.

23. Forbes, "About Representative Ocasio-Cortez…" by Howard Gleckman, Janury 8, 2019. https://www.forbes.com/sites/howardgleckman/2019/01/08/about-rep -ocasio-cortezs-70-percent-tax-rates/#129ce043bbff. Accessed June 25, 2019.

24. Pew Research Center, "Activism in the Social Media Age," by Monica Anderson, Skye Toor, Lee Rainie, and Aaron Smith, July 11, 2018. http:// www.pewinternet.org/2018/07/11/activism-in-the-social-media-age/. Accessed January 30, 2019.

25. Ibid.

26. Twitter, Alyssa Milano, October 15, 2017. https://twitter.com/Alyssa_Mil ano/status/919659438700670976. Accessed May 7, 2019.

27. New York Times, "Harvey Weinstein, Fired on Oct. 8, Resigns from Com- pany's Board," by Brooks Barnes, October 17, 2017. https://www.nytimes .com/2017/10/17/business/media/harvey-weinstein-sexual-harassment.html. Accessed January 26, 2019.

28. The New Yorker, "All the Other Harvey Weinsteins," by Molly Ring-wald, October 17, 2017. https://www.newyorker.com/culture/cultural-comment/all-the-other-harveys. Accessed January 28, 2018.

29. The Social Element, "Is Social Media Changing...," by David Woods-Holder, February 21, 2018. https://thesocialelement.agency/is-social-media-changing-society-for-the-better-metoo-suggests-it-just-might-be/. Accessed January 30, 2019.

30. Pew Research Center, "Activism in the Social Media Age."

31. IT Technology Updates, "Less than 10 Percent...," by David Wiky, May 2018. https://www.itechnologyupdates.com/less-than-10-percent-of-twitter-users-question-fake-news.html. Accessed May 9, 2019.

32. Ibid.

33. Pew Research Center, "Activism in the Social Media Age."

34. Fox News, "NATO Pledges to Boost Defense Spending After Stern Words from Trump," by Brooke Singman, July 11, 2018. https://www.foxnews.com/politics/nato-pledges-to-boost-defense-spending-after-stern-words-from-trump. Accessed January 29, 2019.

35. New York Post, "John Kerry Rips Trump...," by Joe Tacopino, July 11, 2018. https://nypost.com/2018/07/11/john-kerry-rips-trumps-disgraceful-nato-speech/. Accessed March 19, 2019.

36. NATO website. https://www.nato.int/nato_static_fl2014/assets/pdf/pdf_2018_07/20180709_180710-pr2018-91-en.pdf. Accessed January 29, 2019.

37. NATO, "Funding NATO," July 27, 2018. https://www.nato.int/cps/en/natohq/topics_67655.htm. Accessed January 29, 2019.

38. NATO website.

39. USA Today, "Trump Is Having an Impact...," by William Cummings, January 27, 2019. https://www.usatoday.com/story/news/world/2019/01/27/nato-chief-credits-trump/2695799002/. Accessed January 29, 2019.

40. Pew Research Center, "Activism in the Social Media Age."

41. Pew Research Center, "Social Media Conversations About Race," by Monica Anderson and Paul Hitlin, August 15, 2016. http://www.pewinternet.org/2016/08/15/social-media-conversations-about-race/. Accessed March 19, 2019.

42. Ibid.

43. Ibid.

44. Pew Research Center, "A Deep Drive into Party...," April 7, 2015. http://www.people-press.org/2015/04/07/a-deep-dive-into-party-affiliation/. Accessed March 19, 2019.

45. Pew Research Center, "Activism in the Social Media Age."

46. Ibid.

47. Ibid.

48. https://expandedramblings.com/index.php/peloton-statistics-and-facts/.

49. New York Times, "Silicon Valley Nannies Are...," by Nannie Bowles, October 26, 2018. https://www.nytimes.com/2018/10/26/style/silicon-valley-nannies.html. Accessed March 19, 2019.

50. Ibid.

51. https://seths.blog/2018/11/the-digital-divide-is-being-flipped/.

52. Hunt, Melissa & Young, Jordyn & Marx, Rachel & Lipson, Courtney. (2018). No More FOMO: Limiting Social Media Decreases Loneliness and Depression. Journal of Social and Clinical Psychology. 37. 751-768. 10.1521/jscp.2018.37.10.751. Accessed June 25, 2019.

53. Pew Research Center, "A Majority of Teens Have...," by Monica Anderson, September 27, 2018. http://www.pewinternet.org/2018/09/27/a-majority-of-teens-have-experienced-some-form-of-cyberbullying/. Accessed March 19, 2019.

54. Ibid.

55. The White House, "Be Best." https://www.whitehouse.gov/bebest/. Accessed January 31, 2019.

56. Ibid.

57. Twitter, FLOTUS. https://twitter.com/FLOTUS/status/831303325886906368. Accessed May 12, 2019.

58. RT News, "FLOTUS Melania Trump Mercilessly Trolled...," February 14, 2017. https://www.rt.com/usa/377299-melania-trump-twitter-women/. Accessed January 31, 2019.

59. https://twitter.com/realDonaldTrump/status/642788749030608896.

60. https://twitter.com/RandPaul/status/1085673240469663745.

61. *The Power of Story*, by Jim Loehr, Free Press, New York, 2007.

62. https://www.merriam-webster.com/dictionary/narrative.

63. Washington Post, "Hands Up Don't Shoot Was Built on a Lie," by Jonathan Capehart, March 16, 2016. https://www.washingtonpost.com/blogs/post-partisan/wp/2015/03/16/lesson-learned-from-the-shooting-of-michael-brown/?utm_term=.7de7ecbaae56. Accessed January 31, 2019.

64. Ibid.

65. Politico, "'Hands Up, Don't Shoot' Ranked One of Biggest 'Pinocchios' of 2015," by Nick Gass, December 14, 2015. https://www.politico.com/story/2015/12/hands-up-dont-shoot-false-216736. Accessed January 31, 2019.

66. Politico, "Lawmakers Make 'Hands Up' Gesture on House Floor," by Lucy McCalmont, December 2, 2014. https://www.politico.com/story/2014/12/lawmakers-ferguson-hands-up-113254. Accessed January 31, 2019.

67. Department of Justice, "Department of Justice Report...," March 4, 2015. https://www.justice.gov/sites/default/files/opa/press-releases/attachments/2015/03/04/doj_report_on_shooting_of_michael_brown_1.pdf. Accessed March 5, 2019.

68. The Weekly Standard, "It's Time to Kill...," by Edward Halper, November 29, 2018. https://www.weeklystandard.com/edward-halper/its-time-to-kill-our-political-narratives. Accessed March 19, 2019.

69. Ibid.

4: Societal Changes

1. *The High Cost of Good Intentions: A History of U.S. Federal Entitlement Programs*, by John F. Cogan, Stanford University Press, Stanford, California, 2017.

2. National Archives, "Declaration of Independence: A Transcription." https://www.archives.gov/founding-docs/declaration-transcript. Accessed February 2, 2019.

3. Ibid.

4. *The Collected Works of Abraham Lincoln*, "Meditation on the Divine Will." http://144.208.79.222/~abraha21/alo/lincoln/speeches/meditat.htm. Accessed February 4, 2019.

5. Franklin D. Roosevelt Presidential Library and Museum, "A 'Mighty Endeavor;' D-Day," https://fdrlibrary.org/d-day. Accessed February 4, 2019.

6. Gallup Research, "Religion." https://news.gallup.com/poll/1690/religion.aspx. Accessed December 8, 2018.

7. Ibid.

8. Lifeway, "Hope for Dying Churches," by Thom Rainer, January 16, 2018. https://factsandtrends.net/2018/01/16/hope-for-dying-churches/. Accessed December 8, 2018.

9. Gallup Research, "Religion."

10. Gallup Research, "Age, Religiosity, and Rural America." https://news.gallup.com/poll/7960/Age-Religiosity-Rural-America.aspx. Accessed December 8, 2018.

11. National Archives, "The Bill of Rights: A Transcription." https://www.archives.gov/founding-docs/bill-of-rights-transcript. Accessed May 9, 2019.

12. New York Times, "THE SUPREME COURT: Justices Affirm Ban on Prayers in Public School," by Linda Greenhouse, June 25, 1992. https://www.nytimes.com/1992/06/25/us/the-supreme-court-justices-affirm-ban-on-prayers-in-public-school.html. Accessed February 4, 2019.

13. Ibid.

14. Georgetown University Berkley Center, "Santa Fe Independent School…" https://berkleycenter.georgetown.edu/cases/santa-fe-independent-school-district-v-doe. Accessed March 5, 2019.

15. Pew Forum, "Where Americans Find Meaning in Life." http://www.pewforum.org/2018/11/20/where-americans-find-meaning-in-life/. Accessed December 8, 2018.

16. Ibid.

17. Ibid.

18. Fox News, "Dems to Strike 'So Help You God,'" by Gregg Re, January 30, 2019. https://www.foxnews.com/politics/dems-move-to-strike-so-help-me-god-from-oath-taken-in-front-of-key-house-committee. Accessed February 2, 2019.

19. NPR, "Three Hours in Orlando…," by Ariel Zambelich and Alyson Hurt, June 26, 2016. https://www.npr.org/2016/06/16/482322488/orlando-shooting-what-happened-update. Accessed February 5, 2019.

20. Obama White House Archives, "Remarks by the President on Mass Shooting in Orlando," June 12, 2016. https://obamawhitehouse.archives.gov/the-press-office/2016/06/12/remarks-president-mass-shooting-orlando. Accessed March 19, 2019.

21. NBC News, "What Really Happened at…," by Tim Fitzsimons, June 12, 2018. https://www.nbcnews.com/feature/nbc-out/what-really-happened-night-pulse-n882571. Accessed March 20, 2019.

22. Obama White House Archives, "Remarks by the President After Counter-ISIL Meeting," June 14, 2016. https://obamawhitehouse.archives.gov/the-press-office/2016/06/14/remarks-president-after-counter-isil-meeting. Accessed March 19, 2019.

23. Pew Forum, "Demographic and Economic Trends in Urban, Suburban and Rural Communities." http://www.pewsocialtrends.org/2018/05/22/demographic-and-economic-trends-in-urban-suburban-and-rural-communities/. Accessed December 8, 2018.

24. The Guardian, "Obama Angers Mid-West Voters…," by Ed Olinkington, April 14, 2019. https://www.theguardian.com/world/2008/apr/14/barackobama.uselections2008. Accessed February 4, 2019.

25. NPR, "Rural Voters Played a Big Part...," by Danielle Kurtzleben, November 14, 2016. https://www.npr.org/2016/11/14/501737150/rural -voters-played-a-big-part-in-helping-trump-defeat-clinton. Accessed February 4, 2019.

26. *The Politics of Resentment: Rural Consciousness in Wisconsin and the Rise of Scott Walker*, by Kathy Cramer, University of Chicago Press, Chicago, Illinois, 2016.

27. Washington Post, "A New Theory for Why...," by Jeff Guo, November 8, 2016. https://www.washingtonpost.com/news/wonk/wp/2016/11/08/a -new-theory-for-why-trump-voters-are-so-angry-that-actually-makes -sense/?utm_term=.76e0601acb92. Accessed February 4, 2019.

28. Ibid.

29. Gallup, "Americans Big on Idea of Living in the Country," December 7, 2018. https://news.gallup.com/poll/245249/americans-big-idea-living-country .aspx. Accessed December 8, 2018.

30. *Hillbilly Elegy: A Memoir of a Family and Culture in Crisis, by* J. D. Vance, (New York: Harper Paperbacks, 2016), 226 (Kindle edition).

31. Ibid., 163.

32. Ibid., 194.

33. Ibid., 245.

34. United States Census Bureau, Historical Household Tables. https://www .census.gov/data/tables/time-series/demo/families/households.html. Accessed February 4, 2019.

35. Ibid.

36. Ibid.

37. Ibid.

38. Ibid.

39. Ibid.

40. New York Times, "Obama's Father's Day Remarks," June 15, 2008. https://www.nytimes.com/2008/06/15/us/politics/15text-obama.html? pagewanted=print&_r=0. Accessed February 4, 2019.

41. Ibid.

42. City Journal, "Family Breakdown Denialists," by Kay Hymowitz, February 12, 2018. https://www.city-journal.org/html/family-breakdown-denialists -15719.html. Accessed March 15, 2019.

43. Pew Research Center, "Modern Immigration Wave Brings 59 Million to U.S., Driving Population...," September 28, 2015. http://www.pewhis panic.org/2015/09/28/modern-immigration-wave-brings-59-million-to-u-s

-driving-population-growth-and-change-through-2065/. Accessed December 8, 2018.

44. History.com, "Ellis Island." https://www.history.com/topics/immigration /ellis-island. Accessed December 8, 2018.

45. Pew Research Center, "Modern Immigration Wave Brings 59 Million to U.S."

46. Ibid.

47. Pew Research Center, "Facts on U.S. Immigrants," by Jynnah Radford and Abby Budiman, September 14, 2018. http://www.pewhispanic.org/2018/09/14 /facts-on-u-s-immigrants/#fb-key-charts-first-second-gen. Accessed March 15, 2019.

48. Pew Research Center, "Modern Immigration Wave Brings 59 Million to U.S."

49. Pew Research Center, "Immigration's Impact on Past and Future U.S. Population Change," September 28, 2015. http://www.pewhispanic.org /2015/09/28/chapter-2-immigrations-impact-on-past-and-future-u-s -population-change/. Accessed December 8, 2018.

50. Ibid.

51. Pew Research Center, "Modern Immigration Wave Brings 59 Million to U.S."

52. NBC News, "San Francisco Allows Undocumented…," by Benjy Sarlin, July 20, 2018. https://www.nbcnews.com/politics/immigration/san-francisco -allows-undocumented-immigrants-vote-school-elections-n893221. Accessed March 16, 2019.

53. Forbes, "Milton Friedman's Property Rights…," by Ken Blackwell, July 31, 2014. https://www.forbes.com/sites/realspin/2014/07/31/milton -friedmans-property-rights-legacy/#6a36b4ed6635. Accessed March 16, 2019.

54. *The High Cost of Good Intentions: A History of U.S. Federal Entitlement Programs*, by John F. Cogan, Stanford University Press, Stanford, California, 2017.

55. Ibid.

56. Ibid.

57. Ibid.

58. Ibid.

59. Ibid.

60. Ibid.

61. Ibid.

62. U.S. Census Bureau: POV-26. Program Participation Status of Household- Poverty Status of People. https://www.census.gov/data/tables/time-series/demo /income-poverty/cps-pov/pov-26.2017.html. Accessed March 19, 2019.

63. The Epoch Times, "Most Democratic 2020 Candidates...," by Ivan Pentchou-kov, March 13, 2019. https://www.theepochtimes.com/most-democratic-2020-candidates-reject-socialist-label-but-back-socialist-agenda_2836286.html. Accessed May 12, 2019.

5: Tribal Temptation

1. New York Times, "Sentinelese Tribe That Killed...," by Kai Schultz, Hari Kumar, and Jeffrey Gettelman, November 22, 2018. https://www.nytimes.com/2018/11/22/world/asia/andaman-sentinelese-missionary.html. Accessed March 5, 2019.
2. NPR, "Where Did Agriculture Begin? Oh Boy, It's Complicated," July 15, 2016. https://www.npr.org/sections/thesalt/2016/07/15/485722228/where-did-agriculture-begin-oh-boy-its-complicated. Accessed February 24, 2019.
3. *Tribes: We Need You to Lead Us*, by Seth Godin, Penguin Group, New York, 2018, p. 1.
4. *American Nations, A History of the Eleven Rival Regional Cultures of North America*, by Colin Woodard, Penguin Books, New York, 2012.
5. Ibid.
6. History, "Japanese Internment Camps," by History.com Editors, April 15, 2019. https://www.history.com/topics/world-war-ii/japanese-american-relocation.
7. Merriam-Webster Online Dictionary. www.merriam-webster.com/dictionary/tribalism. Accessed December 10, 2018.
8. *Tribes: We Need You to Lead Us*.
9. Ibid.
10. https://blexit.com. Accessed March 25, 2019.
11. Twitter, Chris Barron, February 5, 2019. https://twitter.com/chrisrbarron/status/1092993911042265089. Accessed May 12, 2019.
12. *The Disuniting of America: Reflections on a Multicultural Society*, by Arthur M. Schlesinger, Jr., W. W. Norton & Company, New York, 1998, p. 118.
13. Medium, "What Is Cultural Marxism...," by Samuel Kronen, January 7, 2018. https://medium.com/@samuelkronen/what-is-cultural-marxism-a-liberals-critique-of-the-radical-left-a01b6e004fb4. Accessed March 17, 2019.
14. Jewish Press, "Intersectionality": Code Word for Anti-Semitism, by Alan M. Dershowitz, August 27, 2017. https://www.jewishpress.com/indepth/opinions/intersectionality-code-word-for-anti-semitism/2017/08/27/. Accessed February 7, 2019.

6: Party versus Party

1. Los Angeles Times, "Rep. Levy Beaten in…," from Associated Press, http://articles.latimes.com/1994-09-29/news/mn-44232_1_congressional -primary. Accessed March 29, 2018.

2. Los Angeles Times, "Matthew G. 'Marty' Martinez Dies at 82; Former Congressman," October 21, 2011. https://www.latimes.com/local/obituaries/ la-xpm-2011-oct-21-la-me-1019-matthew-martinez-20111019-story.html. Accessed March 23, 2019.

3. The Nation, "A Congressman's Defeat Spells…," by John Nicols, May 10, 2002. https://www.thenation.com/article/congressmans-defeat-spells -trouble-business-democrats/. Accessed March 23, 2019.

4. Fox News, "Rep. Joe Schwarz Beaten…," by Ken Thomas, August 9, 2006. https://www.foxnews.com/wires/2006Aug09/0,4670,CongressSch warz,00.html. Accessed March 23, 2019.

5. Ibid.

6. CBS News, "Two House Members Lose…," February 13, 2008. https:// www.cbsnews.com/news/two-house-members-lose-in-md-primaries/. Accessed March 23, 2019.

7. Ibid.

8. NBC News, "Bob Inglis, A Republican Believer…," by James Rainey, September 13, 2018. Accessed March 23, 2019.

9. The Daily Kos, "We Unlucky Few: A Look," by Jeff Singer, April 20, 2014. https://www.dailykos.com/stories/2014/4/20/1264682/-We-unlucky -few-A-look-at-the-incumbents-who-lost-their-primaries-1994-2012. Accessed February 6, 2019.

10. "History, Arts, and Archives," United States House of Representatives. https://history.house.gov/People/Detail/22585. Accessed March 27, 2019.

11. https://bluedogcaucus-costa.house.gov/about. Accessed March 29, 2019.

12. https://republicanmainstreet.org/about/. Accessed March 29, 2019.

13. Gallup, "US Conservatives Outnumber Liberals…," by Lydia Saad, January 3, 2017. https://news.gallup.com/poll/201152/conservative-liberal-gap-contin ues-narrow-tuesday.aspx. Accessed March 27, 2019.

14. Congress, "S-2372—VA Mission Act of 2018." https://www.congress.gov /bill/115th-congress/senate-bill/2372. Accessed May 10, 2019.

15. CBS News, "Trump Signs VA Mission Act," June 6 2018. https://www .cbsnews.com/news/trump-signs-va-mission-act/. Accessed February 8, 2019.

16. Washington Post, "President Trump Signs $867 Billion…," by Jeff Stein, December 20, 2018. https://www.washingtonpost.com/business/2018/12/20

/president-trump-signs-billion-farm-bill-into-law/?utm_term=.b
83e87ae55be. Accessed February 8, 2019.

17. Ibid.

18. New York Times, "On an Eventful Day, Trump…," by Katie Rogers, December 20, 2018. https://www.nytimes.com/2018/12/20/us/politics/trump
-megan-mullally-video-green-acres.html. Accessed February 8, 2019.

19. New York Times, "Donald Trump Is Doing Something…Good?" by Michelle Goldberg, December 20, 2018. https://www.nytimes.com/2018/12/20
/opinion/first-step-act-trump.html. Accessed February 9, 2019.

20. Pew Research Center, "The Partisan Divide on Political Value Grows Even Wider," October 5, 2017. http://www.people-press.org/2017/10/05/1-partisan
-divides-over-political-values-widen/. Accessed December 15, 2018.

21. Blue Dog Coalition, "About Us." https://bluedogcaucus-costa.house.gov
/about. Accessed February 6, 2019.

22. Pew Research Center, "The Partisan Divide on Political Value Grows Even Wider."

23. Ibid.

24. Ibid.

25. Ibid.

26. Ibid.

27. White House, "Remarks by President Trump in State of the Union Address," February 5, 2019. https://www.whitehouse.gov/briefings-statements/remarks
-president-trump-state-union-address-2/. Accessed February 9, 2019.

28. Ibid.

29. Ibid.

30. Ibid.

31. Ibid.

32. Ibid.

33. Ibid.

34. Ibid.

35. WJLA.com, "Former Obama Border Chief," by Kristine Frazao, January 25, 2019. https://wjla.com/news/nation-world/former-obama-border-chief
-says-its-simple-the-wall-works. Accessed February 9, 2019.

36. Pew Research Center, "Wide Gender Gap, Growing Educational Divide in Voters' Party Identification," March 20, 2018. http://www.people-press
.org/2018/03/20/wide-gender-gap-growing-educational-divide-in-voters
-party-identification/. Accessed December 15, 2018.

37. Ibid.

38. Ibid.

39. Pew Research Center, "Partisan Animosity, Personal Politics...," October 27, 2017. http://www.people-press.org/2017/10/05/8-partisan-animosity-personal-politics-views-of-trump/. Accessed March 29, 2018.

40. Ibid.

41. Public Opinion Quarterly, "Ideologues Without Issues: The Polarizing Consequences of Ideological Identities," by Lilliana Mason, April 11, 2018. https://doi.org/10.1093/poq/nfy005. Accessed December 18, 2018.

42. Ibid.

43. Ibid.

44. New York Times, "Christine Blasey Ford Prepared...," September 26, 2018. https://www.nytimes.com/2018/09/26/us/politics/christine-blasey-ford-prepared-statement.html?module=inline. Accessed May 9, 2019.

45. Ibid.

46. Senate Judiciary Committee, "Prepared Written Testimony of Judge Brett M. Kavanaugh," September 27, 2018. https://www.judiciary.senate.gov/imo/media/doc/BK%20Written%20Testimony%20-%20Submitted%20Sept%2026.pdf. Accessed May 9, 2019.

47. Ibid.

48. Ibid.

49. Ibid.

50. Ibid.

51. National Review, "Cory Booker: Anyone Who Supports Kavanaugh's Nomination Is 'Complicit in Evil,'" by Jack Crowe, July 24, 2018. https://www.nationalreview.com/news/cory-booker-anyone-not-opposing-kavanaugh-nomination-is-complicit-in-evil/. Accessed May 9, 2019.

52. Ibid.

53. National Review, "Kamala Harris Wins the...," by Jonathan Tobin, September 6, 2018. https://www.nationalreview.com/2018/09/kamala-harris-wins-democrats-brett-kavanaugh-primary/. Accessed February 9, 2019.

54. WSYX ABC 6, "Timeline: A Very Bad Week...," by Stephen Loiaconi, February 4, 2019. https://abc6onyourside.com/news/nation-world/timeline-a-very-bad-week-in-the-life-of-virginia-gov-ralph-northam. Accessed February 6, 2019.

55. Ibid.

56. Ibid.

57. USA Today, "Virginia Gov. Ralph Northam...," by John Bacon, February 5, 2019. https://www.usatoday.com/story/news/politics/2019/02/05/ralph

-northam-gop-no-hurry-force-him-out/2776086002/. Accessed February 6, 2019.

58. Washington Post, "Second Woman Accuses Va. Lt. Gov. Justin Fairfax of Sexual Assault," by Jenna Portnoy, Gregory S. Schneider, Neena Satija, and Laura Vozella, February 8, 2019. https://www.washingtonpost.com/local /virginia-politics/second-woman-accuses-va-lt-gov-justin-fairfax-of-sexual -assault/2019/02/08/19e6bb6c-2bdf-11e9-b011-d8500644dc98_story .html?utm_term=.7f3fde5a3f1f. Accessed March 29, 2019.

59. Ibid.

60. Ibid.

61. The White House, "President Donald J. Trump's State of the Union Address," President Donald Trump, February 5, 2019. https://www.white house.gov/briefings-statements/president-donald-j-trumps-state-union -address-2/.

62. NPR, "Fact Check Trump's State…" by Danielle Kurtzlebam, February 5, 2019. https://www.npr.org/2019/02/05/690345256/fact-check-trumps -state-of-the-union-address#women-congress-34. Accessed February 6, 2019.

63. Public Opinion Quarterly, "Ideologues Without Issues."

64. Ibid.

65. Ibid.

66. *Mistakes Were Made (But Not by Me)*, by Carol Tavris and Elliot Aronson, Houghton Mifflin Harcourt, New York, 2015.

67. "When Red Meant Democratic and Blue Was Republican: A Brief History of TV Electoral Maps," Stephen Battaglio, November 3, 2016. https:// www.latimes.com/entertainment/tv/la-et-st-electoral-map-20161102 -htmlstory.html. Accessed December 15, 2018.

68. Smithsonian.com, "When Republicans Were Blue and Democrats Were Red," by Jodi Enda, October 31, 2012. https://www.smithsonianmag.com /history/when-republicans-were-blue-and-democrats-were-red-104176297/. Accessed December 15, 2018.

69. Ibid.

70. Ibid.

71. American Journal of Political Science, "'I Disrespectfully Agree': The Differential Effects of Partisan Sorting on Social and Issue Polarization," by Lilliana Mason, January 2015, pp. 128–45. https://www.jstor.org/stable /24363600. Accessed December 23, 2018.

72. Political Research Quarterly, "Red and Blue States of Mind: Partisan Hostility and Voting in the United States," by Patrick R. Miller and Pamela

Johnston Conover, June 2015, pp. 225–39. https://www.jstor.org/stable /24371828. Accessed December 15, 2018.

73. Ibid.
74. Ibid.
75. Ibid.

7: Outrageous Outrage

1. Washington Times, "Donna Brazile Admits Leaking…," by Douglas Ernst, March 17, 2017. https://www.washingtontimes.com/news/2017/mar/17/ donna-brazile-admits-leaking-debate-questions-to-c/. Accessed June 25, 2019.

2. New York Times, "Read Attorney General William…," March 24, 2019. https://www.nytimes.com/interactive/2019/03/24/us/politics/barr-letter -mueller-report.html. Accessed April 3, 2019.

3. https://www.merriam-webster.com/dictionary/outrage.

4. USA Today, "Nick Saban Smashes Headset as Alabama Commits Multiple Offensive Penalties Before Halftime," by Jace Evans, December 29, 2018. https://www.usatoday.com/story/sports/ncaaf/2018/12/29/orange-bowl -nick-saban-smashes-headset-over-alabama-penalties/2443381002/. Accessed December 31, 2018.

5. CBS News, "Charges Dropped Against Jussie…," March 26, 2019. https:// www.cbsnews.com/live-news/jussie-smollett-charges-dropped-empire -actor-emergency-chicago-court-appearance-today-2019-03-26/. Accessed March 31, 2019.

6. Ibid.

7. Ibid.

8. The Daily Beast, "Calling Out 'Hate Speech' Too Often Invites Censor-ship," by Nadine Strossen, May 4, 2018. https://www.thedailybeast.com /calling-out-hate-speech-too-often-invites-censorship. Accessed December 30, 2018.

9. American Journal of Political Science, "'I Disrespectfully Agree': The Dif-ferential Effects of Partisan Sorting on Social and Issue Polarization," by Lilliana Mason, January 2015. https://www.jstor.org/stable/24363600. Accessed April 8, 2019.

10. American Journal of Political Science, "Fear and Loathing Across Party Lines: New Evidence on Group Polarization," by Shanto Iyengar and Sean J. Westwood, July 2015, pp. 690–707. https://www.jstor.org/stable/24583091. Accessed December 15, 2018.

11. Ibid.

12. Ibid.

13. Wired, "Why David Brin Hates Yoda, Loves Radical Transparency," August 8, 2012. https://www.wired.com/2012/08/geeks-guide-david-brin/. Accessed December 28, 2018.

14. *Mistakes Were Made (But Not by Me)*, by Carol Tavris and Elliot Aronson, Houghton Mifflin Publishing Company, New York, 2015, p. 25.

15. Ibid.

16. Ibid.

17. Ibid.

18. History, "Iran Hostage Crisis," by History.com Editors, October 14, 2018. https://www.history.com/topics/middle-east/iran-hostage-crisis. Accessed April 1, 2019.

19. *Mistakes Were Made (But Not by Me)*.

20. Ibid.

21. Esquire, "The Crack-up," by F. Scott Fitzgerald, February 1936. https://www.esquire.com/lifestyle/a4310/the-crack-up/. Accessed April 3, 2019.

22. Wall Street Journal, "Justice Holmes' Free Speech...," by Richard Dooling, October 12, 2017. https://www.wsj.com/articles/justice-holmess-free-speech-lesson-1507847318. Accessed April 1, 2019.

23. *The Disuniting of America: Reflections on a Multicultural Society*, by Arthur M. Schlesinger, Jr., W. W. Norton & Company, New York, 1998, p. 162.

24. The Daily Beast, "Calling Out 'Hate Speech' Too Often Invites Censorship."

25. Ibid.

26. The Brown Daily Herald, "Ray Kelly Lecture Cancelled," by Jillian Lanney and Carolynn Cong, October 30, 2014. http://www.browndailyherald.com/2013/10/30/ray-kelly-lecture-canceled-amidst-student-community-protest/. Accessed April 4, 2018.

27. Ibid.

28. New York Times, "Condoleezza Rice Backs out After...," by Emma G. Fitzsimmons, May 3, 2014. https://www.nytimes.com/2014/05/04/nyregion/rice-backs-out-of-rutgers-speech-after-student-protests.html. Accessed April 4, 2019.

29. Ibid.

30. New York Times, "Middlebury College Charles Murray...," by Katharine Seelvy, March 3, 2017. https://www.nytimes.com/2017/03/03/us/middlebury-college-charles-murray-bell-curve-protest.html. Accessed April 5, 2019.

31. The Middlebury Campus, "Allison Stanger Appearances Show...," by Sabine Poux, March 14, 2018. https://middleburycampus.com/38046/news/stanger-appearances-show-faculty-rift/. Accessed April 8, 2019.

32. Beloit College, "Additional Details on YAF Erik...," by Bruce Heine and Cecil Youngblood, March 28, 2019. https://www.beloit.edu/news/stories/?story_id=553841. Accessed April 5, 2019.

33. USA Today, "I Was Assaulted at...," by Hayden Williams, March 6, 2019. https://www.usatoday.com/story/opinion/voices/2019/03/06/berkeley-conservative-students-campus-college-bias-punch-column/3065895002/. Accessed April 5, 2019.

8: Civil War—What Could Happen

1. Foreign Policy, "What a New U.S. Civil War Might Look Like," by Thomas Ricks, October 10, 2017. https://foreignpolicy.com/2017/10/10/what-a-new-u-s-civil-war-might-look-like/. Accessed December 28, 2018.

2. *Civil Wars: A History in Ideas*, by David Armitage, Vintage Books, New York, 2018, p. 7.

3. Ibid.

4. Ibid.

5. Ibid.

6. Ibid.

7. Ibid.

8. Ibid., p. 37.

9. Ibid., pp. 73–74.

10. Ibid., p. 83.

11. Department of State, Office of Historian. https://history.state.gov/milestones/1750-1775/parliamentary-taxation. Accessed December 28, 2018.

12. Ibid.

13. Ibid.

14. History.com, "Patrick Henry's Liberty or...," by Evan Andrews, August 22, 2018. https://www.history.com/news/patrick-henrys-liberty-or-death-speech-240-years-ago. Accessed May 12, 2019.

15. *Civil Wars: A History in Ideas*, p. 142.

16. Battlefield Trust, "The Cost of War: Killed, Wounded, Captured, and Missing." https://www.battlefields.org/learn/articles/civil-war-casualties. Accessed January 3, 2019.

17. American Interest, "The Top 14 Causes of Political Polarization, by David Blankenhorn, March 16, 2018. https://www.the-american-interest.com/2018/05/16/the-top-14-causes-of-political-polarization/. Accessed January 3, 2019.

18. Rasmussen Reports, "31 Percent Think U.S...," June 27, 2018, http://www.rasmussenreports.com/public_content/politics/general_politics/june_2018/31_think_u_s_civil_war_likely_soon. Accessed March 29, 2019.

19. Ibid.

20. Townhall, "America's Second Civil War," by Dennis Prager, January 24, 2017. https://townhall.com/columnists/dennisprager/2017/01/24/americas-second-civil-war-n2275896. Accessed March 19, 2019.

21. Foreign Policy Magazine, "What a New U.S. Civil War Might Look Like," by Thomas Ricks, October 10, 2017. https://foreignpolicy.com/2017/10/10/what-a-new-u-s-civil-war-might-look-like/. Accessed January 5, 2019.

22. Ibid.

23. Ibid.

24. Ibid.

25. Ibid.

26. The New Yorker, "Is America Headed for...," by Robin Wright, August 17, 2017. https://www.newyorker.com/news/news-desk/is-america-headed-for-a-new-kind-of-civil-war. Accessed March 29, 2019.

27. Gallup, "Democrats More Positive About...," by Frank Newport, August 13, 2018. https://news.gallup.com/poll/240725/democrats-positive-socialism-capitalism.aspx. Accessed March 5, 2019.

28. Ibid.

29. CNN, "A Time for Choosing," by Ronald Reagan, October 27, 1964. https://www.cnn.com/SPECIALS/2004/reagan/stories/speech.archive/time.html. Accessed May 10, 2019.

30. Ibid.

31. Ibid.

32. National Review, "Venezuela's Future—And Ours," by Kevin Williamson, June 24, 2018. https://www.nationalreview.com/2018/06/venezuela-economic-collapse-socialism-always-fails/. Accessed March 5, 2019.

33. Ibid.

34. Stratfor, "America's Coming Disunion?" by Ian Morris, November 7, 2018. https://worldview.stratfor.com/article/americas-coming-disunion. Accessed January 3, 2019.

35. Ibid.

36. Ibid.

37. Ibid.

38. Ibid.

9: What We Can Do

1. University of California Los Angeles, "Pause, Reflect, and Give Thanks...," by Joan Moran, October 29, 2013. http://newsroom.ucla.edu/stories /gratitude-249167. Accessed April 6, 2019.

2. *The Wealth Choice* , by Dennis Kimbro, St. Martin's Press, New York, Kindle edition, p. 81.

3. http://www.journalism.org/2014/10/21/political-polarization-media -habits/pj_14-10-21_mediapolarization-08/.

4. Psychology Today, "Can We Create a Flourishing World?" by Michelle McQuaid, July 10, 2015. https://www.psychologytoday.com/us/blog/fun ctioning-flourishing/201507/can-we-create-flourishing-world. Accessed January 11, 2019.

5. Ibid.

6. Ibid.

7. Journal of Applied Behavioral Science, "Generative Metaphor Intervention: A New Approach for Working with Systems Divided by Conflict and Caught in Defensive Perception," Frank J. Barrett and David L. Cooperrider, May 1990, pp. 219–39.

8. CFA Institute, "The Power of Appreciation," by Jim Ware, August 7, 2018. https://blogs.cfainstitute.org/investor/2018/08/07/the-power-of-appreciation/. Accessed March 5, 2019.

9. *Mistakes Were Made (But Not by Me)*, by Carol Tavris and Elliot Aronson, Houghton Mifflin Harcourt, New York, 2015.

10. Foundation for Economic Education, "Check Your Privilege: Social Consciousness or Virtue Signal?" by Tricia Beck-Peter, December 20, 2018. https://fee.org/articles/check-your-privilege-social-consciousness-or-virtue -signal/. Accessed December 27, 2018.

11. The University of Chicago, "Report of the Committee on Freedom of Expression," January 2015. https://provost.uchicago.edu/sites/default/files /documents/reports/FOECommitteeReport.pdf. Accessed April 3, 2019.

12. Foundation for Individual Rights in Education, "Adopting the Chicago Statement." https://www.thefire.org/student-network/take-action/adopting -the-chicago-statement/. Accessed April 3, 2019.

13. The White House, "Executive Order Improving Free...," March 21, 2019. https://www.whitehouse.gov/presidential-actions/executive-order-improving -free-inquiry-transparency-accountability-colleges-universities/. Accessed April 6, 2019.

14. Washington Times, "Trump's Free Speech Order...," by S. A. Miller,

March 28, 2019. http://amp.washingtontimes.com/news/2019/mar/28/trumps-free-speech-order-colleges-gets-support-acr/. Accessed April 6, 2019.

15. Associated Press–NORC Center for Public Affairs. "The American Identity: Points of Pride, Conflicting Views, and a Distinct Culture," March 2017. http://apnorc.org/PDFs/American%20Identity/APNORC_American_Identity_2017.pdf. Accessed December 10, 2018.

16. Ibid.

17. *The Disuniting of America: Reflections on a Multicultural Society*, by Arthur M Schlesinger, Jr., W. W. Norton & Company, New York, 1998, p. 123.

18. The Weekly Standard, "It's Time to Kill Our Political Narratives," by Edward Halper, November 29, 2018. https://www.weeklystandard.com/edward-halper/its-time-to-kill-our-political-narratives. Access January 11, 2019.

19. Ibid.

20. Ibid.

21. Speech by Theodore Roosevelt, delivered at The Hamilton Club, Chicago, Illinois, April 10, 1899. http://theodore-roosevelt.com/images/research/speeches/trstrenlife.pdf. Accessed April 8, 2019.

22. The Weekly Standard, "It's Time to Kill Our Political Narratives."

23. Los Angeles Times, "Nelson Mandela Transformed Himself...," by David Horsey, December 6, 2013. https://www.latimes.com/opinion/topoftheticket/la-xpm-2013-dec-06-la-na-tt-nelson-mandela-20131206-story.html. Accessed May 12, 2019.

24. Psychology Today, "Can We Create a Flourishing World?"

25. Bible Hub, New International Version, https://biblehub.com/john/8-7.htm. Accessed May 12, 2019.

26. "Dan Crenshaw: I Made Amends with Pete Davidson on SNL. But That's...," November 13, 2018. https://www.washingtonpost.com/opinions/i-made-amends-with-pete-davidson-on-snl-but-thats-only-the-beginning/2018/11/13/e7314fb0-e77e-11e8-b8dc-66cca409c180_story.html. Accessed November 23, 2018.

27. Harvard Business Review, "A New Way to Become More Open-Minded," by Sloan Snow, November 20, 2018. https://hbr.org/2018/11/a-new-way-to-become-more-open-minded. Accessed January 8, 2018.

28. Elizabeth J. Krumrei-Mancuso and Steven V. Rouse (2016), "The Development and Validation of the Comprehensive Intellectual Humility Scale," *Journal of Personality Assessment*, 98:2, 209-221, DOI: 10.1080/00223891.2015.1068174.

INDEX

ABOUT THE AUTHOR

Jackie Gingrich Cushman is a syndicated columnist, author, professional speaker, corporate strategist, corporate financial advisor, and board member. She co-authored *5 Principles for a Successful Life: From Our Family to Yours,* with her father, Newt Gingrich. Her second book, *The Essential American: 15 Documents and Speeches Every American Should Own,* covers the key points of our nation's history.

Cushman has extensive media experience. She is a holder of the Chartered Financial Analyst designation. During her years in corporate finance, she ran the financial planning department of a $3 billion wireless company. Cushman earned her MBA in finance from Georgia State University.

Cushman served as a senior advisor and media surrogate for Newt Gingrich during his run for the 2012 Republican presidential nomination, where she not only survived, but thrived under media pressure. Her experience in politics spans four decades and includes volunteering, fundraising, strategy, and public relations/media.

Cushman's nonprofit activities include having served on the Advisory Council for the Alliance Theatre and as president of the Mimosa Garden Club. She is founder and chairman of the board of the Learning Makes a Difference Foundation. She is a member of the Atlanta Press Club, the National Association of Corporate Directors, and the CFA Institute. Cushman co-chaired the Atlanta Botanical Garden's "Garden of Eden Ball" and the Trust for Public Land's "Celebration of Land" with her husband, Jimmy. She serves as treasurer of the Georgia Early Education Alliance for Ready Students (GEEARS), on the board of the Atlanta Society of Financial and Investment Professionals Foundation, on the Trust for Public Land task force for the Chattahoochee, and on the advisory council of Our House.

Cushman lives in Atlanta with her husband, Jimmy Cushman, Jr., and their children.